THE SEXY BEAST COMPANY
SB
2001

Sent Items

Printed in the United States of America

Publisher's Cataloging-in-Publication Data

Library of Congress Control Number 2001119015
ISBN 0-9715028-0-3

The Sexy Beast Company
319 Genoa St. # 8
Monrovia, CA 91016

FIRST PRINTING

SENT ITEMS

A Collection of Emails from a Guy with too Much Time on his Hands

Joe Dino

The Sexy Beast Company
Monrovia

Special Thanks

To my Family who are forever unwavering in their love and loyalty.

To my Friends who patiently indulge my gentle excesses.

We Honor and Remember

Dedicated to all the innocent men and women who died on September 11, 2001.

Know that your sacrifices were not in vain, and we are united and strengthened in our struggle against injustice and intolerance.

May your memory guide us to victory.

Contents

Introduction: Why a Book of Emails?

Section I: The Art of Leisure

Chapter 1 Internet Hell 3

Chapter 2 The Gentleman Gambler 26

Chapter 3 Gluttony 35

Chapter 4 Trivia 46

Section II: All the Pretty People

Chapter 5 Chicks 53

Chapter 6 Social Graces 72

Chapter 7 Waitresses 94

Chapter 8 Grant 104

Chapter 9 Guy Trips 117

Section III: Gentle Musings

Chapter 10 **Lessons in Life** 131

Chapter 11 **A Sense of Righteousness** 140

Chapter 12 **Fruits of Fantasy** 149

Section IV: A Man for All Seasons

Chapter 13 **The Traveler** 169

Chapter 14 **The Motoring Enthusiast** 197

Chapter 15 **The Noble Worker** 207

Section V: The Naked Day

Chapter 16 **Moments & Fragments** 221

Chapter 17 **Our Precious Health** 240

Chapter 18 **Farewell to Fools** 243

The Book

Friendly Encouragement

A little nonsense now and then
Is relished by the wisest men.
— Anonymous

INTRODUCTION

WHY A BOOK OF EMAILS?

> An incurable itch for scribbling takes possession of many, and grows inveterate in their insane breasts.
>
> *Juvenal* - Satires

You're probably wondering what this book is all about. It's a book about my emails.

There's nothing special about these emails. My emails don't preach politics, virtues or any divine message. In fact, they really have nothing profound to say. Some rant and rave. Some are melodramatic and sentimental. Some are funny and irreverent.

The only thing these emails have in common is that they were written by me on a computer in some office, in some apartment or in some forsaken internet café in the middle of the blistering Australian desert.

So why assemble this collection of emails at all? Well, I've always wanted my 15 minutes of Warholian fame. And the only thing I'm moderately good at is to write emails. Not novels, but emails. Not screenplays, but emails. Not poetry, but emails.

So I put together a book of my emails.

I was talking to a friend about my email book, and debated whether or not printing my emails would offend certain people. And he simply said: "So what? You already made them angry the first time you wrote it!".

I think most of my emails are interesting. They may not necessarily have a point, but at least they're interesting. At least interesting enough for you to buy this book and give me that 15 minutes of Warholian fame.

I've included the emails (fondly referred to as "mass emails") which I've sent out to friends over the past seven to eight years. I've tried to avoid including one-on-one emails, and other people's replies as they are more of a private nature but there are some exceptions that are simply worth sharing.

Understandably, I've edited out people's last names and true email addresses to protect their privacy. I've fixed up some obvious spelling mistakes and did some minor formatting for readability, but I've left all the grammatical mistakes and lack of proper punctuation. I feel those imperfections add to the spontaneity and vividness of the emails.

I really haven't tried to analyze my development of writing style and content. I know it can't be too bad because I still laugh when I read these emails.

But enough of airy introductions. I'll let the emails speak for themselves.

SECTION I

THE ART OF LEISURE

All the things I really like to do are
either immoral, illegal or fattening
Alexander Woollcott

The test of pleasure is the memory it
leaves behind. (Die Probe Eines
Genusses ist Seine Erinnerung).
Jean Paul Richter

1

INTERNET HELL

If the human race wants to go to Hell in a basket,
technology can help it get there by jet.
Charles M. Allen

NEW PC

It all started innocently enough.

Date:	Friday, 27 March 1998 10:49AM
To:	Barry; Bruce; Dale; Dodge; Jun; Kevin; Lynn; Roberto; Tom
Subject:	New PC

Finally got the new PC! Yes! It came in two huge boxes, so I was intimidated to put everything together, but I finally got connected to the internet in 1 1/2 hours from the point of unpacking, which wasn't bad. The problem with Gateway stuff is that all the units are pretty big. The 17 inch monitor is practically as big as my 19 inch TV, and the CPU tower itself is massive. But I'm impressed that everything worked including the modem which I didn't have to configure at all.

I tried out the chat conferences, and I watched all the people chatting with each other, and it was really quite a sad spectacle. I didn't want to get involved with chatting so I quickly logged out before I got sucked in by people masquerading as other people. Some guy named WebMaster wanted to talk to me (I used TriviaBoy as my alias) before I could log out, but I escaped the chatroom in time.

Also I saw the nude Jennifer Anniston pic which was a rip-off since she wasn't fully nude anyway.

And then I tried out my speakerphone (I can't use my regular phone unless I plug it back in) and it worked too. I will have to call some of you with it. I already tried it on Yvette this morning, but she speaks really slow, so I couldn't really get the full effect of simultaneous two-way conversation.

But the best thing was that it came with MSOffice SBE, so I can start doing some serious writing now at home now.

Any other ideas what I can do with my PC?

P.S. is it true that most of the ISPs in the US have unlimited usage for a reasonable fixed price? I can't find an unlimited usage deal for a reasonable price here.

SINKING INTO INTERNET HELL

It's addicting, I tell you.

Date:	Tuesday, 7 April 1998 9:04AM
To:	Aldo; Chris; Simon; Davide; Barry; Bruce; Dale; Dodge; Jun; Lynn; Roberto;Tom
Subject:	Sinking into Internet Hell

Howdy Boys and Girls!

Got more sleep last night, but that was only because I was running a slight fever, but I fear I have sunk even lower now into the bowels of internet hell.

Last night I created another nom du guerre on yahoo called BustyBlonde, and boy, it's more fun to be a GIRL (well, I suppose if you're blonde and busty it's better than fat and ugly). BustyBlonde was kicking all these guys around and giving them shit, and they were all taking it just so they can have some precious moments with BustyBlonde. It was really quite sad. There was a guy from Finland who said, "In Europe, we think Americans are dumb, but you are very intelligent. I want to be your friend". Ha! Then there was a Male_Tease who claimed he had a Ferrari in LA, so BustyBlonde asked him how much car insurance he was paying, he said $4800. Liar! BustyBlonde was one wicked bitch! Male_Tease even said he was a computer designer, but that was the wrong move to make with BustyBlonde because BustyBlonde quickly asked him what happens when 16 bit apps run with 32 bits apps on Windows 95, no answer from Male_Tease. They just don't their homework, these chatters.

It was amazing how much abuse they took, BustyBlonde was telling IM2FAST4U, "Hey, I'm talking right now, I'll slap you around later", but they came back for even more, hey, when you're 5'8 weigh 130 lbs (I think BustyBlonde should lose 5 lbs, but she's a tough momma) and market computer systems all over the world, you can do that.

I think the next step is to create another id called FATnUGLY and compare it with last night's results. What an experiment in human psyche!

NET CONVERSATION

Sometimes you do learn something useful from the internet.

Date:	Tuesday, June 23, 1998 8:42 PM
To:	Bruce; Barry; Brooke; Dodge; Davide; Dale; Jun; Joe O.; Kevin; Greg; Roberto; Tom; Simon
Subject:	Net Conversation

Sorry guys, but I just had to share this with you as this is a great example of classic net conversation. This happened last night in the chess chat room.

By the way, I was Porky Pig instead of my usual BustyBlonde

SalaciousCrumb:	Genkaos, are you a girl?
Genkaos:	No, but I can be for you.
Genkaos:	Why do people care if you're a girl or not?
Porky Pig:	Because this is the only place ugly guys can talk to girls who are really guys pretending to be girls.
Porky Pig:	I'm pretty good-looking though, I just come here to play chess.
Genkaos:	And I'm gorgeous!
Highlander:	I'm butt ugly
Porky Pig:	Nothing wrong with being ugly, but are you fat?
Highlander:	I'm so fat, I can't get out of bed

Porky Pig:	If you can't get out of bed, how can you change the porno tapes on your VCR?
Highlander:	Don't need porno tapes, I get all the porn from the net.
Porky Pig:	How do you do that?
Highlander:	Because I have all the passwords for the xxx sites
Porky Pig:	Okay, give me some...

And that my friends is how I discovered the hacker sites where they give you the user ids and passwords for the adult sites.

GREATEST CHAT ROOM EXCHANGES

I thought Nepotutu was a very exciting name. I'm only making conversation.

Date:	Monday, 12 October 1998 9:08
To:	Grant; Barry; Bruce; Dodge; Joe O.; Jun; Kevin; Roberto; Tom; Dale; Davide; Brooke; Greg; Aldo; Nicole; Simon; Mark
Subject:	Joe Dino's Greatest Chat Room Exchanges

Please note: Nepotutu is the latest net persona, and events usually take place in the Romance or Religion chatrooms.

GrandmaKaren:	Hi everybody!
Nepotutu:	Hi Grandma! You got big tits?
GrandmaKaren:	Nepotutu is on ignore
Conrad:	Hello!
Nepotutu:	Hi Conrad, you got big tits?
Conrad:	Im a guy, asshole
Nepotutu:	So you got big tits or not?
Conrad:	Nepotutu is on ignore

KoolKat:	Hello!
Nepotutu:	Hi Fag!
KoolKat:	Im not a fag, bitch!
Nepotutu:	Well, you talk like one
KoolKat:	Bye, ho!

Nepotutu:	Hello! Anybody want to talk about porno?
Disciple:	Are you a born again christian?
Nepotutu:	No, IM A PORN AGAIN CHRISTIAN

Nepotutu: PORN AGAIN CHRISTIAN, get it?
Disciple: Everybody, put Nepotutu on IGNORE!

note: there are many more such exchanges but they are rather graphic in nature and unacceptable for general consumption

ChristianWarrior: Jesus loves the sinner, but hates the sin.
ChristianWarrior: So gay people must turn away from their homosexuality or else they will go to hell.
Nepotutu: Are we talking about fags?
KiwiBoy: In New Zealand, fags are cigarettes
Nepotutu: In Los Angeles, fags are people who throw good parties and cut good hair
ChristianWarrior: Are you gay?
Nepotutu: No, but you are

note: homosexuality is a very contentious subject in the chatrooms, and unfortunately Nepotutu has to fight the homophobes with his amazing wit and brilliance, often stunning the homophobes into a dazed state with a barrage of double-entendres and loaded statements

MissDamnPerfect: Hello!
Nepotutu: Hi, you got big tits?
MissDamnPerfect: Shut up
Nepotutu: Dont worry, I'll still like you, you know what they say, small chest, big heart
MissDamnPerfect: Nepotutu is on ignore

Mel: ** sings a happy song **
Julee: ** does cartwheels **
Marine: ** highfives everybody **
Nepotutu: ** ejaculates in coffee mug **
Mel: Nepotutu is on ignore
Julee: Nep, why?
Marine: I'll kick your ass Nep!

And there you have it, I have tons more but I have to work now...
Darn it, I wish I got paid soon so I can do some other activities!

CAM STUFF

It's a good thing I'm not an exhibitionist. I did build up a small yet risque collection of live homoerotic images during this shameful period in my life.

Date:	Sunday, November 08, 1998 7:51 PM
To:	Barry; Bruce; Dodge; Joe O.; Jun; Kevin; Roberto; Tom; Dale; Davide; Brooke; Greg; Aldo; Nicole; Simon; Mark
Subject:	Cam Stuff

Hey, this cam stuff is very entertaining!

This weekend, I did a variety of things with my cam. I had the cam on for an hour or so, so people on netmeeting could watch me iron my shirts LIVE! Of course, I had the occasional perverts who wanted me to show them my wiener on the net, but I refused.

Speaking of wieners, I hardly ever put myself on the cam. Instead I put my little greek statue in front of the cam instead. You guys familiar with my Greek statue? Its the one of the little satyr Pan. Anyways, when people connect and see my little statue, they immediately think: "YES! I FOUND A PERVERT!" and they'll strip down or put their dicks on their cams. Really quite bizarre. I wonder if they know that I can copy and paste that and send it by email throughout the internet?

By the way, you dont need a cam yourself to view my statue. Probably a mike and loudspeakers would help so we can chat on-line. For some reason, when I talk to Aussie folks, the line is clearer. USA line is okay too, but they can hear me better.

So if you guys want to chat with me, just look for Porky Pig on uls.bigpond.com or ils5.microsoft.com after working hours Australia time. It's really very easy, just go to IE4, under Go.., Internet Call... or just go to NetMeeting 2.1.

Okay, I gotta finish up my work so I can go camming on the internet, and talk to MY REAL FRIENDS WHO CHAT WITH ME!

DINOSAURS AND UFOS

I love talking about dinosaurs and UFOs.

Date:	Thursday, 4 February 1999 11:29 AM
To:	Davide; Peter; Grant; Barry; Bruce; Dodge; Joe O.; Jun; Roberto; Tom; Dale
Subject:	Chat Hell #217

Donald Duck and Lisa of Pisa would like to share some of their recent experiences in the chatrooms.

The Dinosaur Debate (this goes on and on)

Donald Duck:	Can we talk about dinosaurs?
JosephK:	What do you want to know?
Donald Duck:	Why do people think dinosaurs existed?
JosephK:	They found fossils and dinosaur bones
Donald Duck:	But God put them bones there
JosephK:	No, they carbon dated it, theyre millions of years old
Donald Duck:	Scientists did the carbon dating, and everybody knows that scientists worship Satan
Donald Duck:	If dinosaurs really existed how come they never found a frozen dinosaur?
JosephK:	Frozen dinosaurs?
Donald Duck:	Yeah, they found frozen mammoths but never frozen dinosaurs
JosephK:	Maybe it was because dinosaurs didnt live in the ice age?
Donald Duck:	How do you know dinosaurs didnt live in the ice age? Were you there?
JosephK:	How old are you?
Donald Duck:	12

UFO Mystery

Donald Duck:	So where do UFOs come from?
PrazeBabe:	UFOs are sent by Satan to deceive people
Donald Duck:	I always thought that UFOs come from the future and they go back to the past so they can analprobe us to get genetic material to save the human race in the future.

More UFO Analprobing (it all makes sense now!!!)

Albion:	So what about UFOs?
Donald Duck:	So are UFOs sent by Satan?
Albion:	Yes, UFOs are the devil's work
Donald Duck:	Is that why UFO people analprobe humans?
Albion:	What do you mean?
Donald Duck:	Well, once you get analprobed, you may end up liking it and become a homo, and once youre homo and take it up the butt, you go to hell. And isnt that what the devil wants?
Albion:	How old are you Duck?
Donald Duck:	12

Iraq (standard staple of mine in addition to the 100 holy crystals)

Wataki:	How old are you Duck?
Donald Duck:	12
DancingGirl:	Why are you so angry and bitter Duck?
Donald Duck:	I cant help it, I live in Iraq so thats why Im so angry
DancingGirl:	Really?
Donald Duck:	I hate Iraq, for xmas we got cruise missiles from Santa
Wataki:	How's Saddam?
Donald Duck:	I hate Saddam, Saddam killed my son Ali
DancingGirl:	Youre not old enough to have a son
Donald Duck:	We get married very early in Iraq, we dont live very long because of the cruise missiles
DancingGirl:	Why did Saddam kill Ali?
Donald Duck:	Ali petted Saddam's dog because Saddam's dog looked like our dog Lightning, and Saddam got mad and killed Ali. I hate Saddam
DancingGirl:	You're kidding right?
Donald Duck:	I miss Ali, I miss Lightning too
Wataki:	Where's Lightning?
Donald Duck:	Lightning tried to catch a cruise missile with his mouth
Wataki:	I hope you catch a cruise missile with YOUR MOUTH!
DancingGirl:	Well, its your own fault because you dont kick Saddam out, besides Iraq invades other countries so you only have yourself to blame.
Donald Duck:	DancingGirl, can I ask you a question?
DancingGirl:	Yes
Donald Duck:	So you got big tits?

Armwrestling

Lion of Judah: I'd like to see you go to hell Duck
Donald Duck: That's it, I'll have to armwrestle you now, except I only have flippers
Lion of Judah: Duck tastes good
Donald Duck: I better not armwrestle you though, the feathers on my arms might turn you on, and you might become homo and go to hell

Indecision

CherryGirl: Im really going to pray for you tonight, you are so full of shit, you need it!
Donald Duck: Make up your mind, are you going to pray for me, or hate me?
CherryGirl: I'll pray for you, but you really know how to make people angry, dont you?
Donald Duck: Im the DUCK
CherryGirl: Sometimes you have a point, but you have to say it another way
Donald Duck: Youre falling in love with me already, arent you?
CherryGirl: Yes
Donald Duck: Well, as long as you recognize me for the sex machine that I truly am, we can date
CherryGirl: Why?
Donald Duck: Because I hate it when CHICKS JUST DIG ME FOR MY BRAIN, THEY JUST WANT ME TO MAKE THEM LAUGH AND LAUGH! THE PRESSURE I TELL YOU!
CherryGirl: And?
Donald Duck: So who makes the CLOWN LAUGH???? I ASK YOU, WHO MAKES THE CLOWN LAUGH?

Superheroes (this never fails to surprise me how theyll gang up on a certain group)

Bob: Catholics have a lot to answer for.
Delia: Mormons and Jehovah's Witnesses are also deceived.
Donald Duck: I wish I was Mormon
Delia: Why is that DUCK?
Donald Duck: Because when I die I want to become a superhero and fly around and see through women's clothes with my xray vision
Delia: How old are you DUCK?
Donald Duck: 12

Peanut Butter (love peanut butter)

Aryrya: So what do you smell like?
Lisa: Peanut butter
Aryrya: Do you apply it?
Lisa: No, my daddy does

Just Plain Weird

Aryrya: How old are you?
Lisa: 12
Aryrya: You dont sound 12. I saw you call other people fags
Lisa: That wasnt me, that was my sister. I just play chess, she just types stuff on the keyboard
Aryrya: How old is your sister?
Lisa: 17
Aryrya: Put her on
Lisa: Okay
Lisa: Hi Fag!
Aryrya: I hate being called that!
Lisa: She's gone now
Aryrya: I think you havc a split pcrsonality
Lisa: Im only 12 and I just come to play chess

More Homo Stuff

Joker: What do you have against homos
Lisa: I dont have anything against homos
Joker: So why do you keep on asking to play with fags?
Lisa: I like to play with fags, homos are very friendly and dont yell
Joker: Im a fag
Lisa: I know you are

Thank you, thank you very much

HOLY CRYSTALS

The holy crystals, they sound so...holy. It's amazing how I remembered all of this. I used to type up my routine in the chatrooms. But later I just kept all the best lines in a Word document and just cut and paste the lines I needed. It got much better and detailed as time went on. I even found a verse which references the holy crystals.

Date:	Friday, 26 February 1999 11:53 AM
To:	Kirsten; Davide; Peter; Grant; Barry; Bruce; Dodge; Joe O.; Jun; Roberto; Tom; Dale
Subject:	Holy Crystals

Sometimes I wonder if I go too far with my holy crystals routine on the internet, if any of you are christians, pentecostals, catholics, mormons, or homos, no offense and many apologies. Im sure you'll be able to decipher the basic gist of the 100 holy crystals.

Presenting that notoriously irreverent yet profound Donald Duck...

The intro...

Donald Duck:	Hello dear dear friends!
Prazebabe:	Hi Duck
Preacher:	Oh no, its the Duck
Wataki:	Loads his gun for duck hunting
Rhiannon:	Hi Duck

June 19...

Donald Duck:	Im so happy today!
Prazebabe:	Why are you so happy?
Donald Duck:	Because I already have all my crystals ready for June 19
Coralee:	What's June 19 and what do crystals have to do with it?
Donald Duck:	June 19 is the day of the rapture, that's the day when us pentecostals will rise up to heaven but you need 100 holy crystals to get into heaven, otherwise you go to hell.

The doubters of the holy crystals...

SuziWithKids:	Ive never heard of holy crystals, and Im Pentecostal

Donald Duck: Youve never heard of holy crystals? Well, when you die, your holy crystals float up to heaven and the angel Briasus counts them and if you have 100 or more you go to heaven

Getting holy crystals...

Coralee: How do you get the holy crystals, Donald?
Donald Duck: Well, you have to do christian things like speaking in tongues, thats why us pentecostals are halfway there, because we get 50 holy crystals for speaking in tongues.
Albion: How can you get the other 50 holy crystals?
Donald Duck: For every sin that you repent, you get 5 holy crystals. But the bigger the sin, the more holy crystals you get.
GayBlackJewishNazi: So if I shoot a muslim abortion doctor, how many holy crystals do I get?
Donald Duck: 20 holy crystals, but only if you repent. If you just sin, you get bits of black coal in your blood. Thats why its important to sin and repent, after all we're all born sinners and we all fall short, so its okay to sin and keep on sinning as long as we repent! Its beautiful!

Black bits of coal...

Coralee: Black bits of coal?
Donald Duck: Yeah, if you have 100 bits of black coal in your blood, you go to hell, that's why a lot of muslims and hindus are darkskinned because they have too many black bits of coal in their blood. Thats why us Pentecostals are mostly white, because we have a lot of holy crystals in our bodies. Heaven will be mostly for white folks, but you know that.

Catholics...

Katholiko: Heaven isnt for white people only!!! A lot of catholics are nonwhites. Theyll be in heaven too!
Donald Duck (DO I HAVE TO REMIND ANYONE, IM CATHOLIC???): oh no, catholics will burn in hell along with the mormons, homos and witches. Catholics worship weird saints like St. Cauliflower of the Sacred Wheelabrators.
Katholiko: You are racist and a bigot DUCK! YOU WILL BURN IN HELL!!!
Donald Duck: Im not a racist, anyone of different color can enter heaven as long as they have 100 holy crystals before June 19.

Back to June 19...

SuziWithKids: What is this with June 19!!! No man knows the day, so says the bible. Where do you get your info from Duck?
Donald Duck: The day of the rapture was revealed to our pastor Brother Bill, thats the advantage of being pentecostal, we have a direct hotline with heaven, and we get all kinds of neat things revealed to us, like the secret password to heaven.
Albion: Whats the secret password to heaven?
Donald Duck: 100 HOLY CRYSTALS

Doubters again...

Coralee: I think Duck is seriously deluded, Duck you should read the Word instead of listening to your pastor
Donald Duck: Brother Bill never lies, he told us about the Principle of Weeding too, that too us pentecostals must follow
JCSoldier: Im pentecostal but Ive never heard of the Principle of Weeding, whats that?
Donald Duck: Heaven is like a big garden, but we have to get rid of the weeds like muslims and hindus and mormons, so there will be more room for us beautiful flowers like pentecostals. Thats why its important that muslims and hindus and mormons not go to heaven, there wont be enough room for us pentecostals.
Reverend: What have I stumbled upon here??? This is not christian talk!!! WE ARE ALL GOD'S CHILDREN!!
Donald Duck: Thats true, we're all God's children, but some of God's children will choose to go to hell, just like homos and mormons. Especially mormons, since they think theyll become superheroes and fly off to other planets when they die.
Homolover: What do you have against homos, duck? Are you a homophobe?
Donald Duck: I LOVE HOMOS, but if homos take it up the butt or munch carpet, they go to hell, simple as that!

Request for proof...

Coralee: SHOW ME SCRIPTURE WHERE IT SAYS ABOUT HOLY CRYSTALS!!!
Albion: Where is it in the bible about Holy Crystals!
Donald Duck: Okay okay, you can find holy crystals right next to the part where it says its okay to hound and discriminate homos until

they blow their brains out, and you can also find a reference to the holy crystals under the passage where it says its okay to shoot abortion doctors, and of course, you can find the holy crystals right above the verse where it says its okay to beat up your wife in an alcoholic rage because wives must submit to their husbands. And I think you can also find holy crystals next to the bit where it says you can have slaves like they had before the Civil War. And thats where you can find the holy crystals.

Coralee: I havent read that.
Albion: There's no such thing in the bible.

Fingering out the Troublemaker...

JCSoldier: Ignore Donald, he's just here to make trouble with his holy crystals
TeddyBear: Holy crystals, what are that?
JCSoldier: TeddyBear, dont ask about holy crystals, they dont exist
Donald Duck: Dinosaurs dont exist but holy crystals do
Wataki: Here we go again about dinosaurs... Hey duck, how come dinosaurs dont exist?
Donald Duck: If dinosaurs existed, how come they never found a frozen dinosaur?
Wataki: Duck, what happens if you have more than 100 holy crystals?
Donald Duck: You can use the extra holy crystals to buy wings and harps
Coralee: How many holy crystals do you have?
Donald Duck: 25,300 holy crystals, that's enough to buy a ferrari.
Wataki: Gee, I only have 5 holy crystals extra, can I buy a Big Mac with that?
Donald Duck: Nope, no meat in heaven, animals dont have souls, thats why there wont be any cows in heaven for beef. Just vegetables will be in heaven. Veggie burgers I guess.

Going to HELL...

Coralee: Ill pray for you duck, because if you dont turn your ways you'll go to hell
Albion: Youll burn in hell for blaspheming against the holy sprit
Wataki: Youll be in good company with the homos and witches in hell, duck!

What a horrible horrible person that Duck is.

The sad thing is, I now have around probably 10 people who wait for me everytime I log on the net to hear about the holy crystals. Truly the internet is the work of the devil. Some people have even gone as far as to tell Ive changed their lives and brought happiness to their existence. How weird is that!!!! IM A FALSE PROPHET NOW TOO!!!!

EVEN I HAD TO LAUGH ON THIS ONE...

Sometimes I laugh so much my face hurts for hours...

Date:	Wednesday, March 31, 1999 10:57 AM
To:	Grant; Peter; Barry; Bruce; Dodge; Joe O.; Jun; Kirsten; Roberto; Tom; Dale; Davide; Brooke; Greg; Aldo; Nicole; Simon; Mark
Subject:	Even I had to laugh on this one...

I just had to write this one up since even this made the unflappable Donald Duck laugh...

Same routine, on a rampage in the chatrooms.

My_Jesus_Is_Lord:	Hello everyone!
Donald Duck:	Hello!
My_Jesus_Is_Lord:	Has anyone heard of Terence Rose? He is a preacher from England.
Donald Duck:	Terence?? Why yes, Ive heard of Terence!
My_Jesus_Is_Lord:	You have, really? Terence is a wonderful man! How do you know Terence?
Donald Duck:	Well, I fell asleep on Terence's sofa and when I woke up, I had my shorts down to my knees, and Terence was dabbing his mouth with a napkin.
My_Jesus_Is_Lord:	What are you talking about????
Donald Duck:	Terence said that a snake had bit my groin and he had to suck the poison out.
My_Jesus_Is_Lord:	You are on ignore Donald Duck!!!!!!
Donald Duck:	I love Terence. Terence is a wonderful man. He saved my life.

I love Donald Duck!!!!

INTERNET ADDICTION

Forewarned is forearmed! I liked the bit where I bought all these little digital clocks and taped them on my monitor.

Date:	Tuesday, April 06, 1999 1:39:19 PM
To:	Peter; Grant; Barry; Bruce; Dodge; Joe O.; Jun; Kirsten; Roberto; Tom; Dale; Davide; Brooke; Greg; Aldo; Nicole; Simon; Mark
Subject:	RE: Check this out

Hey Bruce, I cc'ed my special circle of buddies (there are some Aussies now too, dont mind them), you dont mind right? I didnt want to type everything up again...

Regarding internet chatting, I think you need some practice on the internet chat thing, I thought about it, you have to go through several stages properly before you can take full advantage of it, kinda like a ten step process:

The 10 Stages of Internet Addiction

1. Interest

at this stage you are genuinely amazed at the social network the internet has to offer, and you are curious about learning more. you probably just got a new PC and have a 56K modem. Youre still debating between IE4 and Netscape Navigator.

2. Experimentation

just a couple hops in and there, listening to chats, sometimes piping up to give your own opinion on the war in Iraq or why lesbians should be treated like people too.

3. Honesty

youre probably still using your real name and youve got your age and location and a real email id in your profile too!!!! when chatting with people on the net, youre giving away your real information like your height, weight, where you work etc. Sometimes you'll even tell them how many bros and sisters you have, and what you like to eat. And maybe, if youre really really naive, you'll tell them that you'd like them to be your friend.

4. Back to Experimentation

experimentation has taken a twisted turn and youre now trying out some serious stuff as in talking to single females, and youre reading their profiles and youre matching up their interests with your interests etc. Sometimes if youre really daring, you'll even engage in a little cybering.

5. Realization

pretty soon you realize that the internet is populated by a lot of sick fucks who just go around and pretend theyre chicks and get off telling you theyre guys after youve cybered with them for 2 hours straight. also all those meaningful chicks youve met couldnt really give a rats ass if your dog Lightning died during a cruise missile attack on Iraq. plus you find out all those chicks are fat and ugly and married. when you're sitting at home at 2:00 am in the morning, all naked and covered with peanut butter and youve got a zucchini in your left hand, you know, its time for the next stage, acceptance.

6. Acceptance

now youve accepted the fact that the internet is a sick place. now you can do something about it. Since they hurt you, you can now hurt them. And what better way to fight your enemy by joining them!!!

7. Preparation

start getting little digital clocks and stick them on to your pc so you know all the different time zones, so you can pretend to be Helmut from Germany, or Mei-Mei from China. get a variety of logins, half of them being female nicks such as BustyBlonde or Greta22. Brush up on your foreign languages, you'll need them as the internet has no borders, and you have to abuse people regardless what continent theyre from. Make sure you have your profiles ready in a word document on your desktop so you can have easy access them when you need them. If youre going to be quoting something really complicated such as holy crystals, have them ready in a special document for cut and pasting.

8. Lying

now that youre all set, you can begin lying through your teeth on the internet. join the chat rooms and make sure you sound as believable as you can be. it helps if you dont curse, and you use college vocabulary, they take you seriously. you will be surprised how many positive responses you get. Try and get as many guys as you can to fall in love with you. However, never reveal that you are a guy yourself (hey, you dont want to hurt other guys like those perverts did to you!!!!). And of course, try and get as many girls to fall in love with you too (dont romance them, just be totally outrageous, if you want to be sappy, go buy flowers for your workmate youre infatuated with). Try and get sympathy by telling them that youre too fat to get out of bed so youve hired a midget to change your porno tapes. They love that one!! Remember, people want to believe in what they want to believe in - people dont necessarily want to believe in the truth.

9. Justification

since youve been lying and wreaking havoc on the internet for hours, nay, even DAYS, on end, you will have to justify your demented behavior. Write it up to a mission, such as exposing evil hypocrites or helping lonely people who are deluded into thinking that the internet is a social alternative. that way you'll feel so much better when you get your internet bill.

10. Pain in the jaw or Repentance

at the end of all this, sometimes you get this horrendous migrainlike pain extending from the top of your right eye to your jaw. It could either be punishment from God for messing with people's minds, or it could be because you go to sleep with a perpetual grin on your face because you just told some guy in the chess chat room that you were gonna rip off his training bra and put his panties on his head. This is when you say you'll never be mean again, and please please please let the pain go away so you can eat solid food again.

I hope this helps for those of you interested in internet chatting...

MATCH AND WIN!

Creating cute, inoffensive internet chat nicknames is an art. I always ranked Donald Duck up there with Nepotutu and Magic Koala.

Date:	Sunday, April 11, 1999 5:05 AM
To:	Bruce; Tom; Dale; Joe O.; Barry; Nicole; Mark; Aldo; Greg; Simon; Peter; Grant; Roberto; Dodge; Jun; Kirsten
Subject:	email from that unemployed guy in Sydney

So now that Im bored, I guess I just have to amuse myself in my own special way.

See if you can match up these Donald Duck's responses to the original questions or greetings.

Donald Duck's Response

1. So you got big tits?
2. Sometimes when I take off my clothes, I realize how beautiful I am
3. I'm going to rip off your training bra and put your panties on your head.
4. Im only 12, please dont hurt me.
5. I only wear a pointy crown just in case I get visitors.
6. I already jerked off 10 minutes ago.
7. I love you too.
8. The rubber hose doesnt break any skin.
9. Can we date?
10. Only on Wednesdays.

Original Question/Greeting

A. Hi Donald!
B. How are you Donald!
C. Hello Donald
D. Donald, youre a shithead
E. Donald is on ignore.
F. SHOOTS DUCK.
G. Are you a pervert?
H. Are you for real, Duck?
I. Are you a fag?
J. Im going to pray for you.

Dont worry, I have a lot of stuff I want to do in my free time, make travel plans, straighten out my finances etc., and of course start my book projects, GIMME 10, here I come again!!!

MORE HORRIBLE LIES

I think I reuse my Star Wars material in a later email. Jeanna is such a tramp!

Date:	Tuesday, June 22, 1999 4:56 PM
To:	Bruce; Tom; Dale; Joe O.; Barry; Kirsten; Roberto; Jun; Dodge; Brooke; Aldo; Davide; Grant; Greg; Mark; Peter; Simon
Subject:	More Horrible Lies

Sorry, I've been busy with secret stuff, so I've been lax on my email rampages.

However, on occasion that incorrigible and irreverent Jeanna Walters still manages to get in the action. From recent internet excursions...

Star Wars - The Phantom Menace

Jeanna_Walters:	Hello!
Smiles9000:	Hi Jeanna!
SithLord:	Hi Jeanna!
Jeanna_Walters:	I think The Phantom Menace sucks!
Smiles9000:	Why is that?
SithLord:	No way, TPM is great!
Jeanna_Walters:	Star Wars is full of unbiblical stuff and is evil!
Jeanna_Walters:	Quigon and Obiwan are homo lovers
Jeanna_Walters:	Amidala and Anakin have sex, and Amidala is 4 years older than Anakin! That's like child abuse and rape!!!
Smiles9000:	Quigon and Obiwan aren't gay!!!!
Jeanna_Walters:	If they aren't gay, how come they're always holding their light sabres like penises? Why don't they use guns instead?
SithLord:	I think you're sick Jeanna!
Jeanna_Walters:	That's a funny name you have, ShitLord! That makes me laugh!
SithLord:	That's SithLord not ShitLord, BITCH!!!!
Jeanna_Walters:	Why do you have a pottymouth ShitLord? I think it's because you worship Satan like George Lucas does. Look at Darth

Maul, Darth Maul has penis horns coming out of his head like Satan.

Smiles9000: I think you're reading too much into the movie, Jeanna...

Jeanna_Walters: The original star wars is just as bad, Luke and Leia have sex and that's incest!!!! That's why Darth Vader chopped off Luke's hand because Luke was diddling Leia and Darth Vader got mad at his son!

SithLord: Luke and Leia don't have sex!!! They just kiss!

Jeanna_Walters: And what do Han Solo and Chewbacca do when they're all alone in their spaceship? They have homo bestiality sex!!!

SithLord: BITCH!!!!!

JediKnight: You're full of crap Jeanna!!!

Smiles9000: I think Jeanna is probably just an old guy!

Peanut Butter and the Bakery

Jeanna_Walters: I'm not a guy, I'm a girl and I'm not old, I'm 14

Smiles9000: Oh yeah?? describe yourself

Jeanna_Walters: I'm very pretty and I have big breasts even though I'm just 14.

SithLord: How big are your breasts?

Jeanna_Walters: 36C and they're firm, and the nipples are right in the middle, and they don't have funny hairs.

SithLord: Wow! Can I touch them?

JediKnight: Where do you live Jeanna?

Jeanna_Walters: You can't touch my breasts, that's unbiblical. But my breasts are just the right size and they fit just right in a guy's hand, so my dad says.

Smiles9000: Your dad???? Why does your dad touch your breasts?

Jeanna_Walters: Well, he's got to, how else can Dad put the peanut butter on my breasts?

JediKnight: Peanut butter?

Jeanna_Walters: Yeah, Dad's friends pay 5 bucks to lick the peanut butter off my breasts. Or 10 bucks off my armpits, 'cause it's messier. I make 200 bucks a week, I can buy a lot of CDs and shoes with that money.

SithLord: That's not biblical! And your dad shouldn't be touching your breasts!

JediKnight: Shouldn't you be doing something else other than pimping for your dad?

Jeanna_Walters: I work in a bakery with my dad, it's so hot in the bakery that I usually work without my top on. That's where we got the idea for the peanut butter.

Smiles9000: Which bakery is that?

Jeanna_Walters: Tasty Tops
JediKnight: Which city and state?
Jeanna_Walters: Warren, Michigan
SithLord: I'll see you there, BITCH!!!!

Monkey People

Jeanna_Walters: I think you like to curse and insult, because you're a monkey person and you have satan in your heart.
SithLord: Monkey people?
Jeanna_Walters: Yeah, you know, Asians, Africans, Arabs etc.
SecretAgent: That is bullshit!!!! white people come from monkeys too!
Jeanna_Walters: No way, white people come from Adam and Eve!
SecretAgent: So where do monkey people come from?
Jeanna_Walters: Ishmael had sex with monkeys and that's where monkey people come from.
SithLord: Are you racist Jeanna?
Jeanna_Walters: I'M NOT RACIST!!! I've got nothing against monkey people, my best friend is Indonesian and she's a monkey person.
SithLord: Did you tell her she was a monkey person?
Jeanna_Walters: Yeah, Dewey cried when I told her she was a monkey person and that she won't go to heaven because monkey people don't have souls.
SecretAgent: YOU BITCH!!!!!!!!
Jeanna_Walters: I felt bad too, but maybe there's a monkey heaven for monkey people so I told her she might go to monkey heaven.
SithLord: You're so full of shit!!!
SecretAgent: BITCH!!!!
Smiles9000: BITCH!!!!!
JediKnight: Jeanna Walters is the BIGGEST BITCH IN THE WORLD!!!

There you go, I probably managed to insult 70 - 80 percent of people from all walks of life. That will teach these people to be hanging around the internet!!! It's a sick world out there!!! Don't go to the net! It's satanic!!

I MADE A LOT OF PEOPLE CRY ON THE INTERNET YESTERDAY

I nearly cried myself.

Date:	Wednesday, July 18, 2001 7:18 AM
To:	none *(blind copy)*
Subject:	I made a lot of people cry on the internet yesterday

Last night I was on internet chat again, and I was asking if any girls would like to date a guy in a wheelchair.

A lot of people asked me how I lost my legs. So I gave them a very sad story (I elaborated on my gulf war routine). Most of them wanted to be my friend afterwards.

I told them I was in an infantry unit in Iraq. Our unit had adopted a stray dog, and we called him Lightning. One day, our dog ran out into the desert where we knew there were mines. So I chased after the dog to save him. When I was carrying the dog in my arms back to camp. I accidentally stepped on a landmine. The landmine took my legs below my kneestumps. But luckily, the blast didn't take away my dingdongs.

Then I told them how my girlfriend broke up with me when I got back from the war because I didn't have legs. I said that before the accident, my girlfriend and I used to go jogging together, but now I couldn't keep up with her because I was in a wheelchair. So she broke up with me because she's really into sports.

A lot of the people got mad at the "girlfriend".

Then I told them that now for kicks I go to the park and do "wheelies" for a couple of dollars for tourists. But I assured them I was well taken care of because of a huge insurance payout for my legs. Which is how I could afford my customized BMW with special brake and accelerator pedals for my knee stumps.

One girl said I sounded like a really nice person and wanted to be my friend. Sniff.

If only the magic_koala could find a way to make money off his special talent.

2

THE GENTLEMAN GAMBLER

> There is but one good throw upon the dice
> which is to throw them away.
>
> *Chatfield*

> If you were born lucky, even your rooster
> will lay eggs.
>
> *Russian Proverb*

TRIPLE SEVENS

Sydney's Star City Casino will always have a special place in my heart.

Date:	Monday, 4 May 1998 9:23AM
To:	Barry; Bruce; Dale; Dodge; Jun; Kevin; Lynn; Roberto
Subject:	Casino Drama

Despite a paper loss of $12/share for my EDS stock in the last 4 weeks (and I've got a lot of it), I remained optimistic about my financial situation. Determined to offset my financial setbacks, I obtained several different kinds of blackjack programs to sharpen my gambling skills.

Unfortunately, as blackjack is played with 8 decks here, and I'm pretty much hopeless when it comes to counting cards, I relied on my usual technique of applying the rules, and backing the good players.

Sunday was the showdown, so I got to the casino and made sure there weren't too many old crotchety people who have x-ray vision or psychic powers and who bother me when they tell me their idiotic reasons on why they didn't pull a card on a 16 when the dealer was showing a 10, or why they look at me strangely when I pull on a 16 and the dealer has a 10. By the way I was playing on a table that had super sevens (if you place an extra buck out, and you get 2 sevens, you get $100, if you get three sevens, you get $500).

I was situated between a Chinese guy, and an Australian-Asian guy. I might as well have replaced the two with the crotchety old people I was talking about, as the Chinese guy didn't know how to play the rules, and played in super slow motions. The Aus-Asian guy had x-ray vision, so whenever somebody didn't play the rules, he'd pipe up and say how the wrong pull messed him, but then he'd do something stupid like stand on a 16 on a non-dealer bust card!). Plus he had bad breath.

The first drama came when after twenty or so hands (and everybody on the table places an extra buck for the super sevens, but I don't because nobody ever gets it), I got one seven. Everybody went "Oh, you didn't put a buck!", then I got another seven and everybody went "You should've put a buck! You would've gotten $100!", the dealer says: "You gotta pull another one just so we'll know". But the dealer had a bust card showing, and I was in no mood to split, so I stood. So everybody's screaming now "oh, c'mon pull another card!". Then the guy next to me hits and he gets my seven! The table just goes nuts now, and everybody's yelling "That's $500 mate!", the Asian girl (kinda cute) was shaking her head and saying: "Why didn't you take another card? $500! Give me the $500!". Later somebody had to explain to her that I didn't put the extra buck out anyway. But I won my $5 on that hand anyway. The whole night the table reminded me of my super sevens drama.

The second drama came when the crazy Chinese guy next to me started banging on the table on his fist when the dealer didn't let him place his bets after she started dealing the cards out. The Asian guy was just yelling and asking to see the supervisor and rerun the videotapes. But customer service isn't very big in Australia (the dealer really was at fault, she was too quick and impatient), so after 15 minutes (and I wasn't making any money) of play stoppage, they took away some of his bets, but the funny thing was, he got 2 sevens, and he got $100! Everybody was kinda upset because he made such a big stink and he got rewarded for it.

Anyway, the biggest decision that night was if I could walk away from the table with my winnings, and since I had enough of bad tempered fist-banging (Ashok-type) Chinese guy and the x-ray vision guy, I cashed in my winnings and left. Now I only have to go back to the casino 120 more times and win $100 each time to make up my EDS stock loss. I can do it, BABY!

MR. NUTTYBUDDY PLAYS BLACKJACK

Just fun and games, of course.

Date:	Tuesday, June 16, 1998 4:24 PM
To:	Bruce; Barry; Dodge; Davide; Dale; Keith; Jun; Joe O.; Kevin; Chris; Greg; Roberto; Tom; Mark; Simon
Subject:	Casino Action

Hey Boys,

Thought you guys might like to know the latest casino action story. As you know, the Dino magic has been going strong at the blackjack table for the last two weeks. After last night, I remain undefeated with 5 wins and 1 draw against the Star City casino (the Sydney casino). With a staggering $400 in profit (okay, it's not a lot, but as we all know, it's hard to get away with any money at all).

Remember, 'The Goose' from Mr. NuttyBuddy's Soapbox? Well each time we go to the tables, guess who 'The Goose' is now? ME! Except of course, I play by the book. Usually now, we'll sit at the last two boxes and dominate the game play. Last night some people met up with us (us means me and Dave, little Irish-Australian guy), and apparently Dave and I were so loud, they could hear us yelling and hooting outside the Coral Room before they even entered the Coral Room.

I especially enjoy it when the table starts blaming me if I pull a card and cause them to lose their money. This Asian woman was giving me dagger-eyes because she had double-downed on a couple of hands, and I had pulled on a 13 versus a dealer's 2 (hey, the book says pull!). She was waving her hands, hitting her forehead etc. And the best part was I simply scrunched up my face, shrugged my shoulders, and gave her the Mr. NuttyBuddy smile: "Aaaawwwww, I'm soooorrrry". Ha! Pretty hard to distinguish between Dino and Mr. NuttyBuddy now, as last night I unconsciously started performing subtle psychological warfare against my fellow table players. So a lot of the times when the table lost, who do they blame? The anchor, or as I'm affectionately called, 'The goose at the end'! So what did Mr. NuttyBuddy do? Everybody had stacks of money sitting on their boxes, and the dealer had a bust card, and I had two 2s. Naturally everybody was waiting for me to make my move since this was just a classic textbook play, so what I did was I turned to the woman backing me, and said" Your call, lady". The table turns pretty silent, because at least with me they could predict what I was going to do (by the book you know). So the lady does her moves (nearly textbook but not quite). And the whole table loses (I only lost $5 so who gives a rat's ass, but the table didn't fare as well). And then Mr. NuttyBuddy pipes up and says: "See what happens when the anchor doesn't play?" What an asshole, huh? And for the rest of the night, nobody complained anymore. LOVED IT!

ACCUSATIONS

A fine example of Star City customer service.

Date:	Monday, June 29, 1998 4:52 PM
To:	Bruce; Barry; Dodge; Davide; Dale; Jun; Joe O.; Kevin; Greg; Roberto; Tom; Simon
Subject:	Nearly Got Kicked Out

Whew! I am extremely disappointed in the Sydney Casino! Last night I was nearly escorted out! I was just minding my business (and I wasn't my usually loud boisterous obnoxious casino asshole personality "the goose"), and having a rum and coke playing the $10 table with a fellow from work, when this pit boss comes around and asks me and this lady to give back $10 to the dealer. Apparently, the dealer had mistakenly paid us out some 5 minutes ago and we weren't supposed to have won the money. Well, Mr. NuttyBuddy doesn't exactly cater to accusations without any evidence, so Mr. NuttyBuddy pipes up and says: "I'll pay you the $10 when you show me the video". And the bastard replies: "Sir, we really don't want to take this any further than necessary". ?????? The punk is threatening to kick me out! What the heck? Mr. NuttyBuddy messed around for another 5 mins before giving in, but was very disappointed. Isn't it like when they scan something wrong in the supermarket, the product is free?

The iniquity of it all!

SIDE INCOME

Always take somebody with you to the casino. So you can borrow from that person when you lose all your money.

Date:	Wednesday, July 29, 1998 4:04 PM
To:	Bruce; Barry; Dale; Joe O.; Tom
Subject:	More Casino Action

The titanic struggle between good and evil continues! We were supposed to have some kinda department social activity last night celebrating end of year stuff. So Dan and I head off to the Republic and get there at 5:45 pm (drinks supposed to start at 5:30 pm). But nobody's there! So we said, screw this, let's go to Star City Casino instead! It was an incredible battle, at first I was feeling pretty upbeat winning the mediocre sum of $25 with a $100 stake. But the decks turned, and I was down to $2.50 from a peak of $125. It was desperate times, and I had to double down with $2.50 remaining on a $5 bet. So I had to borrow $2.50 from Dan to double up.

From $2.50 I managed to build up to the glorious pot of $350 in one hour or so! And I stopped at that and took my profit of $250! Money to pay the bills! I love it!

MAKING MONEY FOR CHICKS

I must defeat Star City Casino…

Date:	Friday, 31 July 1998 8:25 AM
To:	Bruce; Barry; Dale; Tom; Joe O.
Subject:	Casino Action Part V

So again, it was another session of blackjack at my beloved Star City. Knowing that my winning or losing streaks are usually 5 runs, last night's session was still guaranteed to be a winning night, before I begin the 5 sessions losing streak.

In the end I won a paltry a $35 but probably more since I had 2 - 3 rum and cokes, bringing my 5 sessions total close to $500. However, mediocre as my profits were, the most interesting event of the night was this Chinese Indonesian woman who was backing my puny $5 bet with $125-$150 bets. She was quite attractive for a mid-30s kinda woman, and her geriatric father was standing behind her. Apparently she had lost $10,000 the night before. Typical superstitious Asian she berated my fellow gambling addict friend Dave for opening up more than 5 boxes (claiming that 5 boxes is better than 6 or 7 boxes), but she was attractive so I didn't defend Dave. She was also quite devoid of social graces and would call the next person to her stupid because he wouldn't pull on a sixteen But again, she was attractive so I didn't really mind. I must've played my best blackjack ever with the pressure mounting on me to deliver wins for my $125-$150 back-better. There was spine-tingling moment when I had to split 8s (always split 8s), so now she had $300 sitting out. And then I doubled down on one of the 8s, so now she had $450 sitting out (I had $15 out). AND WE WON! I must've won $1500 - $2000 for that woman. But she didn't even give me any money for my troubles, or pinch my ass or anything.

Maybe tonight I'll go again.

THE PERFECT NIGHT

I can't seem to get away from this place.

Date:	Friday, 7 August 1998 9:46
To:	Bruce; Barry; Brooke; Dodge; Davide; Dale; Aldo; Jun; Joe O.; Kevin; Greg; Roberto; Tom; Mark; Simon
Subject:	Casino/Drinking/CHICK Action EXTRAVAGANZA

Hello My Friends!

Unfortunately, the casino stories just keep on rolling in! I just love Australia! Where else in the world do you have casinos within walking distance from your work (Adelaide, Melbourne, Sydney... I rest my case).

Being on support this week has been a little hectic, and the GREAT ONE desperately needed some action similar to Trivia Night to liven up the week. Thankfully, Star City Casino was there to help! It was 5:30 pm, and I rounded up the posse (Grant and Dave) to get to the casino by 6:00 pm. Unfortunately it was raining buckets and we didn't get there until 6:30 or so.

My favorite room, the Coral Room was packed and this rude Asian guy didn't want me to play my favorite position, the ANCHOR, instead he offered to let me back-bet him. Screw that, Mr. NuttyBuddy plays HIS OWN BOX, BABY! So

Dave finds his box, but Grant and I are left box-less, so we head off to the main gambling area, and we settle at the midget table (it's a table where the chairs are really really low, for handicapped people really). We each put out a $100, and began placing the bets. The Anchor was this Japanese guy who was even a better textbook player than I am, so I could rely on him to make the hard calls. It was a tough slog in the beginning, but when the dealer CHICKS arrived, Danielle (perky little fake blonde), and Mary (cute little brunette with a very light mustache), we started raking in some bucks! As the Sydney water poisoning has been remedied, the casino started putting ice again in their rum and cokes, which of course, watered down the alcohol content. I remarked to Grant, "Gee, the drinks sure are going fast, aren't they?". It took us 6 - 7 rum or scotch and cokes to get to that zen-like state. By this time, I was betting/backing boxes with chipped up bets, and had nearly $200 in profit.

I must've been getting really loud because the pit boss and dealer were evaluating my condition (dealers can't deal to drunk people). I was high-fiving, and shaking hands wildly with the Japanese anchor who was raking in the big money, and was betting $75 on three boxes as well (he later lost everything, he never chipped down). By this time Samantha, tall blonde with rabbit teeth with a pushed-up bra starts back-betting me, and we all start to lose. I say to Grant, "Grant, we've been here for 5 hours, and we still haven't lost, let's go get dinner and leave". Grant just bet the last of his winnings, so he agrees. So I take my $170 profit, and we head towards the sports bar restaurant. At this stage, we had totally forgotten Dave, the third member of the posse.

Being the winner of the two, I magnanimously offered to shout for dinner (when the GREAT ONE wins, everybody rides for free MAN!). So I get the prawns and fries, and Grant goes get some other junk food. We leave the food on the table, and go get some condiments and cutlery (leaving the fine feast unattended!). From the corner of my eyes, I see these two hussies in black coats walk past our table. Incredibly, the tall hussy picks up one of my french fries and eats it! She turns around confident that no one saw her, but in there she is mistaken, for being a persistent gambler, my eyes have developed the uncanny ability to pick things out of order, and what I saw, WAS JUST NOT RIGHT! So I yell out (she's 10 yards away from me) "Hey hey hey!". And she turns around, realizes she's been caught and waves at me. At this point, I can see that the two hussies are somewhat attractive. I start pointing fingers and shaking my head at her, while she keeps on smiling, waving and saying thank you. So she leans over the railing, says thank you again, we shake hands, and do a thumb-lock just to show that there were no hard feelings (no double-entendre there!). So the two CHICKS come round again with their own food, and ask if they can sit with us. One of them is Kate, who looks like Ginger Spice, and the other is Kylie (the one who ate my french fries), who doesn't remind me of anybody but she was mighty fine looking Australian girl. Kylie started eating my french fries again, and Ginger Spice wanted some of my prawns but said she can't eat them because of the heads. So I took off the heads, peeled the prawns and fed Ginger Spice some prawns. Kylie is still eating the french fries. Kylie and I start talking about the gambling problem in Australia, and Katie tells us how they nearly got into a fight with two American girls who called them white Aussie trash (shame shame). Suddenly Kylie's mobile rings, and it's her boyfriend asking where she is. Katie says Kylie's boyfriend was in the Olympics as a boxer. Well, that pretty much ruled out any future action that night. Why bother messing with the girlfriend of a skinhead boxer (whom we later saw when we were walking out, he kinda looked like a brute). Kylie sounds a little confused, and she starts asking me if being an Olympic boxer was "good". Kylie still doesn't want to let go of me, and says she wants to buy me a drink, I tell her, we've already had 6 or 7, but if she finds me later, she can buy me a drink. To which Kylie replies "and if I can't find you, my loss, huh?". YES BABY, YOUR LOSS!

Hmmm, I myself was getting confused now what the hell the vibes were. The girls stood up, and Kylie's still insisting she wants to buy me a drink, I politely decline (heck, there's a freaking boxer lurking somewhere), so Kylie kisses me on the cheek instead. YES! I'VE STILL GOT IT! JOE DINO, SEX MAGNET EXTRAORDINAIRE! WHOOOHOOO! When they left, I grabbed the drink Kylie was drinking from, and drank from it, explaining to Grant that that was nearly the same as kissing Kylie on the mouth. And since it was midnight, it was a good time to pick up our coats, catch a taxi and go home, with my winnings in my pocket.

What can I say? I won $170, had 6-7 rum and cokes, had some CHICK action, and didn't get beat up by the boxer. FANTASTIC!

I FINALLY WON A SUPERBOWL BET

For once, I'm a winner... The sex store story is actually pretty funny.

Date:	Sunday, January 30, 2000 8:28 PM
To:	Bruce; Dale; Barry; Joe O.; Tom; Simon; Aldo; Brooke; Davide; Greg; Helen; Yvette; Maria; Kirsten; Dodge; Jun; Roberto
Subject:	I finally won a SUPERBOWL BET!!!!

SuperBowl

Yeah, I finally did it!!!! After years of placing a bet with the casino on a team, I finally won. The Rams did it for me!!! I won 67 dollars off a 50 dollar bet!!! So thats a big profit of 17 bucks!!!

So after $15 taxi, $18 breakfast, $40 pokies, $6 fare back home, so thats only a 62 dollar loss today!!! DAMN YOU STAR CITY!!! DAMN YOU TO HELLL!!!!!!!

And the worst thing, I gotta go back to Star City collect my money.

Porno

Hey, you know the situation when you go into an adult store and youre always scared that somebody you know might see you walking in or walking out of the store? Well, this Saturday, Dan and I went to Chinatown to have all-you-can-eat BBQ, so after that we went to the bakery to get some pastries, then while we were carrying the pastry, we passed by this adult store, and I asked Dan if he had ever been to one. And Dan said he never did because he was too scared to go and that somebody might see him go in/go out.

I said "NONSENSE!!!! WHAT ARE THE CHANCES!!!".

So we go inside the adult store and I show him all the interesting sections: the bondage, the granny, the ethnic, the homo, the big dildos etc. Anyway, that was all fun and games, and weve had enough so we walk out. And Dan is saying "good thing that nobody saw us", then we started talking about prostitutes and brothels and were walking up the street when somebody slaps my head from the back! I turn around and its Rowena (from my old work) and her husband!!!! Ha ha ha!!! So she asks us what were doing, and I just wave my bag of pastries at her, and say "oh were just buying pastry!" I dont think she saw us go to the adult store though.

Deuce Bigalow - Male Gigolo

I saw that yesterday and walked out halfway through the movie. It was just very lame. I paid full-price too.

3

GLUTTONY

Eat, drink and be merry, for tomorrow, ye diet.
William Gilmore Beymer

Never eat more than you can lift.
Miss Piggy

ALL YOU CAN EAT RIBS

First crack at Tony Roma's ribs...

Date:	Friday, September 17, 1999 10:34 AM
To:	Dodge; Jun; Roberto; Rowena; Nicole; Karen; Helen; Alicia; Brooke; Aldo; Dan; Davide; Derryn; Greg; Mark; Peter; Simon; Kevin; Kirsten; Bruce; Dale; Barry; Joe; Tom; Maria; Yvette
Subject:	All-You-Can-Eat-Ribs

Hello Dear Dear Friends!!!!

I had the distinct pleasure last night of engaging in the ever-favorite all-you-can-eat-ribs at Tony Roma's last night, but before that...

PROBLEMS AT WORK

So after a long day at work in which I had to resolve some internal issues with the company. Basically, my company (GDI Australia) in Australia was refusing to set me up/pay for my temporary lodging when I returned to Sydney. I, however, contested that flagrant violation of my ideal of company-employee relations. I sent off a long and verbose email (similar to the emails I send you guys) with lots of difficult words worthy of Rogets and complex sentence structures declaring my displeasure of being financially penalized for an obvious blunder and poor planning and mismanagement on the company's part. Anyway, I sent off the tirade and specifically said that I was "NOT HAPPY" with the unprofessional arrangements being offered as options. And of course, we all know what "NOT HAPPY" really means to someone who is as one-track minded on personal happiness as I am.

VICTORY

So just as I was about to leave the office (around 4:30 pm or so, I come in at 7:00 am), my manager grabs me and asks me to stay until he has a chance to talk to me. So I hang around until 5:30 pm during which I did nothing but send off emails to my favorite people. Finally, the manager and I meet and discuss the above issue, and the only thing he says is "I AGREE WITH YOU". YES!!!! IN YOUR FACE, GDI AUSTRALIA! You don't mess with the MAN!!!!! So the manager said he'll take care of it, and all he wants to do is make sure that there is nothing that will make me NOT come back to Los Angeles.

RIBS

So after that I went off to the mall to check out some gift ideas at the Borders bookstore, but it got really confusing because they had thousands and thousands of books, and I only got away with one book. After which I picked up fatboy, and we headed off to Tony Roma's. Unbeknownst to us, they had just started their All-You-Can-Eat-Ribs specials. They didn't list the price anywhere but it's actually just the cost of a full slab of ribs (15-17 bucks for a full slab depending on the type of ribs). So what can you lose? I remember going there with Bruce and I don't know how many ribs we finished off but it's not that easy.

But they trick you, they offer you all the appetizers, stuff you with salad and bread and potato, and of course fill you up with unlimited ice tea and coke. So by the time the ribs come out, you're full!!! So the full slab comes out, and we just stick the rib in our mouths and suck the meat straight off the bone (pretty soft those baby back ribs).

I even got the big plastic bibs that fatboy didn't want to put on at first. I had around 15-16 ribs on that slab, but I'm just a machine so we just order some more. The next batch was 5-6 ribs each. They went down okay but I noticed that I had rib taste all the way up to my chest now, and they weren't going down as fast anymore.

The next batch was another 5-6 ribs each again, but this time the machine was breaking down, and I couldn't get the ribs down below my throat without wanting to vomit all over the place. There's only so much sweet smokey meat that you can chow down.

LESBIAN PORNO

To give our stomachs some breathing space, we discussed one of my favorite tenets of believing in what is right and not necessarily what is legal. He really didn't quite understand it, so I had to give him some examples of society's fleeting fancy with the law. For example, slavery was legal 200 years ago but that wasn't right, now was it? Lesbianism was classified legally as deviant behavior less than 30 years ago in the US. Similarly, porno was unavailable legally in many US states. But today, most everyone can enjoy an afternoon of lesbian porno videos in the privacy of their homes. Not that I'm condoning or promoting such issues; far be it from me to walk where angels fear to tread.

GAVE UP ON THE RIBS

We were contemplating going "Roman" so we could put away some more ribs, but that would've been really debaucherous, so we just gave up. But next time, I'll be better prepared. Next time, three slabs each, minimum.

Thank goodness it's Friday today.

KICKED ASS!

I had to go back and teach them a lesson.

Date:	Wednesday, September 22, 1999 10:10 AM
To:	Dodge; Jun; Roberto; Rowena; Nicole; Karen; Helen; Alicia; Brooke; Aldo; Dan; Davide; Derryn; Greg; Mark; Peter; Simon; Kevin; Kirsten; Bruce; Dale; Barry; Joe O.; Tom; Maria; Yvette
Subject:	KICKED ASS!

Hello Dear Dear Friends!

I feel I just had to share this monumental achievement with my dear dear friends, so please indulge me with this short yet satisfying account of two men's battle against all odds.

So yesterday was a sad and unpleasant day in the personal life of the Great One, but thankfully I had some plans for the evening which would paint back the smile on the clown's frown (look, it rhymes, will the clown never stop?). As you all remember last week, Grant and I experienced all-you-can-eat ribs at Tony Roma's. And I had around 24-26 ribs (that's just a slab and a half), and I faulted that mediocre performance to unfair tactics used by the restaurant personnel to fill us up with appetizers, soups, salads, breads and drinks. Lying in bed and thinking about how I was deprived of my true potential by Tony Roma, I was determined to return to that fine establishment and teach Tony Roma a lesson he'd never forget.

So I made plans with Bruce, a dear dear friend, to head over to Tony Roma's after work. We got there just before six, and this time no monkeying around. George, our waiter, attempted to cheat us early by offering those silly chicken wings and onion loafs. No go, George! Just give me the baby back ribs and let the machine do its work. George tried to give us a salad and soup. I said NO SOUP AND NO SALAD! JUST GIVE ME RIBS! But I somehow got the meat soup anyway, but I didn't touch any of that. George brought out some bread too, but he might as well have been bringing chicks to Keanu Reeves, it just wasn't gonna happen, GEORGE!!!!! BRING ON THE RIBS, BABY!!!!!!!!

George, knew he had some serious customers here, and unlike last time when I waited more than 10 mins for the first slab to come out, the first slab of 14 ribs came out in a minute or two. So Bruce and I dug in with slow and meticulous bites. Fortunately, I had just eaten one taco for lunch, just enough to expand my stomach for tonight's ordeal. The ribs were piling up, baby!!!!! Pretty soon, the little ribs were piling up. George came by and wanted to take away the gnawed ribs, but I said: "We're still counting". So George left the plates of bones. Truly George was in for the service of his life. George was great though, as soon as we were down to the last 2-3 ribs, he'd come out with 2 racks of 4 ribs each (one rack for me, one for Bruce). I'm not gonna bore you with all the glorious and gory details, and the number of trips we had to take the bathroom to wash our faces and hands (we didn't go Roman though!), but suffice it to say. We reordered 7 TIMES. Finally George, couldn't stand it anymore with the huge pile of bones on our table, and the bus boy came out and took the ribs. And George came by and gave us a receipt on how many reorders we did. We had 28 ribs on the original order, and 56 ribs on reorders. Making that a grand total of 84 ribs. However, as can be expected, the taste of ribs had now skyrocketed to the roof of my mouth, and should Bruce have said a really funny joke or pinched my arm, I would've been hurling all over the table, and I had to call it quits after 42 ribs. Bruce was more machine than man, and requested another 8 ribs to make it an even 50 ribs for the evening. It's too bad I couldn't keep up, because it would've been great to do 100 ribs. 42 RIBS! THAT'S 3 SLABS! A slab being the length from my elbow to my index finger.

IN YOUR FACE, TONY ROMA, IN YOUR FACE!!!!!!!

After we had finished, and started entering that catatonic phase where nothing else mattered, there was this extreme feel of contentment. Quite frankly, after that experience, I don't feel like eating ever again. Any future case of colon cancer, I can surely attribute it to the night of Sep 21.

Sleeping that night was quite painful, as digesting that much food is quite stressful. And I could hardly walk to work without breaking out into a sweat. I think I'll just eat fruit today.

COMPETITION ANNOUNCEMENT

Challengers wanted!!!

Date:	Monday, May 15, 2000 3:20 PM
To:	Grant; Helen; Aldo; Brooke; Davide; Greg; Simon; Maria; Yvette; Bruce; Barry; Joe O.; Tom; Kirsten; Craig; Dan; Derryn; Grant; Karen; Rowena; Dodge; Jun; Roberto; Julie; Eunice; Devin; Belen; Oscar; Nancye; Alison
Subject:	Australia vs USA

It is with great pleasure that I can announce the upcoming blockbuster event!

DATE & TIME: MAY 18, 2000, 6:00 PM
VENUE: TONY ROMA ON VENTURA BLVD, ENCINO, CALIFORNIA
TONY ROMA - ALL-YOU-CAN-EAT-RIBS CHALLENGE

AUSTRALIA VERSUS USA

AUSSIE Challenger:

Name: Grant ("Sex-Magnet")
Home Town: Walla-Walla Outback, Australia
Age: 30s but says when he was younger he looked like Kirk Douglas
Weight: Impressive
Hobbies & Activities: Audio/Video, Exotic Movies

Past Record: Unknown but we can see what he's capable of

USA Challenger and Current Champion:

Name: Bruce ("Boy")
Home Town: Cornfields of Simi Valley, California
Age: 30s - but blond highlights make him look so much younger
Weight: Fluctuating but can be impressive
Hobbies & Activities: Rollerblading & Cats
Past Record: 50 ribs (without vomiting)

SURPRISE Challenger (representing his Shaolin Temple):

Name: ("Crazy") Albert
Home Town: 7th Shaolin Temple of the 5000 Laughing Buddhas, Wu-Tang, China
Age: 30s - but has the energy of a nubile sixteen-year-old medieval wench
Weight: 170 lbs of compact lap-chiong
Hobbies: Ballroom Dancing and People's Leftovers
Past Record: Unknown but his appetite is legendary

HONORARY Challenger:

Name: Joe ("Filipini-Weenie") Dino
Home Town: Star City Casino, Sydney
Age: Mild yet Evocative
Weight: A cunning 130 lbs
Hobbies: Comic books and creative furniture making
Past Record: 42 ribs (without vomiting)

HAS-TO-YET-MAKE-UP-HIS-MIND Challenger:

Name: Devin (the Devil)
Home Town: Woody Hills, California
Age: Comfortable with himself
Weight: Makes Joe Dino's car creak
Hobbies: Oiling his 20-inch chainsaw
Past Record: CLAIMS he can do 3 slabs (42 ribs) - unsubstantiated

This is by no means the complete list of challengers, and last-minute challengers are welcome to rise up to the task (it's around $17 for all-you-can-eat on Thursdays).

Spectators are encouraged to drop by to show their support, and perhaps dab dry the perspiring foreheads of these brave fellows willing to increase the risk of unnecessary colon cancer.

Historical Note: On September 21, 1999, the current record of 50 ribs was set by Bruce B. versus Joe Dino's 42 ribs at Tony Roma's, thus defeating Philippines and keeping the title crown in the USA.

RIB EATING PREPARATION

Strategy is needed to win the war.

Date:	Thursday, May 18, 2000 10:51 AM
To:	Bruce; Devin; Albert; Joe O.; Grant; Oscar
Cc:	Maria; Yvette; Barry
Subject:	cleared up my bowels today!!!

whew, I had to do some intense preparation last night for the rib fest today I went to Pollo Loco for dinner, put down some of their salsa (always gets me going), and then went home and ate two giant mangoes and drank orange juice - I had to lie down on the sofa and not move for a while and let the mangoes do their work this morning, as expected, the foul poisons were cleansed from my body in all their entirety now I feel expanded yet delightfully empty

RIBFEST 2000 – THE RESULTS

It was epic.

Date:	Friday, May 19, 2000 10:56 AM
To:	Vinh; Belen; Lesli; Oscar; Albert; Devin; Sandra; Manuela; Bettina; Dodge; Jun; Roberto; Rowena; Karen; Derryn; Dan; Grant; Charles; Craig; Kirsten; Bruce; Barry; Joe O.; Tom; Yvette; Maria; Eunice; Keith; Chris; Mark; Nitin; Helen; Aldo; Brooke; Davide; Greg; Simon; Nancye; Alison
Subject:	RibFest 2000 - The Results

Dear Dear Friends,

Some of you may have already been aware that last night, a battle was raging at Tony Roma's, Burbank, California for the All-You-Can-Eat Rib-Eating Championship Crown.

A field of combatants from all over God's Green Earth was assembled to showcase their prodigious talents. The entries were (including their nom du guerre):

USA Challenger: Bruce "Boy" - record: 50 ribs - current champion

Aussie Challenger: Grant "Sex-Magnet" - record unknown - has done all-you-can-eat before

Mexico Challenger: Oscar "Macho" - record unknown but talked a lot of pre-competition trash

Kung Fu Challenger: "Crazy" Albert - record unknown but highly rated as he calls himself the "Garbage Meister"

Philippine Challenger: Joe "Filipini-Weenie" Dino - record 42 ribs - runner-up from last time

Sri Lanka/Sweden Challenger: David "I like to give a rat's ass about other people's salaries so I can complain about how overpaid/underpaid they are, and then I can bitch about my own sorry-ass job to people who don't give a rat's ass about it either"

It is with some regret that some notable challengers who may have been serious contenders dropped out last minute, perhaps in light of the high-caliber contestants. I won't mention Joe O. by name because it might embarrass him, but needless to say, we knew who the real HEROES were that night.

As we had originally built this up from an Australia versus USA challenge to an international event, some of us did some preparation for last night's event. My technique was to expand my stomach yet empty it by the next day - this consisted of dinner being mexican chicken with plenty of hot salsa, and two giant mangoes downed with orange juice. This resulted in bloating that night, and of course, a purging of the foul poisons the next morning. Bruce made a careful selection of lunch - fish - light yet filling but which made him hungry as dinnertime approached. The suitable loose pants and belts were also considered by the contestants. I tried some mind-games with Albert as I had Maria send over my meatball sandwich and a slice of pizza to Albert for lunch - to fill him up with slow-digestable food. But Albert ate that and his own lunch, and even thanked me for it. Oscar talked trash for a couple of days, and even made silly bets because he was positive he'd kick everybody's ass. However, we did take up Oscar on "losers pay for the winner's meal".

The original location was Tony Roma's, Encino, but as I called two nights prior, I was disheartened to discover that the manager (silly Asian woman!!!!) had cancelled all-you-can-eat-ribs on Thursdays because of some bullshit that "rib prices went up last month". She even lied that no Tony Roma's offered all-you-can-eat-ribs on Thursdays anymore. Maybe she had recognized my voice as I had eaten all-you-can-eat-ribs there 3 times prior already. But I called up Tony Roma's in Burbank and being that Sweet Baby Jesus looks upon us with great favor and love, we were blessed that Burbank was still offering all-you-can-eat-ribs.

I booked a reservation for 8 people (two spectators were coming) for 6:30, and we all finally got there at around 6:30-6:45.

So six of us ordered the all-you-can-eat-baby back ribs (at around $17-$18 bucks/apiece). The first slab was 10 ribs, and subsequent ribs came in racks of threes. Albert spurted to 3 ribs ahead of us, so clearly Albert was the man to beat. We reached 20 ribs each (two slabs) with no problems, and at this time Tony Roma decided to play their little mind-games with us and slow us down by serving us reorders every 15 minutes at 3 racks each (this took forever!!!). Albert had to leave at 8:30 to go dancing and he was up to 38 at 8:15 pm. I was at 32 at this time. Finally, Tony Roma couldn't stand us anymore and chose to overwhelm us by giving us two plates of 3 slabs each. And this was the amazing part, Albert ate 13 ribs in 10-15 minutes to give him an unsurpassable lead of 51 ribs (thus breaking the current record of 50). Each time Albert picked up a rack of three, it sent shivers down my spine as I could hardly tear off any more meat off the rib without gagging. Bruce conceded with 40 ribs to Albert's 51 ribs, and I eventually gave up with 40 as well. At 8:30, Albert stood up, smacked his lips and said: "Gotta go dancing! Bye bye!".

Albert humbled us mere mortals.

We were there till 9:00 pm and if Albert had stayed past 8:30, goodness knows how many ribs Albert would have eaten. The amazing thing was, Albert never left his chair for the two hours except for the one time when we sent Albert to the restroom to look for Bruce who had dubiously disappeared for 10 minutes. Considering that the first slab tastes the best, the second slab loses its flavor, the third slab tastes like paper, and anything after the third slab is simply disgusting, anything more than 3 slabs is worthy. Albert did 5 slabs without breaking a sweat. The last slab (10 ribs) consumed in under 10 minutes.

We paid the bill (paid for Albert too, that's the least we could do for the Garbage Meister), and staggered out of Tony Roma's. I barely made it to the car as walking wreaked havoc with my stomach. I nearly passed out when I got to the car and tried to spew forth the evil spirits in the parking structure but only succeeded in getting rid of some iced tea. I thought "Oh crap, I'm gonna vomit in my car driving home", but I made it home okay and managed to throw up 4 times to get rid of some of the 40 ribs sitting like bricks in my upper intestines. That night, I had nightmares and dreamt that Albert had died from eating too many ribs.

The final tally (may be slightly inaccurate but who cares, Albert kicked everybody's ass):

1st Albert: 51 ribs
2nd Bruce: 40 ribs
2nd Joe: 40 ribs
3rd Grant: 35-36 ribs
Oscar: 30 ribs
Dave (bowed out later of competition): high 20s

Although, there were some excuses floating around that night (e.g. "ate a big lunch", "ribs didn't taste good anymore after the 1st slab" etc.), all of us agreed that Albert, in all his sick, twisted and depraved gluttony deserved to be called a champion, a hero of heroes, and a man for all seasons.

WE LOVE YOU ALBERT!!!!!!!!!

Thank you, thank you very much.

I HAD TO INCLUDE JOE O.'S RESPONSE...

Date:	Re: RibFest 2000 - The Results
To:	Joe
Cc:	Vinh; Belen; Lesli; Oscar; Albert; Devin; Sandra; Manuela; Bettina; Dodge; Jun; Roberto; Rowena; Karen; Derryn; Dan; Grant; Charles; Craig; Kirsten; Bruce; Barry; Tom; Yvette; Maria; Eunice; Keith; Chris; Mark; Nitin; Helen; Aldo; Brooke; Davide; Greg; Simon; Nancye; Alison
Subject:	Re: RibFest 2000 - The Results

Okay... okay... let me set some things straight...

What Mr. Dino (Mr. Fabulous as he would prefer to be known) failed to report in his little recounting of last night's activities is that the reason I couldn't attend the competition last night was that I was serving my community by attending a meeting of volunteers wherein I was being honored and being given the title of Grand Chief of the Ga-Sioux Nation Indian Guides and Princesses for the year 2000/2001. It was quite an honor and, more importantly, an acceptance of responsibility for the shaping of the young minds possessed by the urchins that are part of the Father-child program. I accepted this position, humbled yet gravely reverant to the task at hand.

That being said.... I smiled when I read that Albert had eaten 51 ribs, and was declared "rib king". Why, I eat 55 ribs routinely for breakfast on my drive to work. Just the other day, I ate 75 ribs while reading the Sunday paper on "the throne". And last Sunday, I consumed 103 ribs while building some shelves in my garage. It is a shame that we hold so dearly those who attain glory untested. Would you still be heralding Albert's accomplishment had he suffered defeat while still eating 51 ribs? Would that number "51" mean so much if he was in second place? I think not.

So... glorify your "paper lion." I'm sure his reign will last. But know this... my day will come! I will rise! I will overcome!

4

TRIVIA

Little minds are interested in the extraordinary; great minds in the commonplace.

Elbert Hubbard

There is much pleasure to be gained from useless knowledge.

Bertrand Russell

TRIVIA NIGHT VICTORY!

I knew Davide was good for something. I've been trying to win the Trivia prize for weeks.

Date:	Monday, August 31, 1998 5:13 PM
To:	Mark; Aldo; Davide; Brooke; Greg; Nicole; Barry; Bruce; Dodge; Joe O.; Jun; Kevin; Roberto; Tom; Dale
Subject:	Trivia Night Victory!

As the subject suggests, Team Good-Looking has finally reached the Grand Final and crushed the paltry opposition!

After making Davide pay for dinner , Brooke, Davide and I headed off to Scruffy Murphys to meet up with Grant, Madelyne and Paul who had reserved a table for us. I could sense a little tension/sizing up between Davide and Paul as Brooke sat between them. I myself prayed that the two guys could control their raging hormones and keep a cool head so we could finally bring home the coveted carton of beer.

The questions of the first session were not too difficult, and we were able to pull out some beauties such as which character did Natalie Imbroglio play in "Neighbours" (Beth), what ancient country was Memphis the capital of (Egypt), and Paul managed to use his ethnic background to recognize "Boom Boom Shake the Room" by Jazzy Jeff and the Fresh Prince. We tied for first place in the first session.

Brooke in the meantime was selected to represent Team Good-Looking by going up to the stage and compete with two brutish blokes. The emcee gave each a wheatbix and asked them to start eating it. All hesitatingly began eating the wheatbix as most of these games have some kind of sexual involvement, but then the emcee said: "Now whistle!". Alas, poor Brookie with her mouth all stuffed up with dusty, grainy wheat particles couldn't get a tune out of her mouth no matter how hard she tried! One of the brutish blokes (mighty impressive I must say) finally got a whistle out and won.

The second section (by the way, Davide was buying all the drinks, good on ya matie!) began and we were pretty confident and upbeat! Again, we managed to pull of some remarkable answers such as recognizing a line from Pulp Fiction, identify Kosmo Kramer from his high school mug shot (Davide did that), and which part of the tin man needed lubricating first? The Mouth.

Another of the stage games was held, and Davide and Brooke went up. The emcee gave everyone a carrot, and the girls a condom. The girls and boys were then asked to put the condom on the carrot without using their hands. The team was in trouble already, as I could see Davide floundering (probably because of some homophobic fear of sticking a penile shaped object in his mouth), by weakly holding the carrot (it was flopping!) in his mouth. Brooke however wasn't that sharp either as she had the condom inside out, and the two started to argue whether or not the condom was inside out!

Needless to say, our reps didnt win, and the blonde girl with the big tits and her partner won.

However, as the final scores were counted, TEAM GOOD-LOOKING CAME AHEAD WITH AN AMAZING 36 1/2 POINTS! 4 POINTS AHEAD OF OUR COMPETITORS! And we won the carton of beer along with some phone cards.

Go Team Good-Looking Go!

TRIVIAING FOR THE COMPANY

It's too bad they don't have full-time jobs for people with my skills.

Date:	Thursday, 15 October 1998 1:49 PM
To:	Barry; Bruce; Dodge; Joe O.; Jun; Kevin; Roberto; Tom; Dale; Davide; Brooke; Greg; Aldo; Nicole; Simon; Mark
Subject:	Little Story

Hello DEAR DEAR DEAR FRIENDS

Some of you have expressed some concern about my recent indoor activities specifically the internet chatting thingy. And although I really dont find anything wrong sitting buck naked in my office chair, eating potato chips and discussing Euro porno with the lonely people on the internet, I do go out on the rare occasion. Deciding to forego the nightly ritual of talking to my net girlfriends on Wednesday night (yeah yeah, so these girls could be guys, but hey, who am I to judge????), I participated in the company sponsored trivia night at the University of NSW. So there were 20 teams or so from all different companies (I didnt see any EDSers because if I had, I wouldve asked them for the $5000 they owe me, those bastards!).

I primed myself with 3 rum and cokes at the pub, before Paul picked me up to catch a taxi to the uni. My companions were definitely quite unattractive, but that's okay because one of them turned out to be a trivia buff so he had all the answers. Not that I'm saying there's a direct correlation between ugliness and good triviaing, because after all, I AM PRETTY HOT! At the uni, we were a little early so went to the bar and got beer at uni prices (good tip there). After downing two schooners, we went back and to the main trivia area and got more beers.

The trivia buff guy wasnt drinking so that was good. Trivia started, and as the trivia buff guy knew most of the answers, there was no pressure on me to perform. But I did yell out the odd non-sensical thing to throw others off. Which the cute girl in the little blue shirt with the hot bod would often laugh at. Other than trivia buff boy, the other trivia folks in my team were pretty hopeless as they rejected two or three of my answers. And of course, I WAS RIGHT. Everybody knows ADAGIO is slow! And that the IMF is based in Washington DC! But with trivia buff boy and the occasional accepted answer from the drunk guy (me), it was enough to secure victory.

Unfortunately, half the team left before we were declared winners, so as the cute blonde announced called out Team Donut's victory (I didnt get a chance to name our team TEAM GOOD-LOOKING as tradition demands it), I RAISED MY ARMS IN VICTORY (doing the Satanic devil horns things with my fingers) and shook the beer bottle with much flourish. The cute CHICK with the hot bod giggled at my shameless exhibition much to the dismay of her sissy-looking poof boyfriend.

So we got gift vouchers, I got one, Paul got one, and the trivia buff boy took the rest to distribute.MISTAKE!!!! I was accused a couple of times now that I had an extra gift voucher because someone didnt get theirs. If anyone's the suspect, it's that trivia buff boy. As if I really care for something of so little value that I would bother to steal it. Heeesh. What do they think I am? POOR? But I digress.

When I got home, I had to drink a lot of water and 4 tylenols because my head was spinning, andnow I have a terrible hangover. But today is payday, so that's okay.

bye bye

NEPOTUTU

Section II

All the Pretty People

There are four varieties in society; the lovers, the ambitious, observers, and fools. The fools are the happiest.

Hippolyte Taine

5

CHICKS

> In the beginning, said a Persian poet - Allah took a rose, a lily, a dove, a serpent, A little honey, a Dead Sea apple, and a handful of clay. When he looked at the amalgam - it was woman.
>
> *William Sharp*

GERMAN GIRL

There's just something about euro chicks... I think her name was Cecilia.

Date:	Tuesday, 24 March 1998 8:43
To:	Aldo; Greg; Davide
Subject:	German Girl

Here's a good story of the German girl which I sent to some other people, I think you'll like it (oh yeah, I'm over her already, so these are just fond memories):

I can't even begin to describe my German princess. She's just so classic German. Tall, blonde, and a little gangly. But her voice, umm! Like a real woman's! Here's a little tidbit which you will enjoy.

I was drinking beer with her and doing conversation, when she saw the book I took home from work. It was about the Australian financial markets, and I explained to her I was new to the finance industry. So she asked if she could take a look at the book, and she flipped it to the first page where I had written my name and the date I bought the book. She looked at me and said: "You wrote your name so people wouldn't steal it, right?". I nodded in agreement. And then she said: "My father has a lot of books with other people's names in it, it didn't help those people unfortunately."

AND THAT WAS THE MOMENT I FELL IN LOVE WITH HER. Now let me explain my thought process:

1) Interest in a book (you know how I feel about literature)
2) A brilliant deduction on my name on the first page (this girl is not afraid to show off her BRILLIANCE!)
3) A brilliant display of dry humor of which I myself am a keen practitioner
4) Ability to bring in her father, and A MORAL to the story (double bonus!)

In other words, she said all the things I could've said if the positions had been reversed!

THE DAY DUSTY SPRINGFIELD DIED

Maybe she was lesbian, like Dusty was.

Date:	Friday, March 05, 1999 4:37 AM
To:	Dale; Bruce; Barry
Subject:	CHICKS

Hey guys,

I just remembered this story, just so you guys don't think Ive lost my CHICK-SHMOOZING skills. So I was at Ryan's with Dan and just talking about life in general, when we noticed the music started playing. They had some live performers, a girl and guy. The girl was playing the guitar and she looked a littler peculiar, so naturally I was attracted to her. They were playing the blues, and then I realized that Dusty Springfield (e.g. son of a preacher man) had died that day. So I told Dan I was going to do a special request, so when she finished her song, I waltzed up to her and asked if she could do a Dusty song. She got all serious because obviously she knew something about Dusty, and made a sad serious face. She asked me if I was gonna hang around, cause she'd play a Dusty song in 15 minutes. So I hung around some more and downed some more rum and cokes. Bloody beers cost nearly as much as spirits at Ryan's!! (it's a fancy yuppie place where all the bank people go). True to word, she sang a beautiful rendition of Son of a Preacher Man. So when it was time for her break, I staggered towards them and offered to buy them both a drink, the boy looked a little bit like a poof and he said he had a beer. But the girl said she'd take a Cascade (one of those low class beers, versus the Coopers that I get). So I got her a beer and rocked up to her. So we started chatting about Dusty and what a great loss she was to the world. She looked like an attractive lesbian, a little bit disproportionate from the waist down, butt a little big, a little bow legged, and I think she had a tummy somewhat. Not as bell-fat like Yvette if the way you describe Yvette is accurate. But of course, I found her quite HOT, especially with the 4th drink in me. She didn't have butch hair though. Anyways, were talking about Dusty and by this time, Im literally 2 inches away from her face, it was weird because I realized how close I was to her because from that distance, she was pretty goodlooking. Anyways, its going okay, and all of a sudden, I get this tug on my arm. And its Madeleine, Grant's girlfriend, Madeleine's been sitting at Ryan's for 6 hours now since lunchtime (never went back to work) and she's really pissed (pissed can mean really drunk in Aussie diction). So she's tugging at my arm and says: "Hi Joe, I just wanted to say goodbye!!" Then she turns to Tania, and says: "Do you work for Macquarie too?" and Tania says "No, I was just singing here". Then Madeleine starts a bloody conversation!!! Dusty died, Madeleine's sick of MacBank people etc. Blah blah blah, and more blah blah blah. So anyways, I see Dan and Grant milling around, so I said I have to get back to my buddies. So Im walking back to the guys, and Madeleine says to me: I didn't interrupt anything, did I? Were you chatting up to her? (chatting up means like making your moves). Now, Madeleine's like part-catholic or something cause she always feels guilty, so I say "na na na, no worries", but of course I secretly blamed her. Tania sang some more songs, and once in a while she'd point to us, who were on our nth round of drinks, and I'd be thinking, who's she pointing to? Me or Madeleine? Damn, competition with a girl!!!

After her last gig, she and her buddy took off for a break, but I couldn't find them anymore, so I wrote my number on an ATM receipt and left it on her stool. How sad. But Tania never called.

VIOLATED

I was outraged!

Date:	Monday, October 25, 1999 2:53 PM
To:	Dodge, Jun; Roberto; Brooke; Alicia; Helen; Karen; Rowena; Simon; Greg; Derryn; Davide; Dan; Aldo; Keith; Kevin; Kirsten; Bruce; Dalc; Barry; Joe O.; Tom; Maria; Yvette
Subject:	More Uncivilized Behavior!!!!!!

Hello Dear Dear Friends,

I'd just like to share this traumatic experience I had yesterday. As you all know,

I don't go to work on Mondays, and I often use this day to go about taking care of personal and finance stuff. Some of you are aware that I'm a big believer of Given's "Wealth Without Risk", and one of the basic ideas is that you must have 10% of your yearly income available to you in cash at anytime. Reason being, should you have to kill somebody and leave the country, you can just take the money and run, versus having to put your house on the market, wait for a buyer etc. But I digress! So I was planning the rest of the year's finances when I realized that I was getting ripped off with 0.25% interest I was getting on my savings & checking account at my Commonwealth Bank.

So I thought, hey, I'll just move the money into an ING or Macquarie Bank Cash Management Trust (like a money market account). But before I did that, I decided I'd give Commonwealth Bank one last chance. So I walk in the bank and this guy asks me if he could help me and I said: "I want to move my money from Commonwealth to ING or MacBank so it can earn 4.25%, can you match it?". And the guy checks with this girl, and they say: "We can give you 4% variable with a CMT". So I think, that's fair enough. At least the money is all in one place.

So the little chickie takes me to one of the customer studios to do the paperwork. And this is how it went (condensed version)...

Myrna: So you're Filipino?
Joe: Yep, are you Filipina?
Myrna: Yes.
Joe: That's wonderful. Then we must know each other already or we're related.

Myrna laughs

Myrna: Are you saving for a house? *(after checking out my account balance)*
Joe: No, that's just my emergency cash in case I kill somebody and leave the country.

Myrna chuckles

Myrna: Kill somebody? Aren't you a good Catholic boy?
Joe: Yes I am, but I don't go to church *(speaking in Filipino now)*
Myrna: I don't go to church either (*also speaking in Filipino)*

what is Myrna hinting, we both don't go to church so we can do UNBIBLICAL NAUGHTINESS????

Myrna punches up something on the computer

Myrna: Your birthday is next month. I'm only a month older than you.

Joe is wondering what this has to do with his cash management trust

Myrna is looking at the computer some more

Myrna: You work in computers?
Joe: Yep, I'm a propeller-head.

Myrna laughs again

Myrna: You must make a lot of money.

Myrna verifies my income bracket and monthly deposits on her monitor

So then she takes me to the teller to do the withdrawal/deposit, asks for my atm card to swipe it, and then now we're concluding our business.

Myrna: You'll get your statement in the mail...blah blah blah...
Joe: Thanks, it was nice doing business with you.
Myrna: Your welcome, and WE SHOULD HAVE LUNCH together sometime.

Good grief! What a hussy!

Joe: Thank you, and can I have my atm card back?

That's right mister, get to the point and get the hell outta there!!!

Myrna: Oh I'm sorry, it was stuck to my security card.
Joe: Commonwealth Bank must be paying you very little to want to steal my atm card.
Myrna laughs: Ha ha! Your account is empty now.
Joe: Thanks again!

shakes Myrna's hand again for the umpteenth time

Myrna *(not letting go of hand):* Come by and say hello when you're around!!!!
Joe: Buh-Bye!

Whew! Needless to say, I was severely scarred by that experience. It almost felt like as if she was undressing me (financially and physically) with those cunning eyes of her!

Thank you all, I await your heart-felt sympathies in the coming hours and days.

BEST OF MORE UNCIVILIZED BEHAVIOR

The responses were even funnier.

Date:	Tuesday, October 26, 1999 2:46 PM
To:	Rowena; Karen; Helen; Alicia; Brooke; Maria; Yvette; Bruce; Dale; Barry; Joe O.; Tom; Kevin; Kirsten; Keith; Aldo; Dan; Davide; Derryn; Greg; Simon; Dodge; Jun; Roberto
Subject:	Best of More Uncivilized Behavior

Dear Dear Friends,

I was indeed touched by the OVERWHELMING response of my dear dear friends who took the time to comfort and console me in my time of emotional need.

This mass email must've struck a nerve because I got more responses than any of my other emails, it even beat Nepotutu and Donald Duck! Really really overloaded my inbox this time.

However, I must admit, a lot of the responses were extremely funny, so I thought I'd share the most interesting ones. But be warned, there is a whole lot of crudeness (by the way, the married people had the most unbiblical comments). No names are mentioned and it's in order of received date.

Don't miss the lengthiest response! It's a classic.

Was she hot!??!!

What don't you like about her? And please don't tell me something was too big! You know sometimes you can't have everything you want in a girl.

YOU FOOL! You had her tongue on the tip of your pickle! My Christian boy my foot! HAHAHAHA!

What other made up stories do you have?

I say you tickle her tonsils with your six-inch lumpia.

This email begs several questions:

Was she hot?

Do you have a problem with a Filipina?

Did she have nice breasts?

Did she seem intelligent? One would have to be to keep up with the great one, eh?

Was she hot?

Did she has good child bearing hips? Can't have them too skinny, because then she won't be able to have a vaginal birth, and would have to result to a C-section, which leaves nasty scars, which would then become a sore-spot for you since every time you'd see her naked, you'd see the scar and start thinking about clinical things like C-sections or menstrual-cramps and that would turn you off and you'd start having sexual disfunction which would then lead to a messy divorce and she'd clean you out financially and you'd end up having to come back to the States and sleeping on my couch a miserable, pathetic, lonely little man who cries daily in his Post Toasties and watches re-runs of Batman and Marcus Welby, M.D. until all hour of the night, only to wake up in a pool of your own vomit and urine, which would only serve to further depress you until you finally hang yourself from a nearby yucca plant, which would cause all your dear, dear friends to become very depressed, thereby starting a whole cycle of self-loathing, deprecation and ultimate personal-collapse for all those involved!

Was she hot?

Let me know, because then I'll be able to help you more with answers to my vital questions. Did I ask you about her breasts?

You Fool Joe, your leaving the country and your not going to take advantage of a poor Filipino girl?

This girl was abusing her privileged access to your information so you should abuse her.

What are you doing DINO!
I didn't think you would reject advances from a CHICK!
Oh well, I guess you are ALL TALK and NO ACTION!

Sounds like you need therapy...

Now you're just showing off!

It's funny how you guys get scared if the girl is a little aggressive.

And that's about it! All I can say is, what's the big deal? Yeah, well even the sun shines on a dog's ass.

HANDICAPPED CHICKS

Have to use the chick magnet skills once in a while!

Date:	Wednesday, November 24, 1999 12:58 PM
To:	Brooke; Helen; Karen; Rowena; Simon; Greg; Derryn; Davide; Aldo; Dan; Yvette; Maria; Bruce; Dale; Barry; Joe O.; Tom; Kirsten; Dodge; Jun; Roberto; Nitin
Subject:	Chatting Up the handicapped CHICKS!

So yesterday was a busy day as I moved out of my apt in Kirribilli and moved into a hotel in the city. During the day I also had to pick up my tripod from Derryn (the fishing guru), and order a new leather strap (for my travel bag, and to spank chicks with in Tasmania). Also my dear dear friend Nitin K. had just moved from Adelaide to Sydney, so I promised to meet up with him for dinner or so (not that we're homo and had a date, he's married and has a kid, and I think Janet F. and Lisa B. are HOT!!!! not that many of you would know those FINE HONEYS).

So I came back to N Sydney from the city. Along the way, I saw all the work guys leaving work, and they were inviting me to go to the pub with them for a beer or so (I'm pretty popular at work for some reason - much more popular than Fat-Boy - must be my Star Wars thing and my diatribe on the preferred profession if I could do it all over again - porno star, of course, good working hours, good working environment and friendly work people, medical benefits etc. but I digress!).

But I denied them all as I had to meet Nitin in the foyer of the Novell building.

I was a bit early so I just sat down in one of those big cushiony lounge chairs and made myself comfy. Across from me was a young lady, fairly attractive I suppose (if I noticed her, she must be attractive, right?) who had her arm in a sling. Having a morbid personality, such physical inconveniences (I sadly confess) does arouse my interest. So we're just smiling at each other, both waiting for someone, but I just can't figure out a clever icebreaker for that moment. Luckily, Craig, a coworker who suffers from some form of skin disorder which makes his head look like a roma tomato (very red), was on his way out and he started talking to me. He was eyeing Mary (yep, I got her name later) so he stayed for a while to check her out (from earlier discussions it was revealed that he was getting desperate for some boinking). So during the conversation, I told Craig that I was waiting for someone at 6:00, blah blah blah. Then he left. So now it was 6:00 pm and Nitin still hadn't showed up. So of course, this was the icebreaker.

I shook my head, animated my harms and said: "WHY CAN'T THESE PEOPLE BE ON TIME????!!!!". So of course, that amused her, which led to "are you waiting for someone also...".

From that point on it was fairly easy to get the conversation going with her. So it turned out her name was Mary, she's a radiographer (I wonder how much that job makes, 70%?) at some kinda hospital with Martyr in the name (I'll have to look up which one), and she was waiting for Sarah (she's cute too) who works for BME in the same building. Of course, I had o ask how she got her arm all slinged up, and she said she broke her collarbone while playing touch football. To which I replied "I thought that was the point of touch football, not to get hurt". You notice, how I always have a clever reply to everything? And then she said: "I was going for a try". My my my, pretty aggressive CHICKY! So I said: "well, I bet there were some medical staff on your team". Which there were, apparently, she just went back to the hospital and xrayed herself. Mmmmm, xrays. So we just blah-blah-blahed on until Sarah came down. I think Sarah was jealous because she just stood there wondering what was going on and Mary saying "bye Joe". Oh yeah, the names!!! I forgot to mention how I got the name. So after describing the accident, I just said: "we'll probably never see each other again, but my name is Joe!". Isn't that brazen! So of course, she was obliged to tell me her name was Mary. Mary, the blessed mother of sweet baby Jesus. And of course, she probably thinks Joe is short for Joseph. HOW BIBLICAL!!!!! Anyways, I thought this little episode would amuse some of you.

And then Nitin showed up 1 hour later, very apologetic. As my old EDS team in Adelaide would say: "BLOODY NITIN!!!!". Just kidding Nitin!!!!

OUTRAGED

But I was still amused.

Date:	Sunday, February 20, 2000 9:51 PM
To:	Dodge; Jun; Roberto; Derryn; Dan; Rowena; Eunice; Bruce; Dale; Barry; Joe O.; Tom; Maria; Yvette; Helen; Greg; Davide; Brooke; Aldo; Simon; Kirsten
Subject:	Outraged!!!!!!

I usually wouldn't reveal this but I thought this was pretty amusing...

So as usual, my Sunday morning adventure to Star City turned out to be a disaster. Dan was lucky to escape minus 5 dollars. When I left, Grant was still sitting on the 25 bucks. And I had been soundly beaten on the $10 and $25, and Star City would be ordering a nice new blackjack table courtesy of Mr Dino's expenditure for the day. It's a good thing I had the breakfast buffet before I sat at the tables. It just does not pay to gamble on the Lords Day.

Anyway, so I went home to cry and vent my anger at the faceless internet people, and played endless mindless games with the little people on the internet. That kept me occupied for 3 hours or so. Then my little chubby yet pretty friend got online and she said she'd like to see me again, so I said okay, I'll come over to her place since she's been to McMahons Pt. She lives in a suburb called Dee Why (cool name) which is on the beach.

I grabbed a taxi driven by an amusing Czech driver who had nothing good to say about Germans and said that the reason why multiculturalism exists in Australia is because so many Aussie men marry non-Aussie women. And that's thanks in part to the terrible terrible characteristics of the Aussie woman. I guess he didn't like the independent Aussie woman. I always thought that was a very attractive trait, myself. So when I told him I was off visiting a an Aussie chick, he goes: "I WARNED YOU!!! YOUR TAXI DRIVER ALREADY WARNED YOU!!!!!" I gave him a 3 buck tip, he made me laugh.

So I got to her place, she took me around the beach, ordered pizza, ate at her home, then walked back to the beach so we could check out the moon and stars. In the meantime, I was of course my terribly witty and humorous self, and I made her laugh so much that her head hurt. I don't mind making her laugh, she's quite pretty and not dumb. Anyways, I'll write up my best lines later, but first for the "Outraged" bit. So we're lying on the sand, and we're talking about gun control (I don't know how this subject came up but a couple of Aussie girls have brought up this subject independently the last 2 weeks). Anyway, I gave her my little story on how Ashok, that crazy Indian guy tried to run me over on the freeway, and how I bought the magnum 357 for a little close-combat action should that psychopath try to steal my comic books or worse in Monrovia. So she's listening attentively to the story, and after the story she asks in all seriousness: "were you seeing this guy?"

silence

yep, it was quiet for a few seconds. So I thought it over and said "no, it was work-related". And I look at her, and say something: "sorry, I'm not homo". And she looks at me "you could've been bi". Hmmmm. It would've been funny if she was laughing but she was kinda serious.

So I guess I lost my erection after that, and told her I wasn't bi either. And then when we got to talking again, and it was okay again. But I didn't kiss her after that. Not entirely because of the "bi" incident, but it could have been partially that. Ha ha ha. Just thinking about it is making me laugh. whatever could she have meant? was she perhaps thinking of a possible menage-a-trois? but homey don't share, though!!! I guess I'll see her again and find out. At least she didn't think I was completely gay!!!! at least she gave me the benefit of being bisexual!

Whew, thank goodness for that!

well, here are my best lines...

Joe: so you like trivia?
Allie: I'm not really into trivia, I'm more of a, how can I say it... an emotional person
Joe: what does that mean?? you like to cry a lot?

she later meant she was more into spiritual, healing, self-awareness stuff

Allie: I lost my balance and I fell
Joe: yeah, especially if one of your breasts is larger than the other, it's easier to lose your balance
Joe: we commonly call that offending breast, the "bad boob"

she nearly passed out laughing from that one, she's quite healthy in that area

Allie: we gotta get over there *(pointing to the sand dunes)*
Joe: where? over there in the dark???

Joe:	I gotta walk on the sand?? do I have to take off my shoes?
Joe:	I'm gonna get cramps in my feet

I ended up taking off my shoes

Joe:	you know what would be good on this beach? if they had pillows
Allie:	you can use your jacket
Joe:	ummm, no
Allie:	you don't want to get sand in your million-dollar jacket?
Joe:	yep
Joe:	you like it when I behave like a brat, right?

she loves it

Allie:	here's my fish tank, I've got the filter, the tree, the lights etc. but no fish
Allie:	I gotta get some fish
Joe:	If you get fish, the fish will crap all over in the fish tank
Joe:	I think the fish tank will look better without any fish, just leave it as is

everybody loves Honest Joe

Too bad I can't remember all the other lines. At least I was able to talk to her. Not like some chicks who have the personality of a piece of plywood.

It was a very interesting day.

TAWDRY EXCUSE

Casino or chicks?

Date:	Saturday, February 12, 2000 4:18 AM
To:	Helen; Greg; Davide; Brooke; Aldo; Simon; Maria; Yvette; Bruce; Dale; Barry; Joe O.; Tom; Kirsten; Derryn; Dan; Rowena; Roberto; Dodge; Jun
Subject:	Great Day!!!!

So today was a great day! Well, not really, it was quite a hectic day at the home office with the New York people going crazy and making me work. But today was the day when my little friend and I were gonna go have the big seafood platter at Doyles! Well, guess what??? I got stood up again!!!!!

But wait, this is quite good. Guess what excuse was given? Her Granpa died and she had to attend the funeral tomorrow.

I don't know, but I've heard all kinds of good excuses but this one was pretty good. I mean, am I going to ask for granpa's death certificate? Well!!!!

But it's okay, I didnt want to give up the opportunity for the legendary Doyles experience, so I got Dan to go to Doyles. It was great! Huge seafood platter served by the striking Polish waitress Gosha. Naturally, it cost quite a bit - $150 for both me and Dan. But I didn't ask Dan to put out or anything, since we're not homo.

But I did convince him to go to my TRUE LOVE, Star City Casino. It was a rainy Saturday night, and we only found 1 hour parking on the street, so we reckoned 1 hour was good enough to kick some casino ass.

We sat down at a little $10 table, and I wedged myself between two fat CHICKS, and pretty soon, it looked like the casino was going to rip off my panties and slap me silly until my weewee turned red. Down to my last $40, I managed to use all my cunning and skill to claw back to a magnificent $250! Which of course paid off my $150 dinner. Oh the sweet sweet justice of God's green earth. IN YOUR FACE, STAR CITY, IN YOUR FACE!!!!

I stood up to cash the chips but Dan didn't want to go yet, apparently, he had been stuffing his pockets with the red chips and he was still on a lucky streak. But it was time to go back before the car ticketed and we got away with Star City's hell-bound blood money!

What a great day!

DINNER ACCORDING TO DINO

This was just Margaret's birthday dinner but of course, I had to make a big production out of it. I don't think Margaret was on the mailing list for this one.

Date:	Wednesday, February 28, 2001 11:44 AM
To:	Brooke; Barry; Bruce; Roberto; Dodge; Vahe; Greg; Kevin; Chris; Aldo; Helen; Jun; Joe O.; Rowena; Davide; Tom; Kirsten; Karen; Dan; Richi; Debra; Yvette; Maria; Mark; Dale
Subject:	Dinner According to Dino

I would just like to share my dining/social skills since they've been so successful as of late.

1. email the CHICK and ask if she'd like to get "shit-faced" that evening

2. tell the CHICK to come pick him up at his house when she's finished with her stuff

3. when the CHICK comes over, show photos of other CHICKS and circle the faces with index finger while saying "cutie-pootie".

4. proudly exclaim that you have "up $16 dollars off " coupon for a restaurant

5. drive to restaurant in your vehicle which has the bumper sticker "BITCH MAGNET" on the back (don't tell/remind the CHICK about the bumper sticker)

6. at the restaurant, remind the CHICK that she must order an item close to $16 as the discount is based on the lesser value of the two meals, so no ordering hamburgers or salads.

7. remind the CHICK that you are lactose-intolerant, and you get gas if you eat a moderate amount of cheese, or "explosive diarrhea" if you eat too much cheese (use exact terminology). get the french onion soup since it's covered in cheese.

8. for dinner conversation, say something interesting like why the pope is a pervert for telling everybody to have sex without a condom because the

pope knows it feels better to have sex without a condom. make sure you're catholic before you say this, otherwise, it's bigoted and rude.

9. when paying bill, remind the waiter/waitress to take off the coupon discount if they haven't (gotta get that discount!)

10. before heading to the car, thank the CHICK for riding in a car which has a "BITCH MAGNET" bumper sticker.

MAMMA MIA!

Earlier in the week, Pam had talked to Eunice and Eunice had asked Pam why she would go out with Joe Dino to the Mamma Mia musical. Eunice felt that I was not Pam's type so the thought of Pam and I actually going to an event together was somehow beyond all rational thinking. Pam and I decided to play a little joke on Eunice by hinting something physical had happened between us after the Mamma Mia musical.

I began to "blind copy" the emails after a particularly disruptive episode in which people would perform never-ending reply-alls.

Date:	Saturday, March 17, 2001 12:55 PM
To:	none *(blind copy)*
Subject:	Mamma Mia!

What a great musical!!!! Truly, Benny Anderson and Bjorn Ulvaeus are the musical giants of this century.

As usual, work decides to keep me until 6:00 pm (1 hour beyond my standard 5:00 pm departure time), and I only have 1.5 hours to get to the Shubert Theater to meet Pam. I get there 7:20 pm and valet park for the reasonable amount of $18.00/night (please remember this, future Mamma Mia attendees, there is a parking structure just a little ways off). This just leaves me enough time to get a McRib at the McDonald's below. I conscientiously try and scrape off the raw onions just in case I get drunk and start kissing Pam after the show.

I get back up to the theater and start looking for the tall, skinny blonde foxy CHICK that Pam is, but this is Los Angeles, so the entire area is just floating with tall, skinny blonde vixens, and I just give up - too many of them. I figure she'll just find me instead. After all, how many HOT Filipino dudes are gonna be walking around the Shubert to see the Mamma Mia musical?

Sure enough, I turn around and there is Pam, all dolled up, and sporting a black leather jacket. Grrrrrrrrooooowwwwwwwlllll. May have to break some more promises I made earlier...

Being totally shameless, I actually made Pam pay for her ticket, but hey, we're adults!

We got inside, and we were seated in V27-28 Orchestra. I definitely recommend Orchestra because Balcony is just too high up and weird. We were right smack in the middle and had a great view. We could've sat a little bit closer (maybe rows N, O, P would've been perfect), but it's such a small theater that it was really pretty good.

I won't give the show away, but it was just superb!!!! They inserted all these ABBA songs in the story-line and the audience would break out laughing and cheering whenever they managed to put in the ABBA song to the situation. Lots of dancing and singing in all the scenes. When it came to "Winner Takes it All", I just sat enthralled listening and clapped out my little Filipino hands when it was all over. Sniff. After the main show ended, all the singers and dancers got up on a stage and they did two more ABBA songs, and it was total mayhem on stage with the ABBA frilly glitter costumes. Everybody in the audience stood up and started clapping and singing.

For a brief 3 hours of time, 2500 people forgot about war, poverty and disease and bonded in joyous Harmony. The world owes so much to Benny, Bjorn, Agnetha and Frida. I may have to see the musical again with the next batch of people going.

Walking out the theater, I tell Pam my plans of having an all-out ABBA party complete with costumes. We then head to Harry's Bar which is in the same complex and we have some appetizers, drinks, and talk stuff. Good thing about Pam is that she's never short on stories. They're all kinda edgy stories too. Never realized how HOT Pam can be sometimes. Maybe it's that fine line between danger and common sense that makes her so appealing. Grooowwwwwwwllll. Naturally, after a couple of drinks, I throw all resolutions what I'm not going to do, out the window (I'm really easy after a couple of drinks). But since gentlemen don't kiss and tell, I'll have to end the story right here.

By the way, I thought up a couple of lines Friday night. Not that I'm trying to imply anything happened.

1) even the thorniest rose smells good
2) we're all the same skin color in the dark
3) we're all the same height lying down

On a final note, if Mamma Mia comes to your city, go see it!!!!!!!!!!! You won't regret it.

THE SEXY BEAST

Sometimes it just doesn't get any better than this.

Date:	Thursday, June 14, 2001 7:10 AM
To:	Dodge; Roberto; Aldo; Vahe; Tom; Davide; Dan; Rowena; Debra; Barry; Eunice; Maria; Yvette; Joe O.; Derryn; Jun; Bruce; Margaret
Subject:	Sexy Beast

Must... must... must... take advantage of all Fox benefits...

So yesterday was my first chance to try out the free movie screenings we can go to on the lot. I invited Margaret (already experienced to my previously demonstrated social skills) to accompany me to "Sexy Beast" starring Ben Kingsley as a psychopathic criminal.

"Sexy Beast" was a strange little movie, and it had a lot of questions (who the hell was the Sexy Beast??? we missed the first 5 minutes, so maybe it was explained then). Afterwards I gave Margaret the tour of the Fox lot and showed her all the studios/stages, the NYPD outdoor set, the restaurant where I eat everyday etc. Then we had noticed that there was a little outdoor party going on near the commissary (another cafe/restaurant), and people had these VIP passes around their necks. So we thought we'd barge in and see if we could catch some celebrities. So we took a little secret way so we could join the crowd unobtrusively. They seemed to be all biz people by the way they dressed, and talked. Unfortunately, we didn't see anybody famous. I lined up to get champagne for Margaret, but then I noticed it was a cash bar. Forget it!!!! On our way out, the waiters were standing around with platters of canapes, so I got one little miniature pizza (the size of a raisin) for Margaret and some kinda cracker with stuff on it for me. Then it was enough, so we left the Fox lot.

I hope you all know what this basically all boiled down to: a showcase for my arsenal of gentleman skills.

1) took the girl to the movie
2) took the girl somewhere interesting and nice (tour of the Fox lot)
3) took the girl to a party (hey! by definition, it was a party!!!)
4) fed her (the little canapes)

Granted, I was unable to get her a drink, but that probably worked out best since we had to work the next day and we both have early shifts.

And best of all, it was all free!

We did end up at Denny's for dinner (all the excitement must have made hungry), and the best part about it was, Margaret paid for my meal too!!!! Jackpot!

All this Sexy Beast has to say is, "Who's Your Daddy Now?"

P.S. on another note, I am canvassing suggestions for my future BMW wardrobe (when I plan, I must be thoroughly complete). I am thinking of getting several leopoard-spotted/tiger-stripped silk shirts + gold/silver necklaces, and those wicker/braided shoes that you wear with no socks. I know, I should probably test drive a BMW first before buying the clothes, but finding the appropriate clothes is just as challenging.

Thank you all.

SMOOTH TALKING CHICK MAGNET

I outdid myself this time.

Date:	Monday, August 13, 2001 4:29 PM
To:	Dodge; Roberto; Aldo; Rowena; Jun; Barry; Maria; Yvette; Dale; Bruce; Margaret
Subject:	smooth-talking chick magnet

the HR manager's assistant gave me a call yesterday to reschedule an appointment with the manager for some paperwork

I could never figure out the assistant's name, and all I know is that she's kinda cute, and she's got a tattoo from the small of her back down to her butt. I was confused about her name because it sounds like DJ or BJ. And of course, I didn't want to call her BJ by accident just in case she thinks I'm making some kinda sexual innuendo. So I reminded myself next time I had contact with her, to ask her name. So here goes.

Joe: okay, it's 9:30 am with Becky then

Assistant: yes

Joe is telling himself: "okay, go ahead, ask if her name is DJ, but don't call her BJ... don't call her BJ... don't call her BJ..."

Joe: Say, is your name BJ? (dangit!)

(silence)

BJ (in an ice cold tone): No. It's DJ.

BJ: D as in DOOOOG.

Joe: okay, I get it! DJ as in Disc Jockey.

BJ: That's a better way of saying it.

Joe: okay, I'll see Becky at 9:30 am tomorrow! Bye!

The Sexy Beast strikes again.

6

Social Graces

Man is the only animal that can remain on friendly terms with the victims he intends to eat until he eats them.

Samuel Butler

Good breeding consists in concealing how much we think of ourselves and how little we think of the other person.

Mark Twain

THE ASSET MANAGER

I can't believe I embarrassed my cousin at my sister's wedding!

Date:	8/31/95 10:20am
To:	Bruce, Dale, Debbie, Maria
Subject:	Humorous Story

I just remembered a funny story.

At the wedding, my cousin Cristina and her young boyfriend Matthew were sitting with Max and my friend Roberto and his wife Carrie at the same table.

I hadn't met Matthew yet, so I introduced myself to make smalltalk.

Joe:	I haven't met you yet. You're Matthew, aren't you?
Cristina:	Oh I'm sorry, Matthew, this is Joe, one of my favorite cousins...
Matthew:	Nice to meet you.
Joe:	What do you do, Matthew?

Matthew:	I'm an asset manager.
Joe:	An asset manager? Wow, making money eh? Carrie, what's your title?
Carrie:	Financial analyst.
Joe:	Oh good, then you two can chat! Joe leaves.

So that was that, one day later, Max comes up to me and asks why I insulted Matthew. I asked him why he thought I was insulting Matthew. And Max says I was being sarcastic about him making money. I said asset managers make a lot of money because they invest in stocks, bonds, etc. So how could I have been sarcastic? Max said: He's not an asset manager, he's a gas station manager!

CHICKS DEFENDING DINO

Thank goodness I had chicks to defend me that night.

Date:	Friday, April 16, 1999 9:13 AM
To:	Kirsten; Roberto; Dodge; Jun; Aldo; Grant; Peter; Simon; Bruce; Tom; Dale; Joe O.; Barry
Subject:	Bloody Hell!

So I still didnt finish my travel plans, but I guess I got an idea on what to do. Instead I rolled over my superannuation (deferred comp in Oz), and got my mom to order some Microsoft shares early yesterday morning. I reckon, if I cant decide on my leisure activities, I might as well settle my finances. Anyways, I would just like to share an interesting experience with you all, and perhaps you (guys only) would like try out someday. So Grant and I go to the Rugby Club to meet up with Madeleine and Karen to watch the game. Grant's got to do some silly housecleaning stuff so he goes home and somehow I get a craving to get fish and chips at Kings Cross (notorious place for hookers and strippers).

So the two chicks and I go to the Cross and go to the Bourbon. Now, I guess I havent been out for a while because it was sure annoying for every 10 minutes, some bloke would come up and start coming on to Karen or Mad. I also noticed a strange peak to when the mad rush to hit on the girls came. It was around between 10:00 pm and midnight, when all the guys just went boom boom boom and just came on to the chicks. It tapered off after midnight. Now since I was the complimentary male in the group, naturally all the guys had to eye me with suspicion. And sometime in the night after one of the chicks had rejected one of the guys, this Indian guy (you know my history with Indians...) starts to talk trash to me. Now he was just a little guy in a suit (kinda like me really) who just got rejected, so I guess he was just lashing out with some juvenile talk, so I just ignored him but I guess that just egged him on. But the chicks got really mad, and Karen yelled at him and called him a fuckwit (I like that term). And the guy just left even more humiliated. Poor guy, I felt sorry for him. First he got rejected, then he didnt get his fight with me, and then a chick calls him a fuckwit. Anyways, the night ended okay, the chicks came away unscathed, and there were no more "incidents".

So the moral of the story is, have the chick do the trash talking for you, they cant hit the chick, and it hurts even more when you get insulted by a chick. And thats what I learned last night. Will the daily lessons in life never cease?

Thank you Mr. Dino. thank you.

P.S. I didnt get my fish and chips. I got ribs and chips instead (chips are french fries by the way).

PARTY INVITES

The official welcome back party...

Date:	Monday, August 30, 1999 10:46 AM
To:	Grant; Alicia; Karen; Rowena; Oscar; Dave; Belen; Eunice; Maria; Yvette; Bruce; Dale; Barry; Joe O.; Tom; Julie; Marc; Alison
Subject:	Sep 10

Hi All,

Please plan on making it to:

Perigee Apts, Unit 155, 21041 Parthenia (I think it's Canoga Park but it's close to Chatsworth) on Friday, Sep 10 starting around 8ish. The apt phone number is 818-709-4216.

The cross streets are Canoga if you're coming from the west, or De Soto if you're coming from the east.

Best place to find parking is on Variel or Parthenia. Just ring buzzer, go straight towards laundry room (stairs down), don't take stairs down to do laundry or garage to get mugged, instead take stairs up to have a good time.

Please don't be scared of the apartment complex.

I'm only going to be grilling hotdogs and burgers, so you can eat ahead if your dietary needs find hot dogs wanting. Even though I abstain from unbiblical behavior, may I politely suggest bringing a lot of alcohol with you. You can also bring your swimming trunks if you want to jump into the pool (there's two of them) or hot spa/tub (for those adventurous types). Feel free to crash overnight, but if your wallet is missing, and your underwear has been reversed inside-out, don't be blaming me.

There is no theme to the party, although I was wavering between "Casino Coin Bucket" and "Deliverance" themes. But I guess chasing people around and making them squeal like pigs may not be everybody's cup of tea.

Looking forward to see everybody's smiling (even though by the end of the night, somebody will be crying in the kitchen)faces next week . I LOVE YOU ALL!

P.S. Barry (this is a big ask, but you're pretty organized), can you forward to Linda, Pam, Beth, Nancye, Jenn, Natalie, Dave, Devin, Scott, Clarence, Rico, Jennifer etc. , and anybody else who may get offended if I don't invite them. Thanks!

SUMMER POOL PARTY

A lot of people came for the canola-oil powered "Wheelabrator"...

Date:	Tuesday, June 27, 2000 5:24 PM
To:	Shalauna; Debbie; Mark; Manuela; Bettina; Karen; Nancye; Oscar; Sandra; Chris; Eunice; Nitin; Greg; Craig; Devin; Keith; Pamela; Simon; Vinh; Marty; Belen; Albert; Sung; Charles; Richard; Jun; Dodge; Roberto; Rowena; Grant; Dan; Derryn; Kevin; Kirsten; Dale; Bruce; Barry; Joe O.; Tom; Yvette; Maria; Davide; Brooke; Helen; Aldo; Andy; Alex; Rick; Jeff; Haigaz; Tom G; John T.; Ray; Lesli; Orit; Mimi; Dave; Jenn
Subject:	First Summer Pool Party of the Millenium

Dear All,

We're having a party on Saturday July 8, 2000 at Barry's & Joe's house. There is no theme to the party but feel free to bring your bikinis or speedos as the pool will be available. I'll have the weights and bench ready for the guys who may wish to pump themselves up before then.

Please bring an adequate supply of your choice of beverage/alcohol. Hot dogs, hamburgers and "exotic" treats will be provided throughout the night.

Time: 4:00 pm till late (until everybody starts getting unbiblical and I have to kick everybody out)

P.S. an rsvp would be good so we can figure out how many hot dogs to buy for the evening, and how much canola oil I need to put in the wheelabrator for the night's "special" activities.

HAPPY HOUR

Another classic reply-all to a happy hour invite...

Date:	Tuesday, July 11, 2000 5:07 PM
To:	Jim
Cc:	Michelle; Cara; John; Louie; Andrea; Barry; Belen; Beth; Bruce; Clarence; Cheryl; Crystal; Dale; Eric; Frank; Gloria; Jim; Jodi; Joe; Joe O.; Julie; Maria; Nancy; Oscar; Rico; Stan; Yvette
Subject:	Re: Happy Hour - July 28th

WHASSSSSS UPPPPPPPP!!!!!!!!!!!!!!!!!!!!!!!!

Well, unlike Joe O., I'm really not into family values nowadays and I'm concentrating on getting the largest private porno collection in the San Fernando Valley. Doctor says it's good for my low blood pressure, gets the ol' hemoglobin flowing through those hardened arteries, if you get my drift.

In addition to that, I've taken up to sharpening my knives in the nude whilst listening to some classical music. It's a tantric meditation technique I picked up during my three years in Australia. I'll be sure to tell you all about Down Under when we catch up for happy hour.

In fact, I'll be bringing my friends (if you all don't mind), Pepe and Pei. They're midgets from Peru and China but they get drunk really fast since they don't have a lot of weight to them. But they're plenty fun and can run really fast when we chase them with rolled-up newspaper and try to smack them on their little heads.

Hope you and everyone else are doing well. I'm looking forward to seeing lots of you at the Happy Hour.

Talk to you all soon.

HOLIDAY EVENTS

A rambling email indeed.

Date:	Monday, December 18, 2000 1:04 PM
To:	Aldo; Greg; Davide; Maria; Yvette; Bruce; Barry; Tom; Devin; Vahe; Kirsten; Kevin; Rowena; Derryn; Dan; Karen; Dodge; Roberto; Jun
Subject:	Holiday Events Update - Long Rambling Email

Dear Dear Friends,

My rambling emails have been rather infrequent, and of a sparse nature as of late. So I apologize for not updating my dear dear friends on my latest CHICK action, or of my latest bowel movement (no particular order of importance).

So this is a long one, read at your own leisure or don't read at all - doesn't matter to me, I don't put guns to people's heads and make them do things they don't want to do.

However, I feel it incumbent upon myself to share the good fortune of recent days.

Last week, we were called in for an impromptu staff meeting - it was short and sweet, they laid off 9 people in our Northridge office, 25% of our staff. It seemed that our new CFO wanted to make the company more efficient and streamlined and asked for cuts across the company. So the folks which were unbillable, or didn't have assigned projects were unfortunately let go. Fortunately, my project is a fixed-rate contract for 1 man, so I suppose I was covered since I was 100% billable. But to think that I was requesting a transfer to another group which may have been T&M and consequently a shaky financially-viable project. And to think of all those people who got the bad news, a week and a half before xmas. As a single, skilled, resourceful, good-looking (may I say HOT?) and devilishly charming young man, I wasn't really too worried about the financial impact of being laid off, but it did dawn upon me how fickle and incongruous life can be. But as God's good grace may have it, I spent the following weekend enjoying xmas parties/dinner (more on that later), my Grandmother's birthday celebration, and wrapping xmas presents.

So on to the pleasant stuff!!!

Friday - Michelle's Party

the CHICKS

Saturday evening we had a xmas-get-together-party at Michelle's. Being of festive character, I spread goodwill and cheer around by talking to most of the CHICKS at the party. As promised, the first thing I did when I got to the party was sit on Belen's lap. She complained that I was too heavy, and was trying to get me off, but I would have none of that, and held on like a rodeo cowboy for a couple of minutes. Margaret was there too, she looked very nice and I gave her some chat-time as well. Then it was off to Jodi, a tall skinny blond who was surprised that I remembered her name and face having only met her once (the curse of eternal memory). Most of the guys think Jodi was the hottest girl at the party, but the way she talks reminds me of somebody, and physically she reminds me a lot of that other skinny blond girl in Sydney whom Rowena makes fun of a lot. Jodi's okay, she seems nice. I'd armwrestle her for a jar of peanut butter, if she wanted to.

There were some strange girls there with whom I rapped about their trip to Mexico City and the Mexican pyramids (my latest travel project). They were cousins, one was blond and pretty and her name was Catherine and her boyfriend's name was Brian. And the other was tall, blond, homely and a bit big-boned, and I already forgot her name. But I danced with the tall one because I'm kind to all animals, great and small. But I only danced with her for a couple of minutes, because I didn't want her to get the wrong idea. I even spun her around and touched her waist. The funny thing was, she was in London during the millenium. But she was on the north bank, whilst I was on the south bank. What a coincidence.

Then there was Gloria, Michelle's friend, I think she wants me as she recognized me but I forgot her name (I seem to forget the names of non-beautiful people very easily). Then I made the acquaintance of Sherry, she was rather HOT for an older blond woman, she was with a strange guy who was wearing his black leather trench coat in the apt, it must be so sad to be with somebody you don't love. Then pretty Julie was there with her boyfriend, muppet-voiced bald-headed John, again it must be so horrible to be dating somebody people make fun of. But I'm not bitter or anything.

I had a solo dance with Belen, she looked very HOT doing that latin mumbo-jumbo dance she was dancing. Then there was tall Michelle who started to look pretty HOT as the night wore on. I'm ashamed to say, I may have even entertained unbiblical thoughts about her. But then again, we're all sinners. So that's what happened to the chicks.

Homoerotica

The guys did okay too, Bruce brought some party poppers and exploded them in front of Michael, a very interesting gay guy (flaming, but not used in a derogatory way, he was just really queer). Michael kept us entertained throughout the night, but Vahe, whose homophobic behavior only confirms his latent homosexuality, was being downright rude by sitting across from Michael and pretending to pull the pin from an imaginary grenade and throwing it at Michael.

Later on, Vahe commented how great Devin's cologne smelled and put his arm around Devin. Then Michael tried to hit on Devin. And those were the only three gay people who attended the party that night. It is California after all. We spent some time figuring out what name we should call Dale's puppy – I was all for Heidi or Elektra, but Sasha seemed to be high on the list as well.

A lot of the other guys were all hitting on Jodi, but unfortunately they lacked the high caliber wit and charm of a Dale or Joe, the muscularity of a Barry, the height of a Bruce or the mountain-man ruggedness of a Devin. Vahe has been talking trash now about all the chicks he was going to pick up at the party, and all those wild and crazy things that he does on the weekend, but yeah, it was pretty much proven that it was just all talk since he spent most of his time pretending he got calls on his pager, or made fun of Devin and Michael.

And that was about it, nobody got angry with each other (Devin seems to think I was angry with him, but I already apologized when I mistakenly lashed out at him during the night).

Saturday Night - OAN/EDS Dinner

The next day, I had my Grandmother's birthday celebration to attend to, so I went to Monrovia/Covina for lunch to meet up with the relatives. It was pretty good since I got some money from one of my aunts who was visiting, and my Grandmother loved the framed photo of the Dinos.

I had to rush back to Woodland Hills in the afternoon so I could prepare the place cards. We wanted Vahe to sit across from Pam, so Pam could tear him a new asshole once Vahe starts talking about women, relationships etc. Got home, and took unused xmas cards (18 for 99 cents) and put the names of the guests on the xmas cards. Then I dressed up in my snappy blood shirt and charcoal suit (not black) without a tie so I looked cool. Bruce came by to pick us up, and he looked pretty hot in his black outfit but grey sportscoat. And Barry was muscular again.

Then we drove to Studio City to Sparks. We finally found parking off a side street, and then we saw Devin driving up the street. The reservations were at 6:30 and we got there at around 6:35. The tall blond lesbian restaurant manager was relieved to see us, and showed us the long table for 12. I placed the cards around the table strategically (the lesbian manager thought I was very thoughtful). And then we waited. We waited a long time. Yvette and Varand were 30 minutes late. Maria and Oscar were 40 minutes late. Why can't people from foreign countries be punctual!!!!! But because all the guests actually showed up, we were very happy and pleasant with each other.

The guests were Vahe, Bruce, Pam, Barry, Devin, myself, Varand & Yvette, Maria & Oscar, Albert and Dale. Eunice, Alison and Joe. O. were unable to attend. I entertained Oscar with interesting stories on all the men Maria found HOT at OAN. Maria of course denied everything. One of the funny conversations was when Maria was complaining on how Oscar had the roving eye in Spain and was checking out all the women. And I said, "hey, it doesn't matter where you get your appetite from, as long as you come home for dinner!". And Varand said: "I agree". Of course, Yvette wasn't listening, and she didn't hear Varand say: "hey, I don't even get dinner!". I followed up with: "oh, you make your own dinner, huh?". Finally, Yvette got in the conversation and after everything was explained to her about her husband not getting dinner, she said: "just for that, no dinner and NO DESSERT!!!!". But it was all fun and games. We reminisced about old workmates and friends, dead, alive and crippled.

At the other side of the table, Pam kept the guys amused with her stories. Vahe was keeping up with her because I heard Pam say: "This guy has a comment for everything!". Which is basically true. After that, I saw Vahe checking his imaginary calls on his pager again. Maybe Pam intimidated Vahe. Pam can do that to a man less prepared. Pam also commented how changed and thin Devin looks, to which Devin smiled and took off his sportscoat to show his muscles and rock-hard abs.

The food took a long time to prepare and was very pricey, but it was very good. Having roast lamb reminded me of my days in Oz, particularly the Adelaide days.

We were rather loud as we were laughing out loud quite a bit (I know I was loud), so it may have been a relief to the restaurant that we started paying the bill. Thankfully, the table was devoid of cheap people and we were only short

$10 out of a bill for $400 for 12. The last time we were at Sparks, we were short a couple hundred. And I was able to get $10 without any quibbling.

We headed out to take photos since we were all dressed up. Yvette may have been taking a dump in the toilet so she missed the first couple of photos, but we all managed to take a couple of good shots. I hope Devin's camera took them well being it was night time and outside.

The manager of the restaurant came out to chat with me. We shook hands, and I asked the tall lesbian blond woman her name. Her name was Elizabeth Shaw, one of the owners of the restaurant. So we chatted for a little while and intrigued her with my suaveness and chick magnetism. Had I talked to her a little bit more, I would've probably been able to blanket out all the bad memories she's ever had of men who've mistreated her and caused her to become the aging slim lipstick-lesbian that she is now. But I was a bit tired, and just decided to call it a night.

The dinner party all said goodbye to each other, and we all parted with pleasant thoughts.

It was quite enjoyable, and I enjoyed the weekend immensely.

I hope you all have a merry xmas and a happy new year.

MY FAVORITE KOREAN, EUNICE

Like a fool, I offered practice sessions to people in preparation for the Karaoke Party.

Date:	Friday, January 26, 2001 11:13 AM
To:	Joe O.; Dale; Bruce; Maria; Yvette; Debra; Barry
Subject:	date with eunice + had enough of karaoke practice

so I was still feeling very weak from yesterday's 3x dumping, and I didn't even have enough energy to go to the gym to run on the treadmill.

so I just had dinner and went straight home. eunice was supposed to show up for practice but I thought she wouldn't come anyway because of a little email incident we had

when I got home, I felt kinda tired and had shortness of breath, so I just went to bed around 7:30-7:45 pm

barry must've known something because he didn't go to the gym, and did house stuff first and said he'd go gym later

sure enough, 8:00 pm, Eunice and Sarah arrive

I was just settling in under the warm blanket thinking of what I would do with the superpowers Jesus or the space aliens would give me once they establish their rule on earth when Barry knocks on my door - crap

anyway, I got out of bed, and babysat Sarah while Eunice sang and messed around with the DVD player like a 36 year old with Attention Deficit Disorder. naturally Eunice couldn't stop complaining but that didn't bother me anymore and I just waved off all her criticism with my hand, and told her it just goes in one ear and out the other. Eunice actually sang very well once we found the right songs for her (that took forever), and may have to compete with Yvette on the ABBA songs. She also sang "When I need you" pretty well, but of course, she is prohibited from singing that, as that is my signature song.

barry sang a couple of backup vocals while Eunice was singing and then attempted to escape the house by 8:55 - 9:00 pm. barry had to return to the house as Eunice was blocking all our vehicles (she had parked her car behind my car, and the butt of her car was still on Rawlings Ave. so I said, "just wait 5 minutes, 9:00 pm is the end of karaoke practice, and Eunice will go anyway". Eunice said she'd only be around for 30-40 minutes, and it was 1 hour already. But Eunice said she came late and had to sing a few more songs. So she gave barry the car keys so barry could escape. I began to lie and started talking to Sarah: "Oh Sarah, you're tired and sleepy? oh you want to go home?" but it didn't register with eunice

Finally, after two hours of complaining, criticizing, and fidgeting (she can't sit still!!!!! her fingers always have to touch and move things, she was even throwing around my precious karaoke VCDs!), she finally was able to tear herself away from the karaoke player. Eunice stayed till 9:55 pm. 55 minutes over the prescribed schedule.

that's it, I've had enough, no more karaoke in Woodland Hills until the karaoke party - I can't deal with all these people and their personality quirks that come out when they get a microphone close to their mouths

in fact, I can already see what a nightmare it will be to DJ the karaoke on Feb 9.

KARAOKE PARTY

Having purchased a DVD Karaoke Player, I immediately put it to good use by hosting a Karaoke Party.

Date:	Sunday, February 11, 2001 9:40 PM
To:	none *(blind copy)*
Subject:	Karaoke Party

Dear Dear Friends and Party Attendees!

What a smashing success!

Due to the hammering my inbox received from last week's 2 million reply-alls to my "What Lies Beneath" movie review, I thought the BCC: format may be more prudent this time.

From the last summer party, I've relearned the planning strategy one must consider for a Southern California party which says that one must plan for a 40-50% flake rate. David S. even noted that the flake rate could reach as high as 90%, but that is easily reduced to 40-50% by carefully accounting for the traditionally unreliable and flaky. I had about 35-38 confirmed yeses so that probably meant around 20-23 people which would fit comfortably in the house.

The Guests

The attendees were:

Jodi (hot chick)
Ayaz (guy, sat in chair and checked out the hot chicks)
David S. (guy with digital camera taking pics of hot chicks)
Mike (guy)
Oscar (guy whose claim to fame is the Oscar sandwich at the Cheesecake Factory is named after him)
Belen (wore red shirt because she is muy caliente like a red hot chili pepper)
Bruce (guy - sang "careless whisper")
Yvette & Varand (hot Armenian married couple)
Vahe (big man)
Maria (hot married chick)
Barry (owns the house and sang a lot of songs)

Mo (hot chick, sang "Torn")
Dale (dark and brooding complex guy, sang Radiohead's "Creep" using CD only)
Margaret (hot chick)
Gina (hot chick, loved my wontons)
Hillary (hot chick)
Francoise (hot chick, into nature)
Pam (tall hot chick)
Rand (guy, Pam's friend)
Joe (aka "Magnet")

Bad People

There were some rumblings and grumblings from some folks who had "issues" with the way I removed them from the invite list once they hadn't committed after a certain time, but hey, who did they think they were dealing with? Mother Teresa? Good grief, they're dealing with a guy who sleeps on the floor, and has a combat knife under his pillow. I'll deal with them, and the flake-artists who made me buy extra pop and snacks, later. But enough about my positive characteristics! Let's talk action!

A Lesson in Fried Wonton

I left work early Friday afternoon so I could do pre-party preparation. At 5:00 pm, I began assembling my fried wonton from 2 packs of wonton wrap, 1 lb of ground pork, green onions, 1 egg, salt and pepper and 2-3 tablespoons of dark soy sauce. I started frying the first batch at around 6 pm, so the early folks can have something to eat. I'd fry the rest later at 8 pm when the rest had arrived. Maria was the first to try my wonton, and she said: "Did you put meat in this? Why did you make it so small?". That's funny, that's what the culinary savages like Vahe and Devin complained about also last time. Well, Maria, you see if you make the meat size bigger, it means you'll have to cook it longer, and the wrapper will get too dark and look and taste burnt. Now you may say, fry it on medium heat, but if you do that, it will cook even longer and the wrapper and meat will get too oily. As programmers, we're all trained to think of creative solutions, so how about pre-cooking the meat? The meat will taste different after being double-fried. I hope that settles that.

The Singing Starts

After Maria had downed 10 wontons, and rearranged the food/snacks table efficiently and aesthetically, she settled into the sofa and tried out some of the karaoke songs. Personally, I thought she did a great version of "Feelings". Dale arrived and we belted out some Elvis songs.

The chicks started rolling in, and we got into some signature songs. Barry and Maria did a heart-rending "You Light Up My Life" complete with eye-contact, Dale did "Suspicious Mind", I did "I Started a Joke" which made Jodi cry (it couldn't have been that bad). At first, the chicks didn't want to touch the mikes, but after incessant prodding and realizing that it really can't be that bad, they got to singing too. Yvette even grabbed the mike and started singing a few ABBA tunes. Margaret and her hot chick friends did a Shania Twain song. The songs that were most requested that I didn't have were Grease songs and "I will survive".

Photo Madness

Dave, an entrepreneurial young man, went around taking snaps of the girls with his digital cam to post them on his website. Great job Dave!!!!!!!!

Pumped Iron

For some reason I no longer remember (I had 3 or 4 Smirnoff Ice), I ended up showing Pam, Gina and Hillary my bedroom. Good old punch-me-in-gut Pam said: "So Joe, when was the last time you had a girl in here" pointing to the disheveled pile of blankets and pillows on the floor. Fortunately, one of the chicks believed my line of "not believing in material possessions" and "earthly waste" and correctly figured out that I am a traveler. I like that. Traveler. I wonder who said that, Gina or Hillary?

So as I was showing Gina and Hillary the various chick magnet material I had hung up on the wall, Pam was lying on the ground trying out my abroller. Pam: "Does this thing work??? Do you use it????" I said: "Yes, it does work, but that thing is too small for you. You need a bigger one." Yeah, I liked that reply. So Pam says: "Show me your stomach!". So I lifted my shirt and showed the chicks my lithe and perpetually-tanned stomach.

I was still giving the chicks the tour when Pam had moved to my weights and was trying to lift them. Pam didn't believe I could lift all that iron, and challenged me to lift it. Are you kidding me? In front of two hot stranger chicks????? Of course I'd lift those weights, even I get a brain aneurysm from popping a blood vessel. So I lifted the weights with dramatic ease. I should've taken my shirt completely off, but we're having a cold spell right now in California, thank goodness I was lying on the fake zebra skin to keep me warm. Good old Pam. Work WITH me, woman!!! Not work AGAINST me!!! Funny thing is, I've even agreed to go with Pam to the Mamma Mia concert. Whatever possessed me to do that?

Back to Karaoke & Wonton

We did more singing, but I was losing my voice so when it was time to sing "When I need you", my voice cracked in several places, so I was a bit disappointed, especially after I had been practicing for MONTHS. But the good thing was, I had sung the song a thousand times beforehand to my friends already, so when the song came up, they all joined me in unison, and it was just beautiful. All of us singing together. It's a good group song. Dale did a wonderful version of Radiohead's Creep. We just stuck a regular CD (without karaoke words on the TV), and killed the vocals, and Dale did the rest. The chicks were very very impressed.

The fried wonton was another smashing success, as from a batch of 150-170 wontons, less than 10 remained. Naturally I had to milk it for all it's worth, and enjoyed giving Gina (a little firecracker) all my secrets on how to prepare wonton. Must get more info about Gina and Hillary from Margaret. Actually, it's a good sign if a girl does eat fried wonton and do karaoke. Maybe I should put that on the list of requirements.

Karaoke singing started to die down, and we just lapsed into regular late 20s - 30s party-talk. I tried to explain our internet dating business idea to Margaret and Francoise of how to make specific websites to match unattractive nerdy people with other unattractive nerdy people (by the way, there would be no reason for me to actually use that site, as I am neither unattractive nor am I nerdy) or just a place for people to find unattractive nerdy people.

Finally, it got to the reminiscing stage, when we went back 5-7 years to talk about things in the past, who was hot for whom etc. and that's usually a cue that the party will end soon. So past midnight, it was closing time, and that was that.

And best of all, my beloved karaoke player had survived the night.

THE SEXY BEAST ENTERTAINS

A warning to people in their twenties.

Date:	Monday, August 13, 2001 4:29 PM
To:	none *(blind copy)*
Subject:	The Sexy Beast Entertains

I wrote this on a Sunday evening (so I had more time), so I wrote it a bit longer because I wanted to practice story-telling development and style. Please indulge me as this took 2 hours to construct. This is the second time I'm sending this, apparently my initial sendout failed, so apologies to those who got duplicates.

A Visitor

My good friend Kirsten from Seattle was in town for work this weekend, and since it had been a year since I forced her to take the public bus to the Getty Museum on a sweltering summer day (I must admit it was rather unfortunate that we waited one hour for the bus on the wrong side of the street amongst other eventful details I choose not to share), she braced herself for another fun-filled weekend with the Great One.

Planning

Being of a rather logistically-minded nature, I planned Friday's and Saturday's events to within 90% utilization of the time available. Friday night was dinner and comedy at Miceli's in Hollywood. Coincidentally, Miceli's was not far from the McDonald's on Hollywood where on one of our prior trips ('95 or '96) I had left her alone in her bejeweled finery whilst I visited the little boy's room. Apparently, she felt it was "unsafe" with the unsavory locals milling around. Not my fault she decided to wear the Blue Star of Africa that night. I did not bother to solicit Kirsten's preferences for Friday night's activities as after all, she is the guest and I would be remiss as host to make her figure out the plans. Instead I boldly decided for her it would be comedy night versus movie night at the Fox studio lot. She did tell me that she did not really like crass and crude humor, and would be horrified if we were picked upon by the comedian(s). Well, I'm glad she told me that because those things would be totally out of my control. After all, do I tell the bird how to fly? or the fish how to swim? Those who wield the power cosmic must wield wisely.

Miceli's

In the evening she arrived after a grueling trip on the freeway, and we quickly settled the issue that her 6'1 frame actually fits in the front seat of the BMW. A month ago I told her that I believed she would barely fit in the new car, which I suppose insulted her. So she gets in the car, doesn't move the seat back and says: "See? See? I fit!!!!". I was really surprised. Then we drove off to Hollywood.

When I had the bitch-magnet mobile, I would actually park the car 5-6 blocks from Miceli's just to find free parking, but because it was my dear friend of 11-12 years, I considered her safety concerns from the first Hollywood trip, and I gallantly parked the car in the pay parking lot just next to Miceli's. The well-being of the BMW did not play any decision in anteing up 7 dollars to the parking attendant. Besides, Kirsten paid for parking.

We were all dressed up in our Hollywood evening get-up (I was wearing black jeans with one of the fancy Filipino shirts Max got me in Manila), and Kirsten was in all black with pants that had zippers in interesting places. She had her martini and I had a gin and tonic whilst we mulled over the menu items (food not really great, but okay for that price and the show). Fortunately, we were seated maybe 10 feet away from the comedian's microphone. I assured her we would not be picked upon as there was another row of small tables in front of us. At 9:00 pm, the procession of comedians started, and yes, there was a considerable amount of "ass" and sex jokes (a portly young woman's routine probably had 50% fat-ass joke content). But I suppose, the greatest discomfort came when a young, red-headed comedian was picking on a 60-70 year old silver-haired granny sitting in the front row and telling her how much she "wants" him. Well, it turns out that smiling granny turns out to be the sister of the owner of Miceli's, and just like the emcee said after the act: "hey, we wouldn't be surprised if we found Danny whacked in the parking lot". I don't think he'll be called back for a second performance. To close the show, a comedienne ended her act by talking about how she liked dating her security guard ex-boyfriend because if he was willing to take a bullet for $8.25 just imagine what he'd do for pussy. Did I consider such humor crass and crude? Mayhaps, but the only thing that was really important was that Kirsten enjoyed such high-brow entertainment.

Later, as we got into our car, an elderly black gentleman came up to us and asked: "is that a lamborghini? that's a nice lamborghini!". I hurriedly tried to get the key into the ignition, but it was too late, the man had started spraying and wiping some opaque film on the window. Despite my pleas from within the car: "nooooooo!!!! the car's just washed!!!", and because the BMW has good sound insulation, all he heard was a muffled cry. Well, it was too late by this time, and at this proximity, the safe play is to give the man his dollar. And I did. He actually did a good job. He should've done the rear window too. And that was Friday night.

Jewelry District

Saturday was jam-packed with events. We left the house quite early, but not before Barry took a photo of us in our day-get-up in front of the Sexy Beast. She was dressed in her leopard skirt, and I had a light blue Filipino shirt to go along with the blue car. Unlike some people, Kirsten doesn't mind hamming it up, and goes along with whatever requirements the day's photoshoot is going to need. First stop was the LA Jewelry District. Normally, such an outing would require the advisory services of my mother, but Kirsten was pretty sure she'd be just looking, but I played it safe and got the percentage discounts from my mother, and she also gave me her past receipts to prove to the vendor that we were serious buyers. The LA Jewelry district is really just two blocks of jewelery shops and malls on Hill Street in downtown Los Angeles. You can get anything you want in downtown, diamonds, gold, silver, Rolex watches, custom jewelry, loose stones etc. We were browsing in the first store, and the young lady asked us if we needed any help. Kirsten politely declines, but I know better and I point up to Kirsten's ears (I have to point up, she's a head taller than me): "See those? you got anything bigger than that?". The girl look's at Kirsten's golf-ball sized diamonds, and says: "Diamonds? No, not bigger than that. We have smaller." Smaller? Please, we didn't come to downsize! So after that little incident, Kirsten quietly pulls her hair over ears to prevent such further outbursts.

I had to agree with Kirsten, going through hundreds of jewelry booths and stores was a bit overwhelming. It was just too much gold and jewelry. It didn't even seem valuable after a while because there was just so much stuff. So after an hour, we decided we had enough so I took snaps of her as evidence of the visit and off we went to Rodeo Drive, Beverly Hills.

Rodeo Drive, Beverly Hills

Interestingly enough, my initial plan had called for a visit to the Forest Lawn Cemetary Museum, but I think Rodeo Drive was a better choice. When I finalized the Saturday plan with Rodeo Drive on the itinerary, Kirsten had emailed me about Barney's of New York, so I thought okay, yeah we'll go there. Then on Saturday morning, Kirsten mentioned Barney's another 3-4 times (a couple of those were directed to Barry, but I was within earshot). You know, women have a really SUBTLE way of telling you what they really want. So finally I say: "okay okay, we're going to Barney's! you already told me that in your email you know. I get the hint." Then she follows up with: "oh we don't really have to go there..." Oh pleeeeeeezzze!!!!!!!!

To assure her that we were really going to Barney's, I said: "you know what, I'm going on the internet to find where Barney's is."

So we drove around Beverly Hills. It was kinda neat, we fit right in. I saw two cars next to each other which looked exactly like mine (same color). Good taste was clearly evident in this part of town. As we turned on Santa Monica Blvd to find parking, Kirsten saw Prado's on the corner of Rodeo Drive, and she got all giddy for a moment. We were crossing the street when some tourists complimented Kirsten on her sunglasses. So I guess we were properly attired. We walked on the west side of Rodeo Drive, and hit most of the stores (she seemed to know most of these shops, and I was pretty much oblivious to what was going on around me - let's face it, to any guy this would just like be going to a mall and waiting for the girl to make up her mind, your only hope is that you'll get to see some HOT CHICKS along the way). At the end of Rodeo Drive is Wilshire where Barney's was located. Now I had thought Barney's was just another "store". But clearly I had underestimated the 5 story building which was Barney's. Now I mention the 5 stories not because of the architectural merits of such a construction, but because we would actually be walking up 4 flights of stairs (they were those long winding stairways too). Fortunately, the top 4th and 5th were mostly men's stuff so we went through those quickly. However, on the third floor Kirsten found a very interesting belt to go along with her outfits. It actually looked good with her leopard skirt. So she bought it for the price of a good progressive scan DVD player, and the young man with "fine features" (her words) put it in a clever little Barney's of New York bag for her. Finally she got her fix of Barney's, and I was relieved that we actually walked out of the store with something.

We walked up the east side of Rodeo Drive, and clearly Barney's had satiated her as we didn't go into any stores. As we had ceased window shopping, I thought now would be an opportune time to take photos of her against objects that accentuate her height. We had lunch at a little Italian bistro/cafe. Pretty reasonable prices actually. And that was Beverly Hills.

Fox Studio

On the way home, we stopped by at work so I could give her a little tour of the Fox Studio lot. We even took a photo of her in front of my tinderbox trailer which was next to the "Dharma and Greg" stage. Everything was going according to schedule.

Karaoke Party

We got back to Woodland Hills at around 4:30 or so, and it was blistering. Over 100 Fahrenheit. Barry and Mo had already been working all day to get the turkey and other dishes ready, and I wrapped up the loose ends with a trip to the supermarket for some soda and little necessities.

The place started filling up at around 7 pm, and we probably maxed out at 15 people when Dale and Michelle showed at 10:00 pm. I will say that several core people I was expecting (those who had actually indicated they were going to show), did not show up and flaked which gravely angered me. Unlike the gentle giant Joe Orr who had a similar experience last month and magnanimously did not exact fearful retribution, I will not be as forgiving.

The dynamics of the party was a little bit different this time because of the mix of people. I knew it was going to be exciting when Bruce walked up behind Kirsten and squeezed her shoulder growling: "hey baby". And when Bruce was raising his knee and leg up, and asking repeatedly how Mo's chlamydia was, I realized the benefits of not explaining Kirsten's abhorrence of crude behavior. I was exceptionally overjoyed with Bruce impromptly hugging Kirsten whilst she sat quietly on the living room floor watching us sing. I guess I neglected to mention that she severely dislikes unsolicited physical contact. I later told her "boy, I guess you'll be on muscle relaxants for weeks to come, eh?". I'll have to query Bruce later on those events, and he also made some smashing impressions on some new chicks but unfortunately I was in the living room singing my little heart out, so I'll have to get the details later when everybody's sobered up.

My good friend Vahe had reemerged from the dead, and he stayed for nearly 3-4 hours!!!!! That's way over 15 minutes. Vahe actually had the spotlight on him for quite a while making statements such as: "all Koreans generalize and stereotype!" whilst raising his index finger in the air. He did not disappoint.

Margaret came down from San Jose, and brought 3 friends with her (I think one of them was her young niece who was a bit overwhelmed by everybody). I thought Anne-Marie was pretty cute, and I kinda thought there was some attraction between her and Bruce, but I guess later somebody took a pistol and shot the horse they were riding on.

Cecilia, Marsha, Mo, Kirk and I were in the living room belting out tunes. The only thing that really annoyed me was that they kept on asking for songs I didn't have. They also kept on bugging me why I don't have happier songs, and I only have "suicide" songs. Hey, the world isn't a bed of roses, you know! We all mangled the Neil Diamond duet "you don't bring me flowers" magnificently. By the way, Kirk is Mo's new love, and so far, I approve of him (I don't know about Barry or Bruce, but I guess bringing Kirk over was like introducing him to the "family").

However, the highlight of Karaoke came when Michelle, Dale's young love, said she can do one song "The Rose". Oh my goodness, our jaws just dropped when she started singing. She was absolutely fantastic! All of us were in awe, she clearly had a good voice as any professional singer. Beautiful!!!! We said: "sing the entire disc!".

Kirsten retired early, probably grasping on to the combat knife under the mattress just in case Mr. Chlamydia wanted to sneak in and give her a goodnight kiss.

And that was the Karaoke Party.

Bye Bye

The next morning Kirsten left for the airport to be back in the safe company of her boyfriend Dave, her cat Shy, and her dog Riley. I asked her before she left: "So did you have fun?".

I think she did.

7

WAITRESSES

Do you love me because I'm beautiful, or
am I beautiful because you love me?
Oscar Hammerstein, II

ADULTS ACTING LIKE 5TH GRADERS

What is it with guys digging waitresses?

Date:	Wednesday, September 13, 2000 9:31 AM
To:	Nancye; Helen; Davide; Aldo; Greg; Maria; Yvette; Eunice; Debra; Dale; Tom; Joe O.; Barry; Bruce; Devin; Rowena; Derryn; Dan; Karen; Roberto; Dodge; Jun; Kirsten; Kevin; Brooke
Subject:	Adults acting like 5th-Graders

Some of you were there first-hand, so this is old news to you, but I'd just like to share an example of great juvenile behavior and the resulting intricate discussions we've been having.

We regularly frequent Chi-Chi's, an Italian restaurant where I get my favorite meatball sandwiches. Devin, Vahe (Armenian fellow), Barry and Maria, and I strolled in. And as luck would have it, we had our favorite waitress Amy (this is going to be a waitress story) waiting for us. We all think she's cute and we dig her because she's the friendliest and perkiest of all the Chi-Chi's waitresses, but Devin thinks she's a whore and I think she's a cutie-pootie. Anyway, Amy says: "You're going to my table, because I like you guys!". So we're following Amy, and I notice her different attire, so I say: "Say, you're wearing pants today!". And Amy goes: "Yeah, I have to cover up my fat". She's not really fat, she's just "full" or close to filling out. Maria on the other hand thinks I've blown it by being Mr. Insensitive, so she has to follow up with: "Oh you're not fat at all!!!". Later Maria chastises me for not saving the situation.

So we sit down and order the same food we've been ordering for the last 7 years or so. And we get into our regular inane discussions about gay people, where to buy shoes from: Nordstrom Rack or Big 5, and the reasons we shouldn't be dishwashing after we've ironed or played the piano (Doctor Maria brought that one up). But what we're really thinking about is how to have Amy, our favorite waitress, love us even more.

So we're thinking of cute ways to get her phone number (asking her straight-out for her phone number was of course out of the question as this may result in immediate rejection and make me cry and indicting all my lunch partners guilty by association).

When we get the left-over boxes, Devin says: "Joe, you should look at the box and say - Amy, something's missing from this box - your phone number". I thought that was a great idea! And as Amy is over my shoulder, I'm inspecting the box but I can't stop laughing to myself and I couldn't bring myself to do it. But Maria is paying by credit card, so I go: "Hey, let's slip something in the bill!" But I've got nothing to write on, and the best I can do is grab my ATM receipt with my most recent balance. So I write: "One of us thinks you're cute. Call me!" then wrote the phone number on the back of the ATM receipt.

Maria looks at the ATM receipt and asks: "Is that balance enough? I think you should use another account with more money". Barry looks at it and says: "Oh that's good enough, it's just a checking account". Notice, I hear no dissension or words of discouragement from my FRIENDS (of course, they all just want to see it played out, just like I would - hey, everybody pulls their own trigger and everybody has front-row seats).

But since I didn't leave a name, Amy (if she doesn't rip the ATM receipt up first) has a choice of 4 guys from the table, and technically Maria, but Maria looks pretty straight though.

Of course, if she NEVER calls, WE can ALL go back to Chi-Chi's and we can pretend it never happened and we can all have our meatball sandwiches, so that's okay. But if she does call and it's not fortunate, well, I guess I can never eat meatball sandwiches at Chi-Chi's again.

So we're driving back to work, and Devin says: "Yeah, Amy won't call, she wants someone more strong and take charge - you should've asked her directly". Well, yeah, I agree with that. But then I thought, wait a minute, the last time I was there Amy told me she thought I was the leader because I looked like the leader! So I tell Devin: "Wait a minute, but she thinks I'm the leader so no way will she think I wrote that wimpy note on the ATM receipt! She'll think it's you Devin who was too scared to ask her out directly!". YEAH!!!!!

So now I'm going to get Vahe, Maria and Barry and me to go to Chi-Chi's again without Devin, so Amy (if she doesn't call) will definitely think it's Devin.

I quite enjoyed that.

BLACK ANGUS WAITRESS

My friend Joe O.'s reply convinced me what a small world it really is.

THE ORIGINAL MESSAGE...

Date:	Thursday, September 28, 2000 2:47 PM
To:	Eunice; Roberto; Dodge; Jun; Dan; Rowena; Derryn; Kevin; Kirsten; Bruce; Barry; Joe O.; Tom; Dale; Yvette; Maria
Subject:	Waitress Story #2

Waitresses are just so cute! They're stuck in dead-end jobs, and guys feel sorry for them and want to rescue them from their horrible lives - well, that's my theory at least why guys dig waitresses.

Or maybe it's because if the waitress is a girl, the waitress just has to keep on serving the guy with a big smile no matter what a big brat the guy is.

But I have a nice little waitress story.

So we've gone back to Chi-Chi's and Amy is still our waitress, so it's okay. I can still get my meatball sandwiches. Maria says, Amy is a bit distant now, but I think Maria is just blowing things out of proportion.

But today we went to Black Angus, and the last time I was there, Charlotte (the waitress) was upset that I didn't specifically request for her. So this time, we went there and I scoped the place out, found her, and requested that she serve us. Charlotte digs us because we always come in with coupons and are very entertaining and frugal. Anyway, Charlotte is very busy (she already had enough tables but she still took us), and she comes around and starts asking us questions where we work, what we do. Maria tries to make us look a bit more glamourous and says: "we're all SOFTWARE DEVELOPERS" after I say: "we're just programmers" to which I follow up with: "yeah, but we don't look like nerds, do we???". Charlotte just shakes her head.

So she's tells us she has two jobs and works hard. After she leaves, we wonder what that second job is. And I say: "Medical technician?". I just guessed that. So she comes back, and I give her my guess of "medical technician". She looks at me as if I'm an idiot and says: "well, I have a college degree in psychology and music, and I do opera as my second job". And she then proceeds to tell us about this opera show they're putting together on October 14.

So (I think Maria is helping now but of course it's just all me) I say: "well, do you have any flyers in your locker that you want to give us?". And she says: "why yes, I do have some". So she comes back and gets the flyer and puts it on our table. Maria pays the bill by credit card (no atm receipt this time). And when Charlotte comes back with the receipt, I say: "say Charlotte, how about putting down your phone number so we can call you for any questions regarding the opera show?". So she just smirks and writes the number down on the flyer. YEAH!!!!! I SCORED!!!! Dino ONE - Devin ZERO!

As we're walking back to the building, I remind everybody how fantastic and smooth my operation was. And Barry says Charlotte was touching me all over the place. So I'm looking at the flyer and notice that the last number is missing (she put her last name down too - I don't know about that - that's too hispanic I think). The little games people play, I swear! But if you think about it, there are only 10 possible combinations (0-9) so that is totally unnecessary. And besides, after I looked her up on the internet, the last number is 2. So now I've got the number to call Charlotte and her husband who happens to be the initial J in the telephone listing.

Thank you, thank you very much.

Joe O.'s Reply...

From:	Joe O.
Date:	Thursday, September 28, 2000 2:47 PM
To:	Joe
Cc:	Eunice; Roberto; Dodge; Jun; Dan; Rowena; Derryn; Kevin; Kirsten; Bruce; Barry; Tom; Dale; Yvette; Maria
Subject:	Re: Waitress Story #2

Well... isn't this just a little small world....

That Charlotte you speak of happens to be the youngest sister of one of my college roommates, and is pretty much my little sister too. The next time you're in there, mention that you know Joe O. and she should go on and on about my kids (or how handsome I am or something to that affect).

I've known Charlotte for about 15 years. She's very nice... she's also too young for you. Their father was partially Hispanic, but they're about as white-bread as they come (you should meet her mom.... very sweet, but to meet her, you'd swear she's from some midwestern town). It was not her husband that you found in the phone book... the initial "J" is for her mom... Jeannie. She still lives with her mom in an apartment in Northridge.

So there... don't start talking about how hot she is or what terribly nasty things you'd like to do with her in some pagan ritual you're planning!

- Joe (who's reminding you how much bigger he is than you and wouldn't want you talking trash about a pseudo-family-member!)

LOOSE LIPS

It was a good test for my improvisational skills.

Date:	Friday, September 29, 2000 11:21 AM
To:	Davide; Aldo; Greg; Yvette; Maria; Bruce; Barry; Joe O.; Tom; Dale; Kevin; Kirsten; Dan; Rowena; Derryn; Roberto; Dodge; Jun; Eunice
Subject:	Waitress Story #3

Well, there is follow-up to this story!

But I'm sad to say there was a bit of mischief being played out behind the scenes.

So I give Charlotte a call this morning, and the answering machine is picking up, and I'm leaving a message "Hi Charlotte, this is Joe, the Black Angus coupon guy, hey, do you know a guy named Joe O...." and then the phone picks up and it's Charlotte: "Yes, I do know Joe O.!"

Imagine my surprise when Charlotte queries me on the "email" that's been circulating about the Black Angus waitress.

Oh crap.

So I say: "hmm, Joe O. forwarded you the email?". And Charlotte goes: "Joe forwarded it to my brother who read it to me over the phone! What's this about me touching you all over the place???? And this I SCORED thing? what's that scoring? And how about the last digit missing and the little games I was playing??? And I'm too hispanic for you?????"

Needless to say, I was in a defensive position for most of the conversation, having to explain my stance on waitresses and the touching accusation. But I think I managed to salvage the situation with my wit and charm since I kept her on the phone for a good 30 minutes. I even managed to get her age and where she went to school (she's 24 and went to St Mary's).

Here's a good snippet of conversation (after I told her that Joe O. says she's too young for me):

Charlotte: So how old are you? You look 12.

Joe: No, I only act as if I'm 12. I'm actually 32.

Succinct yet funny. I like that.

I didn't ask her out, yet. I was still in shock from the effects of Joe O.'s mischief.

I just told her I'd come by next week at Black Angus and maybe check her out at Opera Nova.

I think she digs me.

I FEEL SO ASHAMED

Honesty is so overrated sometimes...

Date:	Tuesday, October 03, 2000 9:03 AM
To:	Devin; Yvette; Maria; Bruce; Barry; Joe O.; Tom; Dale; Dan; Rowena; Derryn; Davide; Aldo; Greg; Kevin; Kirsten; Roberto; Dodge; Jun
Subject:	I feel so ashamed...

I already told my first lie to Charlotte's mother Jeannie.

So I figured a couple of days had gone by and it was okay to call Charlotte for a social event.

But she wasn't home, and her mother picks up the phone and is kind enough to take my name and number for a callback. But like a loving mother, she says: "would you like to leave a message?". So I say: "oh this is just about Opera Nova (Charlotte's opera gig on the 14th)".

What was I supposed to say: "yeah, tell your daughter I think she's cute"?

I'm already exhausted from all this CHICK action. I think I'm just gonna concentrate on investments this week.

Tip: Xerox, down to US$12. Buy at US$9 bucks?

CHICK MAGNET DINO

More proof of my magnet skills!

Date:	Monday, October 16, 2000 10:51 AM
To:	Karen; Debra; Eunice; Devin; Nancye; Dodge; Roberto; Jun; Dan; Rowena; Derryn; Kirsten; Kevin; Joe O.; Bruce; Barry; Tom; Dale; Maria; Yvette; Greg; Aldo; Davide; Vinh; Craig; Charles; Brooke
Subject:	Chick Magnet Dino

Well, well, well. Despite the fact that none of my dear dear friends wanted to come see Charlotte's operatic performance in Santa Monica, I braved the ignominy of sitting by myself in the church aisles and drove Saturday night to Mt. Olive Lutheran church. But hey, I have to finish what I started.

There were possibly 100+ people attending Opera Nova, and I got myself a program, and to my dismay I found out that Charlotte's performance was the 13th (4th after the intermission), so I had to sit through 12 performances and I couldn't even escape after the intermission.

As anticipated, there were a lot of good-looking opera girls, and I started grading the hotness of each opera singer on a scale from 0.01 to 1.00. There were a couple of CHICKS that got to 0.8. The performances were varied, and they had some drama and comedy. Mostly lighthearted stuff like "Hansel and Gretel", "Barber of Seville" etc. So when it was finally Charlotte's turn, I was looking forward to something cheery. But then she came out in this totally black dress, complete with arm-length gloves, and had the most somber and serious expression as in a funeral procession. What luck that I chanced on the grimmest choice of operatic performances for that evening! It turned out that she was playing Princepessa, the bitch aunt who took away the son of her niece (and who never told her niece that her son had died). Anyway, it was very good, and her dress showed a lot of neckline and upper arm so I was able to analyze her muscle tone and definition. And her hair was braided and curled which slightly upset me because I prefer her ponytail which is both playful and adventurous.

Well, she and her partner finished their gig (her partner played Christine on Broadway with Michael Crawford, she was kinda hot in a "natural" kind of way), and Opera Nova finished 20 minutes later.

So I didn't want to hang around, so I headed out the door. Charlotte and her cutie partner were walking towards me, so I called Charlotte over, and she didn't recognize me (all Asian people look the same) but she hugged me anyway but then she remember who I was and asked where my deadbeat friends were. I think she was impressed that I was the only one who showed up. Anyways, we parted and I drove back to Woodland Hills.

The next day, I was at home, doing photo albums from 1969-1978 (my current project) when the phone rang. Well, surprise, surprise, if it wasn't Charlotte. Like I always say, "if mohammed won't go to the mountain, the mountain comes to mohammed". And I'm Mohammed, baby!!!!!

She thanked me for coming to her show, and she talked to me for about an HOUR r so (I guess she was enthralled by my wit and charm). She kept on asking me if I was catholic, and how catholic was I. I told her that I'll just go to any church that's nearest of has the biggest selection of single CHICKS. She didn't quite accept my statement that I was a "free-lance" catholic. Gee whiz, when I go to a christian church and they ask me if I'm christian, I say "sometimes" and then they yell: "there's no such thing as 'sometimes" christian!". Can't win! Then I found out she was still working as an opera singer at Macaroni Grill, and I said: "macaroni grill? I've never seen you there and I go there once a month to get my free cake!". And Charlotte says: "Free cake? what do you mean?", and I say: "you know, we pretend it's my birthday and we get free cake!". Charlotte didn't like that at all and spent a good 10 minutes berating us money-making programmers who make waiters/waitresses work harder by lying that it's their birthday to get free cake. I still see nothing wrong with that time-honored practice. Hey, I'm a thrill-seeker, I live on the edge, baby!!!!

The same evening, the guys and I were going to Todai to have Japanese buffet, so I asked Charlotte if she wanted to but she said she had to work at the Angus, but said she'd like to go and take her 23 year old chickie cousin who moved to California with us guys one of these days.

Joe: Barry and Devin are going tonight, you can meet them again
Charlotte: Who's Barry?
Joe: Barry's the guy who said you were touching me all over the place.
Charlotte: Oh Barry, the LIAR, tell him I said hi!
Joe: And Devin's the guy who returned his steak.
Charlotte: Oh, the COMPLAINER!
Joe: You haven't met ALL my friends yet, you'll like them.

I can tell, she digs us.

Anyway, that's about it. I'll probably see her sometime again because she obviously thinks the world of me. But I think there are some issues (religion, free cake etc.) that may be unresolvable, but hey, she's pretty funny. She may make a good addition to the group. And she probably knows a lot of young single hot CHICKS.

8

GRANT

I must be cruel, only to be kind.
Shakespeare, Hamlet.

MY ROOMMATE

Sometimes I think I was a bit rough on Grant. But who can blame me!

Date:	Friday, July 30, 1999 8:18 AM
To:	Dodge; Jun; Roberto; Sandra; Rowena; Nicole; Karen; Helen; Brooke; Alicia; Kareena; Simon; Peter; Mark; Greg; Derryn; Davide; Dan; Aldo; Grant; Kevin; Kirsten; Bruce; Dale; Barry; Joe O.; Tom; Maria; Yvette
Subject:	Alternative Lifestyle Story #23

Dear Dear Friends,

As my good friend from Seattle mentioned the other day, I have now embraced this alternative lifestyle in Los Angeles with that gay-boy Grant C.. I guess it's been a long time since I had a roommate, the last one being in Detroit with a good old clean-cut Christian fellow named Sam from Minnesota or the Dakotas and who used to have a baseball card collection. What a marked difference to Grant, I'd say!

So yesterday we achieved another level of gayness (hey, there's nothing wrong with gay people, we're all God's children and besides, they give the best parties and cut good hair). I had just finished up preparing a magnificent batch of fried rice (making the kitchen smell of garlic and irritating my eyes with the onions), and I also heated up my mother's excellent lumpia shanghai (filipino meat rolls in eggroll wrapper, they look like cigars). Because my mother is thoughtful, she also packed in a little container with sweet sour sauce for the lumpia shanghai. So I'm sitting there, eating the fried rice with some fish in coconut sauce (the fish was all for me, since caucasian boy doesn't like the smell of fish in coco and jalapenos), and then I see Grant stick the lumpia in the sauce, bite the lumpia. AND THEN STICK THE LUMPIA WITH THE BITTEN-OFF-END-FIRST BACK IN THE SAUCE!!!! So I say: "Hey man, whatcha doing? Double dipping with your saliva in the sweet sour sauce?????". So he says some stuff like there's nothing to worry about and I'm being silly. HEPATITIS B & C SILLY MY ASS!!!!! Goodness knows where Grant puts his mouth after he wakes up and before he leaves for work. So I dip out sauce on the pan for ME, so I don't get any more of Grant's love germs. And what does he do, stick more of his bitten-off-end in my sauce. So I said again: HEPATITIS B & C! STOP IT MAAAAAAAN!!!! Anyways, we resolved it and this just means in the future, NO MORE SAUCE FOR YOU!!!!!

So after this gay domestic dispute, we took off for Santa Monica, since that's probably one of the more accessible attractive places to go to in Los Angeles. So we're walking down 3rd Street Promenade looking at all the shops, bars and restaurants, just like any gay couple. Grant's saying that it looks just like Pitt St. Except it's bigger. Hasn't really changed much, the street artists are still there doing their special talents, but there seem to be a whole lot more bums. What was kinda neat was the big Borders or Barnes & Noble bookstore at the end of the promenade where you can just sit and read all the books and magazines (for free) while drinking coffee. No obligation to buy. The smelly street bums were in there too reading magazines. There was also a cool Swatch store, and I was checking out if they had this neat pocket watch I saw on this German dude while I was out in Ayers Rock. But I couldn't find it. Maybe it was a Swiss Army pocket watch. So if any of you know what I'm talking about, you can get it for me as a gift. But in the Swatch store, there was this boy who was trying to impress these CHICKS by saying he had the first Swatch watch and it's now worth 20,000 dollars. I will have to remember to use that line someday.

After the promenade we made a U-turn to go to the beach (it's dark now, so it's even gayer still with two guys walking down the beach). As we're walking, we see the Santa Monica pier with all the amusement park rides lit up in the distance. So I say: "let's walk over there". And Grant's "THAT'S FAR!!!! LOOK, THE BUILDINGS ARE SO SMALL, that must be 30 mins away, let's drive!". Yep, sometimes the physically unfit can be such a drag sometimes. But it didn't matter, 'cause Grant had to follow me because he didn't know where the car was parked and he doesn't know the area. After 15 mins we got to the pier, and they still had the same rides and restaurants as I remembered it. They even had an outdoor concert a couple of minutes prior to when we arrived. Lots of folks streaming out. The surprising thing was that there were so many people fishing. We walked up to the end of the pier, and checked out the big blackness which was the Pacific Ocean. I guess, way across the other end of the ocean was beautiful Sydney, where all my other dear dear friends are - working, goofing off, or doing some other illegal secret stuff that's only 2-3 steps away from going to jail.

By this time, my right ear was splitting from this crazy ear infection I always seem to get. So we drove back to Chatsworth. Stopped by in a fascist drugstore to get some pills for me, whilst Grant bought some ice cream in his quest to break the fabled 300 lb barrier which has always eluded him. I mentioned "fascist" because those authoritarian corporate tyrants at Rite-Aid only sell Pepsi and not Coca-Cola. What kind of freedom of choice is that?????? It really galls me when someone/something restricts me from exercising choice, so we set fire to the trash bin outside the drugstore to register our protest with "the MAN", and left.

Back at home, Grant persisted in more gayness by wanting to eat out of the ice cream box directly. I said "put mine in A BOWL!!!!". Grant made some flimsy excuses that he's used to living with his girlfriend. Probably hinting that if I became his girlfriend, this wouldn't be an issue. JUST PUT THE ICE CREAM IN THE FUCKING BOWLS!!!!!!!! Anyway, the mint ice cream was quite good.

Before going to bed, Grant asked if we could switch comforters afar the next washing since his comforter was all pink/blue and looked like a girl's comforter (mine is a manly blue). I looked at his comforter, and sure enough, it was indeed of a sissy persuasion, and I wouldn't be caught dead sleeping in it. I just looked at Grant and called him faggot (in a nice way), and went to sleep.

And that's about it. I LOVE YOU ALL!!!!!!!

ROLE REVERSAL

Hey, I'm able to poke fun at myself.

Date:	Tuesday, August 03, 1999 8:26 AM
To:	Dodge; Jun; Roberto; Sandra; Rowena; Nicole; Karen; Helen; Brooke; Alicia; Kareena; Simon; Peter; Mark; Greg; Derryn; Davide; Dan; Aldo; Grant; Kevin; Kirsten; Bruce; Dale; Barry; Joe O.; Tom; Maria; Yvette
Subject:	Role Reversal

Grant's been a little bit upset with me since he always seems to be the object of scrutiny in my harrowing tales of the big city and rampant homoeroticism, and since he freely admits he's not a great communicator and doesn't have the tempestuous tenacity of spending a couple of minutes insulting other people, I thought, hey, I'll write up something for him.

Through the Eyes of Grant C.

That crazy Joe Dino! Look at him lift those 100 lb weights, he'll probably get a hernia from lifting those things. And even if he does get a lot bigger, he still won't be as big as me. I gotta admit though, HE'S STARTING TO LOOK PRETTTTTY HOOOOOTTTT!!! But I can't let him know that, Joe already thinks I'm a big fag. Not that there's anything wrong with being gay.

"Hey Joe, you want a Scotch & Coke?". It's kinda pointless to ask Joe that question. Ever since he's gotten back to Los Angeles, he's sworn off all unbiblical behavior including alcohol. But then again, Joe gets kinda silly after 3-4 rum and cokes and starts doing trivia questions, and ranting about his theory about the evils of material possessions and earthly waste. For a guy who has imaginary limits on his bank accounts, he sure doesn't sound like monk to me. Joe's just done his weights and now doing 50 pushups with one hand, and reading a book with the other hand. Joe's got to read 10 books a year, otherwise, he thinks he's a hypocrite since that's in his list of requirements. But then again, maybe he should lay off his list of requirements, I don't see it helping his case. Joe's blabbering something, he says: "No alcohol for me, that's unbiblical. Only water please. The body is a temple, and you have to keep it clean, devoid of all impurities and poison. Remember, cleanliness is next to godliness.". Just more blah and blah. Geeze, for somebody who's always blah-blahing about cleanliness, how come he's always farting? There must be a lot of poison in his bowels that he's gotta get rid of. If only Joe weren't so big and powerful now after weightlifting, I'd sit on him and crush him like an ant to keep him quiet.

"Hey man, can we go to Target?". Joe always laughs at me when I go shopping. He thinks I buy all kinds of unnecessary stuff, but then yesterday he wanted to spend 50 bucks on a garlic crusher, but he didn't want to spend a couple of bucks on coasters for the table. At least Joe doesn't mind eating out except he's always ordering iced teas. He can drink 3 - 4 glasses of iced teas in one session, and he can do it for lunch and dinner. Then he starts crying in the car that his bladder is about to explode. He's kinda bossy too when he's in the restaurant. He wasn't like that in Sydney, I guess it wouldn't have been much use in Sydney with the customer service and all. Here, Joe refuses to sit at a table close to a door (any door! toilet door, exit door, kitchen door etc.), and he treats waiters/waitresses like children and gives them condescending small talk. At least Joe gives me good tips like figuring out how to calculate the tip on a bill. Just divide the bill amount by 7, and you get the tip amount. I guess you could argue multiplying the bill amount by 0.15 would also get you that number, but Joe's just a freaking human calculator!!!!!

Speaking of electronic devices, do you guys remember that Joe never picks up the phone in his apt. Well, he bought himself a mobile/cell phone and half the time, he never answers it or turns it off. What's the point of that??? And when he does use the cell phone, he talks funny. When he calls up his mom, he always :"Hello Mother" instead of "Hi Ma" or "Hi Mom". I think he likes to pretend he's royalty or something like that. He once told me his family are aristocrats, that's why they're always making fun of the proletarian masses. But he's always harping about the corporate fascists, so I don't know how he can reconcile that. Yeah, Joe's got some crazy ideas sometimes. When we go to the mall, ALL the girls that walk past us remind him of TWO girls that he knows. And he points them out and says, "oh look, that's a baby version of ....". "she's a blond version of...". That gets pretty annoying sometimes, especially when he points his finger and starts talking in a loud voice. Everything reminds him of those two girls. I don't even think they're that HOOOOOT!!!!

One other thing Joe is good for, is to find all the places to shop. Meryvn's and Marshalls are pretty good places to get nice clothes for cheap. Joe seems to like the earth-tone colors, like green, rust, grey, beige, khaki, so he's been buying all these clothes that will make him look invisible once he goes to the forests of tasmania. I gotta admit, Joe's got good taste in clothes. But the funny thing is, Joe doesn't really care what other people think of him, so he could be wearing diapers inside-out, and still have that smug condescending look on his face which says: "ASK ME IF I CARE". That's why I'm not sure if Joe will stay with the company because if they do something that he doesn't like, he'll just quit. I hope not, because I don't know how to operate the rice cooker.

LAS VEGAS

A classic Las Vegas story...

Date:	Monday, August 23, 1999 4:17 PM
To:	Grant; Maria; Yvette; Bruce; Dale; Barry; Joe O.; Tom; Kevin; Kirsten; Simon; Peter; Mark; Greg; Derryn; Davide; Dan; Aldo; Kareena; Alicia; Brooke; Helen; Karen; Nicole; Rowena; Dodge; Jun; Roberto
Subject:	Las Vegas

Dear Dear Friends,

So I finally got to see my beloved Vegas since 1996 this weekend. Usually, Vegas is strictly a Dino trip but this time we took caucasian boy Grant C. with us on condition he wouldn't rape my mother, that PERVERT!!!

I'm glad we took Grant with us because it's always good to have a superhero accompany us. You might ask, what kind of super powers does Grant have? All I can say is, I may just have to call Grant Super Self-Conscious Man! But more on that later!

Left Saturday morning shortly after 6 am. Got delayed slightly because Grant needed to eat something even though we were going to have breakfast in Barstow. I told Grant that the McDonald's in Barstow had some kind of world-record or title as being the world's busiest McDonald's, but I'd give it the world's slowest and most inefficient McDonald's after standing in line with 100 hundred other yahoos waiting for their McBreakfasts.

Finally got to Vegas at around 10:30. Our first stop was Excalibur and Luxor because I wanted to hit the end of the strip first. We sat down in Excalibur at a blackjack table to get the feel of the whole Vegas thing, and after showing the dealer that THE GREAT ONE was back in town, and after showing Grant how to order his free alcoholic drinks and tip the hostesses, we moved on to Excalibur. Bear in mind, I've seen all of these casinos before. I'm just doing the tour for SSC-Man. Imagine my surprise when SSC-Man didn't want to go sightseeing anymore. He was getting all crazy, probably got tired from walking and got a little hot from the sun, and said all he wanted to do was sit a blackjack table for hours and just play so he can win all the tens of thousands of dollars that was just waiting for him. So I said "fine, we'll just go to Rio and we can have the buffet for lunch, and then you can gamble after we get to the hotel. No sightseeing for you!"

So we went to Rio, but since Rio is the best buffet in town for the value, there was a huge line. SSC-Man started going crazy on me again and started questioning THE GREAT ONE's lunch plans. Finally tiring of SSC-Man's whining, I just told SSC-Man that he should just go away and sit at a table and play blackjack and come back in 30-40 mins since he doesn't understand how things are done in Vegas. Well, it's a good thing that he did go away and play, because he won 200 bucks and we got to eat the Rio buffet.

The Rio buffet was pretty good, it even had the snow crab legs and calamari. So we sat there for an hour or so while I brought back plate after plate which I hardly finished. The Rio buffet had all kinds of food areas such as Chinese, Japanese, Western, Mexican, Italian, American, desserts, fruits etc. I like the desserts, the key lime pie and chocolate mousse were outstanding!!!! SSC-Man went insane after he dropped some sauce on his polo shirt. He rubbed the shirt with a paper napkin, and the paper napkin kinda got glued on his polo shirt, and he spent some serious time rubbing and trying to rub the paper crap off his polo shirt. This was just the beginning for SSC-Man!

We checked into the Imperial hotel and SSC-Man spent some considerable time trying to figure out what pants to wear for today's schedule. Unfortunately, his pants in the bag got all wrinkled, so he was looking around for an iron to make his pants beautiful so all the CHICKS will MAKE LOVE TO HIM because of those spiffy pants. No iron, just wear jeans instead. So he finally got settled down and we went to the main casino and played blackjack for a couple of hours.

We went to Flamingo a little while later, and we got suckered to play Spanish 21. Nobody was playing at the table, and the dealer CHICK was explaining the rules. Basically, it's blackjack without 10s. The only thing the dealer forgot to tell me was that the game sucked, that's why nobody was playing it. So I lost a quick 50 but she was pretty so that made it all better. But hey, we're all God's children! had thought up of a great gift idea for the Australians while I was at Rio. I figured I'd get coin buckets from the casinos and give everyone a set of casino buckets, which can be used for office, home and any number of unbiblical recreational uses. So I got 5 buckets from Rio, got another 5 from Imperial etc. As we were moving from casino to casino, I was getting more and more buckets until I had buckets from the thigh-level to over my shoulder (kinda like I was carrying rifle of buckets). So I got buckets from Caesar's, Flamingo, Bally's etc. When we were walking to the Bellagio, SSC-Man asked me if I felt the least bit embarrassed about carrying a yard of buckets around in front of hundreds of people and in the glitzy casinos. Not really. What's there to be shamed about? That I'm so caring and thoughtful that I'm taking back all these Las Vegas mementos for my Aussie buddies? Apparently (only SSC-Man would have noticed this) while we were in the Bellagio Art Gallery gift store (they were charging 12 bucks to get in the Art museum!!!! ART SHOULD BE FREE!!!!!), the Bellagio CHICKS and guards were commenting on my prodigious collection of coin buckets. I just say I'm glad that I made an impression on their empty lives! So I bought a lovely calendar of Impressionist paintings for my imaginary special friend who likes Impressionist art. Maybe I should add that to my list of requirements "... must like impressionism" but only Renoir, Gogh, Pisarro and other good ones, and not the guy who did all the South Sea island nudie pics. Unfortunately, calendars have an implied used by date, so my imaginary special friend should best materialize sometime before January 1 to make use of the calendar. I thought the Bellagio was pretty nice. Maybe I'll stay there the next time.

Caesar's Palace still looks pretty good, and they had the movie statues that get angry, wave their swords and yell at each other. They were kinda cool. I think SSC-Man thought the big animatronic CHICK was HOT! It was still in the high 90s at night, so while I was cruising the hotels to get more buckets, Grant was trying to break Imperial's bank by playing blackjack. I finally caught up with Grant at around 11 and he was just having a whale of a time, getting all the free drinks and talking like a fool to the casino people. He was even up 250-300 or so. And SSC-Man said this was just like all old times! Old times? Like the time we lost 2K each at Star City? But SSC-Man was super-happy so I played blackjack for a while. I thought Santiago, our dealer from Cuba was a nice old dork. I was telling them that it was raining outside, and Santiago says: "Raining? You mean raining, like this????", and Santiago flips over his cards and has a twenty and beats our hands. Pretty funny for somebody over 40, I'll give him that.

As for winning at the table, I was playing blackjack earlier, and this girl and I were on a winning streak, and I was raking in the blackjacks but naturally the streak came to an end. During the bad run, the girl was wondering out loud what had happened, to which I replied "The Good Lord giveth, and the Good Lord taketh". I left SSC-Man and went to the room to sleep at around midnight. 5 hours later, SSC-Man comes in, and collapses on the bed. When we woke up at 7:00 am, SSC-Man was still passed out but he managed to mumble out that he got us free meals at the buffet. So what was the damage? Grant was trying to get a total of $1000 in chips, and he was a hundred bucks short. Then the pit boss "fooled" him to double down on some bad calls. And it all went downhill from there on. So he lost everything. But the pit boss felt sorry for him and gave him

3 buffet passes. Not a bad deal for 500 bucks!!!! Like I said, "The Good Lord giveth, and the Good Lord taketh". It was all pretty biblical.

I left SSC-Man to sleep some more on his misfortune, and I walked all the way from Imperial to the far end of the strip where Mandalay Bay and MGM was. On the way, I picked up buckets from Monte Carlo, Excalibur, New York New York, Luxor, Tropicana, MGM and finally Mandalay Bay. I was dead-tired from walking in the heat, so I took a taxi from Luxor back to Imperial. The Luxor guy looked at me when he was getting a taxi and said: "Sir, you're only supposed to take one of those buckets..." I guess carrying 35 buckets was a dead giveaway (the Mandalay buckets are beautiful, you can put your head in it). Beautiful!!!!

So I went back to the Imperial, picked up SSC-Man and we had brunch at the Emperor's buffet. Piled on heaps of food again on the plate. SSC-Man was a bit down I think, he was very quiet and was just sighing and panting. I guess he was doing some reflection on last night's events. After brunch, we headed for Circus Circus so SSC-Man could take a picture in front of Circus Circus and send it to his parents. Circus Circus is such a big zoo that we got lost and we spent so much time trying to find the entrance. So I took some pictures of SSC-Man, stole some more buckets from Circus Circus, and we headed for the long trip back to Los Angeles. Unfortunately traffic was miserable and plenty of accidents and combined with the Sunday rush, it was just horrible. I may just have to fly next time if it's a weekend trip. SSC-Man was asking me why I did most of the driving, and he asked if it was because I don't trust his driving with my mother in the car. So I said yeah. Then SSC-Man was asking me how many accidents I have had, and that he was a better driver because he never had any accidents. I don't follow that empirical logic, but SSC-Man is just a little too wound-up when he drives. But I was so dead-tired from the stop-and-go traffic on the I-15 that by the time I hit Barstow, I succumbed and let Mr. No-Accidents-Man get behind the wheel. He did okay.

Finally got back to Monrovia, picked up some more free weights since SSC-Man has been lifting weights, and then drove back to Chatsworth. In Chatsworth, I laid out all my buckets for display on the dining table, and I figured out that I got an even 100 buckets from 20 casinos. NOT TOO SHABBY!!!! Oh yeah, I only lost $120-$130 or so playing slots and blackjack. I had some nice wins on the slots, but they all eat it up again anyway.

Maybe I should have a big Margarita party and we can drink margaritas from the coin buckets.

DEAD CAT

I question my involvement to this day.

Date:	Friday, June 16, 2000 9:22 AM
To:	Dodge; Jun; Roberto; Grant; Dan; Derryn; Karen; Rowena; Kirsten; Kevin; Bruce; Dale; Barry; Joe O.; Tom; Yvette; Maria; Eunice; Helen; Aldo; Brooke; Davide; Greg; Simon
Subject:	Dead Cat

Dear Dear Friends,

So I've nearly got all the scenes (just vague outline - no detail yet) I wanted to do for "Raising Hell", my screenplay about 3 computer guys who unleash the biblical Hell on Earth and ultimately must defeat the Lord of Flies, the great Satan himself.

But my screenplay book says that for an action-comedy, one would probably need 45 scenes. So I have about 50 now, but some of them will probably fall out when I start putting them together, so I probably need 60 or so, so I needed some more ideas for some scenes. Well, I've been working hard, and it's been slow progress to get the 10 spare scenes I need. But yesterday, I managed to add in the "dead cat" scene to my list.

As luck would have it, life is more interesting than fiction, because yesterday Grant came running into the office, and started crying that Jim's (his roommate, the guy who owns the house) ailing cat had finally passed away. And he needed to contact Barry (my roommate) because Nancye (Jim's partner) had talked to Barry about burying the cat in the backyard. Yeah, all these names and relationships sound like as if this is an episode of Melrose Place, but that's really how it is around here.

So anyway, I gave Grant Barry's number to contact and told Grant that Barry's parents were here from out-of-town so he may not have time to do it. And Grant says,"well if he isn't coming, you'll have to help me bury it". And I say, "why does the cat need to be buried?? why can't we just throw the cat in the dumpster and turn the earth around a little bit in the backyard, so it looks like we buried it?". Then Grant starts crying again and says that Jim might want to dig up the cat and see if we actually buried it. So I say, "okay, if Jim wants to see the cat then why don't we just put the cat in a plastic bag and put the cat in the freezer? then Jim can take care of it when Jim gets back." I thought those were two excellent ideas. My third idea was to put the cat on the barbecue pit and burn the cat away (you know, like they used to do in the wild west before, or the vikings...), but Grant would have none of that. So it looks like we were stuck to burying the cat.

So Barry calls and says I have to go with him to Grant's/Jim's house to bury the cat. I don't know how I got involved in the first place - I don't even like cats. They don't have souls so they won't go to heaven with me (I had an argument with someone today about cats having souls, and the guy goes: "how do you know cats don't have souls???" and I shot back: "because cats don't play chess. Have you ever seen a cat play chess?" that shut him up right there, baby!!!!). Then we arranged to meet at the house at 5:30 pm. Grant was late again and he wasn't home so we went in anyway and started shoveling a hole in the garden. We wanted to finish up early because Barry's mother was cooking this pot roast and it smelled absolutely fantastic, and I wanted to get back home and eat it. Of course, the ground was rock hard, and there were big fat roots in the ground. I dropped my cellphone on the ground, and we did a little dance on the phone before we realized where the phone was, but it was still working. Then crazy Grant arrived.

So we nearly had the hole finished (Barry did most of it - since he's stronger), and Grant brought out the cat which he had wrapped in a towel. We didn't even know what the name of that cat was. Then we had this big gay conversation on how we were going to put the cat in the hole. Grant wanted to wrap the cat in the towel (oooohhh like a little baby, so the little cat will be kept warm in its journey to the afterworld). Then someone thought (probably me) about putting the cat in a plastic bag, but then the bag won't bio-degrade. So finally we came up with newspaper. So Grant wraps up the cat in newspaper and puts it in the hole. But then they notice that the cats legs and tails are sticking out of the hole (rigor mortis), and the two guys don't want to touch the cat anymore and don't want to rearrange the limbs. So it's up to the GREAT ONE who has climbed Ayers Rocks to do the deed. I said: "okay okay, I'll do it!!!!!" I bend down and start putting the joints in place (if I had my Gurkha knife, I could have done it a whole lot faster), until I got all the extremities all bended in the right place. There, the cat fit snug in the hole. Grant pipes up from the back, and says: "what about the head, man????", so I say: "what about the head???" Grant: "the head's sticking out of the newspaper, it's going to get all dirty, we should cover it in newspaper to protect it!", so I say: "explain to me again the purpose of this newspaper????", but I wanted to go home and eat Barry's mother's pot roast so I grabbed some more newspaper, wrapped the head in it, rearranged the limbs some more and placed the mummified-newspaper cat in the hole. I put the dirt over the cat, jumped on the dirt to pack it in, put some more dirt and jumped on the dirt to pack it in and repeated that a couple more times. DONE!!!!!!!

Whew!!! Took three guys to do one cat burial. We briefly stopped by in Grant's room to check out his $2,000 digital TV/DVD set-up (it only took him 15 minutes to get a DVD to start playing), stole some lemons and grapefruit from the next-door neighbor and headed back so I could swim before dinner, and then eat the pot roast!!!! Yeah!!!!!!

INSTANT REBATE

Grant finally got laid off in February. But that had still given him 10-11 months in the USA to accumulate an assortment of expensive electronic equipment. I didn't think it would be reasonable for him to handcarry a 128 lb television on the plane.

Date:	Monday, April 02, 2001 10:07 AM
To:	none *(blind copy)*
Subject:	Funny Story

Hi All,

I just had to share this tragicomical story as it so representative of the complex and irreverent, yet morally justifiable conundrum that is Joe Dino. Some of you already heard this story.

You all remember Grant C., right? I used to dedicate whole emails to Grant (I even gave him special pet-names such as Super Self-Conscious Man, and Fat Boy), and his crazy antics. Well, he got laid off from the same company 2 1/2 months ago, and he's supposed to have returned to Melbourne on Friday, Mar 30. Well, he accumulated a lot of high-tech and expensive gear, and he had to get rid some of them. Chief among his possessions was his prized 124 lb Panasonic 32 inch Standard Digital TV (as opposed to HDTV) with Progressive Scan Line Doubler. That would be too heavy to carry on the plane, so I figured I'd end up buying it because none of his friends have the monetary gumption to shell out that kind of money. So I waited till the last minute, and didn't give much hints that I'd be really interested in it (playing hard to get). And sure enough, he calls up last minute and asks if I want his US$1,300 TV with 3 year warranty (2 years left - worth $140) for $700 bucks. Hey, I don't like to rip off my friends, so I accepted that price without haggling. I figured, hey, he needs the money in Oz since he didn't save anything all the time he was here.

Barry and I head over there Thu evening in Barry's truck (because the TV just won't fit in the Bitch-Magnet-Mobile). We untangle the wires and load the monster TV into the truck. I write him out a check (a check because if I gave him cash he'd have a day to spend it all the next day), and then I start looking around for free stuff he'd give me. So I asked if he'd give me an s-video cable (that's worth 20 bucks), and he gave me one for free. Then I asked if he'd give me a DVD, preferably an "exotic" DVD. But all his pornos are packed up, and only the normal movies are still out there. So I ask if I can have Excalibur (the John Boorman classic). And he goes: "yeah, you can have that. I don't like that movie, I think you recommended it to me." So I take the Excalibur DVD, that's worth 10 bucks. So now, I have $730 worth of stuff for $700. His phone rings, and he starts talking while Barry and I are just waiting around. Whilst I'm waiting, I casually open up the DVD box, and I notice a flash of green (the color of US bills, for you Aussies) in the box and immediately close it. Grant finishes talking on the phone, and we say bye bye and drive off.

The TV starts rattling in the car, so Barry decides to pull over to adjust the TV. So we adjust it so it stops bumping around. But before we take off, I say: "Barry, you may get mad at me, but I just have to share this with you." Because Barry is a very honest and uprighteous individual, I was concerned he may not necessarily agree with my actions. So I pop open the DVD box, and lo and behold, there were 3 crisp $20 dollar bills! Grant gave me a $60 dollar rebate on the $700 TV. How nice of Grant!!! What a friend!!!

Barry says: "Great, now we can have dinner". So went to Friday's to have pork chops and shrimp. Thank you Grant for dinner!!!!!

Digital TV, s-video cable, and DVD all for $640! And I got a good story out of it.

Oh yeah, for those of you who know Grant and his friends, let's just keep this between ourselves. I mean, "if a tree falls in the forest and no one's around, does it make a sound?". Besides, I already spent the 60 bucks.

P.S. the picture on the TV is fantastic!!!!!!!

9

GUY TRIPS

> God save me from my friends - I can protect myself from my enemies.
>
> *Robert C. Edwards*

FISHING

It's a guy thing.

Date:	Monday, June 28, 1999 9:45 AM
To:	Derryn; Dan; Kirsten; Roberto; Jun; Dodge; Brooke; Aldo; Davide; Grant; Greg; Mark; Peter; Simon; Bruce; Tom; Dale; Joe; Barry
Subject:	Fishing Trip 2

One of the advantages of being in Australia is the great outdoors spirit that it instills among its inhabitants. Emboldened by our recent fishing success from 3 weeks prior, Derryn, Grant and I decided to venture out this Sunday to the Hawkesbury to challenge the aquatic denizens in a game of cunning angling skills. Unfortunately, Dan T. the Man, was unable to attend and thus Aldo M. was able to wrangle himself into this select and expert group of fishermen.

I started the day at 5:00 am when I received the wake up call from Grant (who somehow managed to wake up this early) and he picked me up, and we headed off to get Derryn. Derryn was ready, and we collected the fishing gear and equipment. We packed quite a bit of stuff this time, and Derryn provided many buckets because we were sure we would be catching fish by the buckets. After loading the trunk with enough gear to capsize the little dinghy we were going to rent, we set off to pick up Aldo at the Mercure Hotel. Aldo managed to steal some of the breakfast muffins and croissants and the complimentary fruit, much to our delight.

We finally got to the boat rental, and naturally, the first of our many indecisive and gay arguments arose. Should we take a covered boat or an uncovered boat? Should we take an uncovered boat or a covered boat? Yes? No? Maybe? Derryn and Aldo even went so far as to demonstrate the mechanical difficulties of casting out your line from within a covered boat, complete with arm motion and imaginary fishing rod to fully exemplify the constrictions a canopy would provide. Fortunately, after 5 minutes of bickering, it started to rain, and I said "okay, I guess we take covered boat, right?". And that was settled. Aldo and I started to unload the car, while the two fishing experts, Derryn and Grant went inside to consult an even greater fishing expert, the rental guy where the best fish were to be had. Armed with a little map with a bunch of circles around the best spots, we set off into the morning sun ready to catch the 2 meter fishies that Derryn always lies to us about.

I had warned Aldo that my two compatriots were notorious for their diametrically opposed fishing/boating philosophies. Grant is adamant on anchoring. And Derryn enjoys in drifting the boat. As I am clueless on either and just like to see how far out I can cast out my bait, I remain impartial to either preference. It was with much hope that Aldo could perhaps be the tiebreaker and maybe add some rhyme and reason to our boating strategy. Aldo came out strong in the beginning, and even gave his reasoning for anchoring and drifting in certain situations.

Unfortunately, as the day would progress, it became apparent that Aldo would turn out to be just like Grant and Derryn, just a couple of loose ball bearings rattling around in the hood of your car, making a lot of noise, but really neither improving or deteriorating the performance of the vehicle.

We motored out to one of the "HOT" fishing spots and cast out our lines. Aldo was somehow selected as the motor man, and he navigated and motored for most of our trip. As Aldo quietly sat near the motor with his line out, a little fart came out of Aldo's butt. Just a little one, but enough to raise the eyebrows of Grant who turned to me and gave me a devilish smile which basically said: "Aldo farted." To which I smiled back and meant "Yup, Aldo farted and now you can fart as well". And with that Grant let out one of his many interesting and timely farts during our trip. And Derryn, well Derryn didn't really care since he had been silently farting for quite a while now. He probably had been farting since he had stepped in the car but we all thought it was stale air. With the fart barrier now broken, we then moved on to pissing overboard, and talking about homoerotic experiences to complete the male bonding cycle. There was much screaming and ballyhooing when Derryn caught Grant pissing inside the boat, but then again, not all of us can be as well-endowed as Derryn who throws his one-eyed monster with such ease over the boat railing. Aldo and I had gone out the night before to Kinselas, and we were privy to watching two men kissing each other with so much passion, that quite frankly, I was envious of their kissing skills. So that was our homoerotic contribution. Derryn managed to throw in a little gay toilet stall story where "supposedly" he didn't do anything, but Grant was suspiciously silent. But we'll leave it at that. Not that there's anything wrong with being gay!!!

We had settled in and we were patiently waiting for the fishies to bite, but no action was taking place. This was a bad sign, because if we weren't catching anything, inevitably, the great anchoring and drifting argument would come up between Grant and Derryn. Which did happen. Grant was getting a bit impatient now with the selection of the locations, and started blaming the rental guy for giving us bum information. Outbursts of "NO FISH HERE!" with a quick fart became even more frequent.

To pass the time, turns were taken to capsize the boat by getting a harmonic oscillation going by several people leaning left and right in unison. Sometimes, one of us would get a bite/nibble and yell "I got a bite" and then the other three would rush to the same end of the boat where the bite had taken place and thus shifting all the weight. I guess Derryn said it the best while laughing out loud after Grant or I nearly fell down during a tipsy maneuver, "it's all fun and games until someone gets hurt". But the best part came when Grant was whining and complaining that there was no fish and all of a sudden you see Grant diving for his fishing rod and falling flat on his stomach on the bow of the boat. Rod and Grant were nearly gone there for a moment. After wiping away the tears from laughing so hard, I thought that a shark had taken Grant's bait and was hauling Grant away. But unfortunately, Grant had just slipped. But same effect anyway.

We lost Derryn's mind sometime before lunch as Derryn proceeded to guide us to the shallow mud flats to do some GREAT FISHING. It was so shallow, I could've stuck my arm out into the water, and it would've been up to my elbow. I think all our lines were dragging on floor. Not only were we fishing in knee high water, we also decided to drift. I guess one of us could've just jumped and held the boat, no need to anchor. It was at this time we decided to settle in for lunch, and I broke out the bread and sandwich stuff of cheese and ham. I neglected to bring in salt and pepper, so as I was spreading mayo on my bread, Grant decided to fart on my bread to give it some of that special flavor. We did managed to catch some little fishies by now. Derryn had caught some really tiny whiting, breem and flounder, and I even managed to catch a little whiting on the mud flats. Aldo and Grant still were unsuccessful.

We were now getting desperate and many farcical attempts were made to find that elusive HOT SPOT of schools of fish. We went in search of the DEEP HOLE which supposedly was brimming with gigantic sauropods. Yeah, right, we must've cruised for over 45 minutes looking for that really deep hole. The funny thing was, everywhere we went, Derryn would always catch something, and the three of us would catching nothing. It got to a point where Grant would stick his line in the water for 30 seconds, and after that say "NO FISH HERE!!!" in the meantime Derryn would be hauling out a little catfish here and there.

Aldo had begun contributing to the drifting/anchoring debate by refusing to motor up the boat to where we could be anchoring or drifting. Actually it was really like a rerun of the last fishing trip when we had 4 guys not listening to each other, but at least we caught a lot of fish last time. But our prize catch came when Grant hauled up this big red octopus. That was impressive. Aldo was for pickling it in white wine. I said stuff the pickling, just breadcrumb the guy and deepfry it. Derryn wanted to chop off the tentacles to take it back and eat and throw the octopus back since the tentacles would regenerate. So what did we do? We threw the octopus back in. It just wasn't our day.

It was raining and cold, and I was telling the guys to head back and return the boat. But Derryn still wasn't finished with his lies of the 3 meter tuna that were calling our names. Derryn told us we should head over to Cow Rock (there's actually a rock that looks like a cow) where the breem were supposed to BE HUGE!!!!! Derryn wanted to throw the anchor out but a little bit closer to the shore. Aldo agreed with the anchoring but not with the too close to the shore bit. Grant had already cast his line out for 30 seconds and had declared that the area was uninhabited by fish. I had stopped fishing for the last hour and was just trying to keep the Akubra hat on my head.

Finally, we had had enough and Grant was given the task of pulling up the anchor. Grant seemed to be having a hard time with the little anchor, and he was straining and grunting, and possibly letting loose a couple of large farts. It took forever to haul it up. I was thinking "what's wrong with him? what a weakling!!", after 2 - 3 minutes or so, Grant hauls up the anchor, and attached to the anchor was another huge rusted out barnacled heavy duty anchor. Ha ha ha! We were laughing at Grant and he was actually really having a hard time with it. Poor guy!

We finally cruised back to the rental place, and drove back home. What a great day. We didn't take one single fish with us.

LAS VEGAS

Another classic road trip.

Date:	Monday, January 22, 2001 10:43 AM
To:	Karen; Rowena; Derryn; Dan; Mark ; Chris; Albert; Aldo; Greg; Davide; Maria; Yvette; Eunice; Tom; Barry; Bruce; Joe O.; Devin; Vahe; Jun; Roberto; Dodge; Kirsten; Kevin
Cc:	Jodi; Belen; Oscar; Margaret; Michelle; Nancye
Subject:	Las Vegas Story #87

Dear Dear Friends,

The weekend of Jan 19 was to be the first Las Vegas trip of 2001. Our intrepid band of Vahe, Bruce, Barry and myself decided to try our luck in the happiest city on earth, and deal the Las Vegas casinos the violent ass-spanking they so richly deserved.

Getting There

Bruce, Barry and myself rented a car to drive the 300 miles to Las Vegas. We left around 3:00 pm Friday and after a couple of stops at the supermarket to stock up on liquors and soda, McDonalds for McRib, and Long John Silver's for fish & chips, we eventually arrived in the fair city of Las Vegas at 8:30 pm. Vahe, of a slightly more frail and feminine constitution opted to fly as it was more expensive and the flight only takes 1 hour. However, as we soon discovered when we finally met up with Vahe at 11:30 pm at the hotel, he had been waiting at the airport since 7:00 pm but due to delays wasn't able to fly out on time.

Ass Kicked

Having had little blackjack action for the last 4-5 months, I was a bit rusty with money management and too liberal with the two boxes I was playing. In a matter of 1.5 hours, I was down a staggering $400. But because I am a manly superhero, I held back the tears as the Riviera casino pulled down my pants and spanked my ass silly. Instead, I brazenly dug deep into some additional ATM withdrawals, and began round 2 with the casino, and began to impress Vahe with my dazzling blackjack skills. Bruce was doing very well with his progression betting technique, a technique I should really apply the next time I am not drunk or showing off my cunning blackjack abilities. But what can you do? All the rum and cokes are free and it would be so impolite not to accept the complimentary drinks. Vahe and Barry did well on the blackjack table as well, and at around 2:00 am, I was able to walk away with $450, leaving me in the hole ONLY around $250-$300.

Roommates

Barry and Bruce shared a hotel room as they were both white. And Vahe and I, as foreigners, shared the other room. Vahe, whose main superpower is to criticize everybody whilst raising his index finger in the air, expressed extremely jealousy at my navy-blue cotton pajamas which I wore smartly to bed. By the way, Vahe is of some middle-eastern terrorist country descent, so I had to remain vigilant even in sleep, lest Vahe dropped a hand grenade in my mouth, as people of his ilk are usually prone to do. The next morning, feeling confident that it would take more than the drubbing I received last night to defeat my spirit, I woke up early and performed my usual 15-20 minute shower which I consider good time considering I brush my teeth, soap, shampoo and shave all in the steaming shower cauldron. But of course, Vahe had to take it to the next level and hinted I also peed and did some other extracurricular activities in the shower since he had to shower after me. Of course not, especially with guests around!!! However, I did neglect to tell Vahe that the hotel soap being of diminutive size sure is convenient to use in hard to reach places. Oh well, personally, I think it's good that Vahe now has a little bit of the little Filipino in/on him.

Breakfast and Downtown

We had all-you-can eat buffet at the Imperial Palace, we hoped that the eggs would be runny as Bruce likes them runny, but unfortunately they were a little big overcooked and hard. But they had lots of bacon, and I just love all things pork. Downed with coffee/milk and all the different kinds of juices and fruit, I was preparing for the lactose-intolerant-roughage-induced-mega-dump I so desperately needed before getting to some serious business on the blackjack tables. But before that, we drove over to this gambling bookstore in downtown to purchase Bruce some card-counting manuals/books. While in downtown, we checked out the downtown casinos and played a little blackjack. I dropped a quick $100+, and Vahe was frightened by Jyoti, an Indian or Pakistani dealer who had a frightful facial tic/nervous tremor and bug-eyes. Vahe wasn't doing too well, and I was down to $60-70 which I knew would not last. So I said: "Vahe, here's my share of the hotel money", and I gave Vahe $65 worth of chips. Vahe didn't want to it take since he knew he'd gamble it right away, but as he had no more cash left, he had no choice. Poof! $65 of hotel money had disappeared.

Bruce did well again. We walked around a little bit, and Vahe wanted to go to a strip club but since it was only 11:00 am or so, we weren't really in the mood. We were a bit surprised that Vahe had never been to a strip club before since he always says he does wild and crazy things and he had done everything in the world, but I said we'd try and see some boobs for him later on that night. Oh these young kids, I hope they learn this is all just vanity, and a chasing of wind (ecclesiastes).

Vahe and Joe

Then we went back to the hotel so I could take care of some "business". Vahe waited patiently for me for 20 minutes, and then we went to the other room to check up on the white people. Bruce was lying on the bed with only his black boxer shorts on, so he wasn't going anywhere soon. Barry was still dressed up but no more shoes, so it looked like he was going back to sleep too. It was up to me and Vahe then. Vahe and I walked 2 miles up the strip, going through some of the older casinos. We stopped by at Mirage to check out Siegfried and Roy's white tigers. Talked about which chicks are hot and are not hot, ate hotdogs at the Imperial and played blackjack at the Flamingo. I lost some more money at the Flamingo, and Vahe lost too. I felt sorry for Vahe, since he lost and he even had to borrow $5 from me which I kept on reminding him to pay up. So being magnanimous I decided to spring for the taxi cab back to the Riviera.

Dinner

Back at the hotel, Bruce and Barry had now fully recovered and rested, and I had gotten $35 worth of comp money from the casino for being such a fantastic blackjack player. So we went to a restaurant, and we used that money up (we went over 35 so the guys had to pitch in extra). Then we had our blackjack competition. Basically, we all start off with $20, and whoever has the most money in 45 mins is the winner. So we went to the Sahara where they have $1 blackjack tables, and played from 8:15 pm to 9:00 pm. Bruce, using his progressive technique was the first casualty, unfortunately his progression technique was sorely hampered by the $20 stash limit so simple math would say that he could not afford to lose more than 5-6 times in a row (1-2-5-10...) as there is not enough money to keep on doubling your bet. Vahe with his irrational and aggressive middle-eastern play severely threatened my lead and at one point was about to overtake me should he win his big bets. But big bets are won by big men, and Vahe is not a big man. And he got wiped out too. The only one left was Barry, whose legendary patience and silent cunning would qualify him as an oriental if he didnt have blond hair and blue eyes. His meticulous $1 bets and appropriate play allowed him to reach a position where I actually had to match his bets so that he wouldn't overtake me. But then eventually Barry cracked and became impatient, and started doubling his bets. Clearly, doubling with progression to recover is a dangerous play, Barry lost his money at 8:45. Which left the Great One, despite a wallet loss of $200-$300 in blackjack, as the undisputed blackjack champion of the universe. By the way, as part of the competition, the losers had to buy me breakfast buffet the next morning.

Strip Club

Then Vahe and I tried to walk around the strip looking for the "Olympic Garden" to see naked girls, but we either didn't walk far enough or got lost, and it was getting cold and there were a lot of scary people out at the time of the night, so we gave up and walked back to the hotel, just contenting ourselves with stripper/nudie pamphlets and brochures being passed out on the street. And we talked about which girls we thought were hot or were not hot.

Back at the Hotel

We played more blackjack, and Vahe wasn't doing too well and kept on blaming me for losing saying that I bring him bad luck. Well, maybe in the old country, they still believe in the evil eye and witches on broomsticks, but we're in America now. Bruce and Barry were playing now too, and we all enjoyed the interesting characters at the tables. It was around 1 am in the morning, and we needed to eat some hot dogs. Vahe said he'd go back to play with 20 dollars and make it 40 dollars. So Vahe played some blackjack and was at $35, but he had to reach 40 before he could leave. Naturally, he never made it to 40 and lost it all. He should have left but by now, two girls were sitting on either side of him so of course he couldn't leave and pulled out more money. I especially enjoyed the pretty latin/middle-eastern young girl on Vahe's left, whose nose stud, and incredibly hairy forearms excited me to high heaven. She smelled so good that I couldn't tear myself away from her and had to give her advice on how to play blackjack whilst looking down her cleavage. I really wanted to take a bath with that girl, that's how good she smelled. I thought Vahe would hurt me when he saw her shake my hand after my brilliant advice saved her $10 from going to the casino's purse. Vahe kept on playing though. But the girls left eventually. Then I watched Bruce play for a while, and witnessed him placing a $300 bet, which he won. Then I went up to the room, where Vahe was still waiting for me so we could discuss like little schoolboys which girls we thought were hot or not.

Bye Bye Las Vegas

It was the morning to leave. So for the last time we sang "When I need you" at the top of our lungs in the hotel hallways, corridors and garage much to Vahe's embarrassment. My free buffet at the Riviera was very good and we came at the right time to enjoy breakfast and lunch menus (the pork chops were excellent). Then Barry took some pics of me grabbing the bronze asses of the Crazy Girl bronze statues outside the hotel, and we packed up our bags, found the car and left.

We dropped Vahe off at the airport, and we drove for 3.5 hours to Monrovia so I could pick up the karaoke player. 1 hour later we were back in Woodland Hills. A weird thing happened, when I was checking my stuff out and hanging clothes up, I found a $100 bill in my coat pocket. I could've sworn that it wasn't there before. And I'm known to keep track of my money pretty well since I'm a human calculator. I immediately accused Bruce of slipping in a $100 from his massive winnings over the weekend as a kind act of generosity but he denied it. So I guess I must've been pretty drunk when I misplaced that $100.

Anyway, a lot of other things happened and were talked about, but I can't really write about it or already forgot about it.

I love you all.

NEW ORLEANS

This was my second time to New Orleans. I really only had soft-shell crab and crawfish on the mind.

Date:	Tuesday, March 13, 2001 9:40 AM
To:	none *(blind copy)*
Subject:	New Orleans

New Orleans!!!!

I'm afraid I got too tired selecting and scanning all the photos, so I don't think I'll elaborate too much.

Wednesday

Bastards at work kept me working until 6:30 pm. Why the heck do they decide to create a backup application on a different server and different database on the day before I fly out to New Orleans? But because I am brilliant, I debugged all problems and achieved resolution. The band-aid should hold till I get back.

Thursday

Flew out early for the 5 hour flight. Took the regular bus to downtown, checked in hotel, and immediately headed to the waterfront to take a ferry to Algiers across the river. Started drinking rum and cokes at the bar in Algiers, and picked off beads hanging from trees for Mo. Went back to the city to eat seafood at ACME Oyster House. Had the soft shell crab and shared couple of pounds of crawfish (yabbies to the Aussies). Drank hurricanes at Paddy O'Brien's which gave Bruce and some of us heartburn. I guess it was pretty bad because Bruce started vomiting like Godzilla on the street. Vahe and I sat down at a tarot reading table, and the fortune teller gave me the worst fortune ever: will lose my job, my friends will betray and cheat me, trust no one, then I also managed to get the death card and the hangman's card as a bonus. Supposedly, the death card isn't necessarily a bad thing. Yeah right!!!!!!!! Then the fortune teller told me I shouldn't hold any grudges. The nerve!!! Vahe and I decided to go to the Hustler strip club and check out the local wildlife. They were having a little game by throwing out cards, and if you got the right card, you get to go to the VIP lounge (upstairs) for a bit more "privacy" and "action". As luck would have it, I drew the Queen of Hearts and I got two wristbands to go upstairs to the VIP lounge. IN YOUR FACE, TAROT CARD READER!!!! We were immediately followed by a slinky brunette who got me to pay for two lapdances (one for myself and the other for Vahe). Because I am a monk, I do not allow myself to get excited by mere titillation of the flesh , a luxury I hold in reserve for my future wife. Vahe on the other hand, after getting the lapdance and some more rum and cokes became excited and quite agitated. I was leaning over the railing, checking the stripper on the floor below when I heard this deep bellowing voice yell out: "HEY!!! WE ARE RICH MEN!!!! LOOK!!!" and Vahe crumpled up a dollar bill and threw it at the stripper below. Previously, I was sending down my dollar bills as sophisticated little airplanes, but my boisterous Armenian friend enjoyed hitting the girls with the little balls made out of dollars. Later Vahe said that he may have thrown down some 20s by mistake. Hey, all US bills look the same!

Friday

Woke up late due to hangovers all around. Headed for Cafe Du Monde, and had the chicory coffee and beignets (the little donuts without holes with powdered sugar). The waitresses were now all little mean rude Vietnamese women, and I must admit, that took a lot of fun out of the whole place. I kinda liked it 5-6 years ago when they were run by little quiet black girls. Anyway, the beignets were still pretty good. We then walked down Decatur to the Flea Market to check out the junk. Later in the afternoon, we split up. Mo, Bruce and Barry went to Algiers with the ferry. I went to Harrah's to spend $50 so I could get $20 worth of casino chips for my friend Dodge who collects casino chips. And Vahe went to see the white alligators at the aquarium. We all met at the casino, and Bruce won dinner money for us by kicking ass at the blackjack table. Free dinner at Arnaud's Remoulade!!! YEAH BABY!!! At Arnaud's, we had the shrimp remoulade, oysters, and I had soft shell crab again but this time on a po'boy sandwich. DELICIOUS. We split up for the night.

Saturday

Woke up to find my camera was broken. Damn. Now I must rely on the kindness of friends. Took the streetcar on Charles St. to Tulane/Loyola universities. Making many stops along the way. Went back to the flea market so I could get presents for my dear dear friends. Then we waited for the streetcar for around 30-40 mins which never came. So we walked back to the French Quarter and had lunch at the Gumbo House. We had gumbo, of course. Also had alligator sausage while we were at it. Went back to the hotel since we were pretty tired from walking. At some stages, Vahe didn't want to walk anymore because he had big blisters on his feet. He used up all my bandaids from my kit. That's what he gets for wearing stiff black leather clown shoes with the seams on the outside. French fashion, my ass. However, when it came to finding toilets, Vahe could run like the flash, so it seemed. For dinner, we just had Popeye's and we walked around the French Quarter to see some breastflashing. Although, Mardi Gras was just a week before, the atmosphere was still pretty Mardi Gras. The girls were flashing their breasts for beads, and the streets were packed. I managed to see 10 breasts (left and right) from 6 different girls (some girls would only flash one breast). Vahe wasted many camera shots trying to get titty-shots. Bruce also got beads by doing his Riverdance Irish jig in the street, and was kicked out of a bar for supposedly trying to start a fight. I left the guys early to go to bed, but I should've just hung around as I didn't get any sleep anyway and missed all the action. Apparently, there was even more flashing after I had left. But Vahe assured me he had gotten many photos of the girls revealing themselves. More on that later.

Sunday

Left for Los Angeles. Went to camera store to get film out of broken camera, and had film developed at Costco, for pickup on Monday.

Drove with Vahe to get the photos. Went through all the envelopes, but couldn't find any photos of breasts. Apparently in all the excitement of topless women, Vahe was clicking his camera with no film inside! How bizarre!

SECTION III

GENTLE MUSINGS

My life has no purpose, no direction, no aim, no meaning, and yet I'm happy. I can't figure it out. What am I doing right?

Charles M. Schulz

10

Lessons in Life

Every man is a damn fool for at least five minutes
every day; wisdom consists in not exceeding the limit.
Elbert Hubbard

IMPORTANT LESSONS

I must admit, the ice cream story was pretty touching.

THE ORIGINAL MESSAGE...

From:	Yvette
Date:	Friday, June 09, 2000 10:32 AM
To:	Joe
Subject:	FW: Lessons.....

Some life lessons from a nurse:

Most Important Lesson

During my second month of nursing school, our professor gave us a pop quiz. I was a conscientious student and had breezed through the questions, until I read the last one:

"What is the first name of the woman who cleans the school?"

Surely this was some kind of joke. I had seen the cleaning woman several times. She was tall, dark-haired and in her 50's, but how would I know her name? I handed in my paper, leaving the last question blank. Just before class ended, one student asked if the last question would count toward our quiz grade.

"Absolutely," said the professor. "In your careers you will meet many people. All are significant. They deserve your attention and care, even if all you do is smile and say 'hello'."

I've never forgotten that lesson. I also learned her name was Dorothy.

Second Important Lesson - Pickup in the Rain

One night at 11:30 PM an older African American woman was standing on the side of an Alabama highway trying to endure a lashing rain storm. Her car had broken down and she desperately needed a ride.

Soaking wet, she decided to flag down the next car. A young white man stopped to help her, generally unheard of in those conflict-filled 1960's.The man took her to safety, helped her get assistance and put her into a taxi cab.

She seemed to be in a big hurry, but wrote down his address and thanked him.

Seven days went by and a knock came to the man's door. To his surprise a giant console color TV was delivered to his home. A special note was attached. It read:

"Thank you so much for assisting me on the highway the other night. The rain drenched not only my clothes, but also my spirits. Then you came along. Because of you I was able to make it to my dying husband's bedside just before he passed away. God bless you for helping me and unselfishly serving others."

Sincerely, Mrs. Nat King Cole.

Third Important Lesson - Always remember those who serve you.

In the days when an ice cream sundae cost much less, a 10 year old boy entered a hotel coffee shop and sat at a table. A waitress put a glass of water in front of him. "How much is an ice cream sundae?" he asked.

"Fifty cents," replied the waitress. The little boy pulled his hand out of his pocket and studied the coins in it.

"Well how much is a plain dish of ice cream?" he inquired. By now more people were waiting for a table and the waitress was growing impatient.

"Thirty-five cents," she brusquely replied." The little boy again counted his coins. "I'll have the plain ice cream," he said.

The waitress brought the ice cream, put the bill on the table and walked away. The boy finished the ice cream, paid the cashier and left. When the waitress came back she began to cry as she wiped down the table. There, placed neatly beside the empty dish were two nickels and five pennies.

You see, he couldn't have the sundae, because he had to have enough left to leave her a tip.

Fourth Important Lesson - The Obstacle in Our Path

In ancient times a King had a boulder placed on a roadway. Then he hid himself and watched to see if anyone would remove the huge rock. Some of the king's wealthiest merchants and couriers came by and simply walked around it.

Many loudly blamed the king for not keeping the roads clear. But none did anything about getting the stone out of they way. Then a peasant came along carrying a load of vegetables. Upon approaching the boulder the peasant laid down his burden and tried to move the stone to the side of the road.

After much pushing and straining, he finally succeeded. After the peasant picked up his load of vegetables he noticed a purse lying in the road where the boulder had been.

The purse contained many gold coins and a note from the king indicating that the gold was for the person who removed the boulder form the roadway.

The peasant learned what many of us never understand. Every obstacle presents an opportunity to improve our condition.

Fifth Important Lesson - Giving When it Counts

Many years ago when I worked as a volunteer at a hospital I got to know a little girl named Liz who was suffering from a rare and serious disease. Her only chance of recovery appeared to be a blood transfusion from her 5-year old brother who had miraculously survived the same disease and had developed the antibodies needed to combat the illness. The doctor explained the situation to her little brother and asked the little boy if he would be willing to give his blood to his sister. I saw him hesitate for only a moment before taking a deep breath and saying, "Yes, I'll do it if it will save her."

As the transfusion progressed, he lay in bed next to his sister and smiled as we all did seeing the color returning to her cheeks. Then his face grew pale and his smile faded He looked up at the doctor and asked with a trembling voice, "Will I start to die right away?" Being young, the little boy had misunderstood the doctor; he thought he was going to have to give his sister all of his blood in order to save her. You see understanding and attitude, after all, is everything.

You have 2 choices now:

1 - Delete this e-mail or
2 - Forward it to people you care about.

I hope that you will choose No. 2 and remember to:

Work like you don't need the money;
Love like you've never been hurt;
and Dance like you do when nobody's watching!

MY RESPONSE...

Date:	Friday, June 09, 2000 1:11 PM
To:	Nancye; Oscar; Dodge; Jun; Roberto; Grant; Dan; Derryn; Karen; Rowena; Kirsten; Kevin; Bruce; Dale; Barry; Joe O.; Tom; Yvette; Maria; Eunice; Helen; Aldo; Brooke; Davide; Greg; Simon; Devin
Subject:	FW: Lessons.....

Some lessons in life from the guy across the parking lot...

FIRST IMPORTANT LESSON

A young and very handsome went to work for a very big company in Adelaide, Australia. One day, the handsome man resigned from the company and even though the handsome man had put in seven loyal years and thousands of extra hours for the company, the company made him pay back $5000 in relocation expenses. The young man took this as a lesson, and moved on to a very small company in Sydney. The man was still handsome but not so young, and eventually resigned from the small company as well. This time, the small company didn't pay his 401K/retirement money and his severance pay, and the handsome man lost out on about $5000 again.

Finally, the handsome man found work for a company which was not as big as the first company but bigger than the second company. Now the handsome man swims every day in his pool after work.

SECOND IMPORTANT LESSON

A charming and friendly man wanted to buy a car. He was tired of driving his friends around and he remembered that when he had a 4-door car, everybody would jump into his car. So the friendly man went to a repo lot and bought a very small 2-door car which only had room for him, and the chicks he would be banging every Tuesday and Thursday nights.

But when his friends saw that he was driving again, they all jumped in his car anyways and made him drive to all the lunch places everyday because they remembered he was a much better driver than Eunice who always got into a car accident or Maria who used to get lost all the time.

THIRD IMPORTANT LESSON

Long long time ago, in Woodland Hills, a man and his family were moving out of the house. His neighbor, a very handsome young man asked him who would be moving into the house. The man said that a worldly Swedish woman was moving in. The handsome man was very excited when he heard that a "worldly" Swedish woman was going to be his neighbor because the young man was a big fan of ABBA and AQUA and other beautiful Swedish people, and he thought the worldly Swedish woman would be easy to go to bed with.

Then the worldly Swedish woman drove up to the house in a brand new Mercedes E320, and when she walked out, she wasn’t that hot. But the young and handsome man still talked to her even though she wasn't as beautiful as Agnetha and Frida. Then the young and handsome young man took a chainsaw and started cutting the big tree in front of his house.

FOURTH IMPORTANT LESSON

A very handsome man was keeping a box of stuff for his friend in his room. His friend finally came over after many weeks to pick up the box. The handsome man picked up the box and handed it over to the friend who wasn't as handsome as him. The friend grabbed the box from underneath with his hands but accidentally overreached and touched the groin area of the handsome friend. The handsome friend took time out and said: "You touched my weewee, you're a homo".

FIFTH IMPORTANT LESSON

A very handsome wasn't finding the right girls in real life, so he decided to find girls through the internet. Finally he found a beautiful portuguese girl who has a palace, tours with a pop band (The Gift), and reads plenty of books a year. The beautiful portuguese girl said she wasn't fat or thin, so the handsome man has to believe her until he gets pictures of her.

In the meantime, the handsome man also had a friend who was looking for girls too. But what his friend would do is try and pull off the skirts off girls who were trying to get out of the car. And everybody thought that was kinda weird.

MORE OF LIFE'S LESSONS

A response to one of those sappy, feel-good, let-there-be-a-moral emails. I prefer to reply with something creative instead of just writing back "Bullshit!"

THE ORIGINAL MESSAGE...

From:	Devin
To:	Moe; Joe; Barry; Vahe; Bruce; Yvette; Maria; Eunice
Date:	Tuesday, November 07, 2000 9:47 AM
Subject:	FW:Thought for the Day

THE CARPENTER

An elderly carpenter was ready to retire. He told his employer contractor of his plans to leave the house building business and live a more leisurely life with his wife enjoying his extended family. He would miss the paycheck, but he needed to retire. They could get by.

The contractor was sorry to see his good worker go and asked if he could build just one more house as a personal favor. The carpenter said yes, but in time it was easy to see that his heart was not in his work. He resorted to shoddy workmanship and used inferior materials. It was an unfortunate way to end a dedicated career.

When the carpenter finished his work the employer came to inspect the house. He handed the front door key to the carpenter. "This is your house," he said, "my gift to you."

The carpenter was shocked! What a shame! If he had only known he was building his own house, he would have done it all so differently.

So it is with us. We build our lives, a day at a time, often putting less than our best into the building. Then with a shock we realize we have to live in the house we have built. If we could do it over, we'd do it much differently. But we cannot go back.

You are the carpenter.

Each day you hammer a nail, place a board, or erect a wall.

"Life is a do-it-yourself project," someone has said. Your attitudes and the choices you make today, build the "house" you live in tomorrow.

Build wisely

MY RESPONSE...

Date:	Tuesday, November 07, 2000 10:32 AM
To:	Devin; Barry; Vahe; Bruce; Yvette; Maria; Eunice
Subject:	Re: FW:Thought for the Day

THE PROGRAMMER

A handsome young man was ready to move on with his career. So he told his manager about his plans to leave the company so he could get a big fat paycheck at some financial institution offering him twice the salary and benefits.

He said he would miss the shiny plaques they would give him every year or so, and the little company pins he treasured so much.

The manager was sorry to see him go since the handsome young man was such a good worker, and asked the handsome young man if he could do one more project. It involved writing the PowerBuilder ancestor classes for all the maintenance windows of this huge vehicle maintenance application program that was going on.

The handsome man said yes, but realized his heart wasn't really into it anymore, and did a lot of hard-coding, undocumented special logic, repetitive code, and inline SQL. It wasn't his best piece of work, and he wasn't really too happy about it.

Another programmer, but ugly and old, on the team noticed his lackluster dedication and berated him on it. But the handsome young man ignored the ugly and old programmer because ugly and old people's opinions don't count.

On his last day on the job, the manager came by to inspect his work. Since all his shoddy work was hidden behind scripts and events, the manager didn't really notice the terrible programming and simply admired the way the buttons and datawindows were wonderfully positioned on the windows.

Then the manager called in the whole team, and presented the handsome young man with another shiny plaque for his years of service, and a $100 voucher at a fancy restaurant. There was a big party afterwards and cake and lemonade was served. He even made out with the receptionist whom he had the hots for 2 years ever since she got off the plane from Sweden.

Two weeks later, the handsome young man got an email from his friends at the old company telling him that old and ugly programmer who lectured him was assigned to support the unmaintainable trash of code he had put in. The handsome young man was very happy, and didn't regret anything at all.

So it is with us, if you ever in life make a big mess of something that you probably are ashamed of, don't worry, somebody else will clean up after you. Just make sure you aren't around when that happens.

ECCLESIASTES

Came back from a Chi-Chi's lunch, and the guys and gals had given me xmas presents. I especially enjoyed the "Bitch Magnet" bumper sticker.

Date:	Wednesday, December 20, 2000 4:04 PM
To:	Vahe; Devin; Barry; Eunice; Maria; Yvette
Subject:	Thank You!

It was a very good lunch and I liked the presents. And naturally I enjoyed being with my dear dear Friends.

Dale turned me on to Ecclesiastes, and here is Chapter 11. King Solomon wrote

Ecclesiastes in his old age after he had gotten all the wealth, power and pleasures of life, and he wondered what was the meaning of life since all people, rich and poor, wise and foolish, prince and slave will all die in the end. And all their accomplishments will be forgotten, and all their possessions taken by somebody else.

Of course, life is not meaningless nor is it limited by the finality of our mortal existence.

And maybe life is a bit uncertain or without purpose (in Vahe's case, wild and crazy), and maybe we try to control our lives too much, and we get disappointed with the results even though as King Solomon says: "Consider the work of God; who can make straight what he has made crooked?". So here it warns us to be cognizant of the unknown future, whether it be good or bad, and to live and enjoy the days of our lives since our youth and health are vanities, and will not last forever.

I should have been a preacher, instead of a chick magnet.

Ecclesiastes 11

Send out your bread upon the waters, for after many days you will get it back. Divide your means seven ways, or even eight, for you do not know what disaster may happen on earth. When clouds are full, they empty rain on the earth; whether a tree falls to the south or to the north, in the place where the tree falls, there it will lie. Whoever observes the wind will not sow; and whoever regards the clouds will not reap. Just as you do not know how the breath comes to the bones in the mother's womb, so you do not know the work of God, who makes everything. In the morning sow your seed, and at evening do not let your hands be idle; for you do not know which will prosper, this or that, or whether both alike will be good. Light is sweet, and it is pleasant for the eyes to see the sun. Even those who live many years should rejoice in them all; yet let them remember that the days of darkness will be many. All that comes is vanity. Rejoice, young man, while you are young, and let your heart cheer you in the days of your youth. Follow the inclination of your heart and the desire of your eyes, but know that for all these things God will bring you into judgment. Banish anxiety from your mind, and put away pain from your body; for youth and the dawn of life are vanity.

11

A Sense of Righteousness

Even the lion has to defend himself against flies.
German Proverb

Beware the fury of a patient man.
John Dryden

STUPID PORSCHE DRIVERS

Bad people are everywhere, I guess.

Date:	Saturday, December 04, 1999 4:30 PM
To:	Dodge; Jun; Roberto; Brooke; Helen; Karen; Rowena; Simon; Greg; Derryn; Davide; Aldo; Dan; Kirsten; Bruce; Dale; Barry; Joe O.; Tom; Yvette; Maria
Subject:	Stupid Porsche Drivers

I guess I live in an area where there are a lot of brash, yuppie, European-car driving pretty-boy fuckers living around. But on this slightly overcast yet pleasant Sunday morning I was walking to work on this quiet, narrow, tree-lined street overlooking the water. I was just clearly minding my own business as I was just concerned about reading my emails at work and seeing if any of my hotel accommodations for London during the end of year came through. I was crossing the road, and although my head was bowed down (I'm always looking for loose change on the street), I knew a Porsche convertible was gunning to the right of me. So Mr. Porsche-Man HAS to brake in order for his 1 ton car to avoid smacking all my 130 lbs/59 kilos (could be less, I've been losing weight for some reason, contrary to what some people may think). That's fine with me, nobody got hurt, he stopped for the Great One, all is well, and the sun will still keep on shining on tomorrow. But as I got to the other side, Mr. Pretty-Boy had to pipe up and angrily tell me to watch for cars when crossing the road! It seems the pretty-boy had his ass-hairs all tied up in a little knot when he took off a couple of minutes off the life of his brake pads when he had to brake. He wouldn't have had to if he wasn't speeding at 50 mph around the corner in a residential street. He was all upset, and his neck was all straining to get his corporate fascist head yelling at me. So that was the last straw, so I had to stop and turn and say: "HEY, YOU'RE THE ONE WHO COULD HAVE KILLED ME. JUST BECAUSE YOU DRIVE A PORSCHE, YOU THINK YOU OWN THE ROAD (cheap shot, I know)". We exchanged verbal blows for a minute or so, and he was getting all angry, and he was backing his Porsche down the road to yell at me some more, then he goes: "YOU DO THIS ON THE HIGHWAY, MATE????". And I said: "THIS ISN'T THE HIGHWAY, MATE." Then he finally got to pissed off, and drove away so I wouldn't see him cry and shed his little girly-man tears all over the leather-seats.

That was just so unlike me!!! So unbecoming of my placid self. I don't know what possessed me, he was a whole lot bigger than me too - private gym-pumping, gel-spreading pretty boy. I guess, it could've turned ugly, and I didn't have any weapons on me at that time either. Definitely unbiblical behavior, I hope the dear Lord forgives me on this one as well.

LAYING DOWN THE LAW

People really get excited at the opportunity to reply-all. But they don't even know each other!! My friend Kirsten said it best, "Familiarity breeds contempt".

Date:	Tuesday, October 03, 2000 5:21 PM
To:	Rowena; Davide; Devin; Yvette; Maria; Bruce; Barry; Joe O.; Tom; Dale; Dan; Derryn; Aldo; Kevin; Kirsten; Roberto; Dodge; Jun
Subject:	Abuse of Reply-Alls

This is what one of my REAL friends wrote in response to the flagrant abuse of the Reply-All button...

"What happened to your orderly world where none of us were supposed to speak unless it was to you directly...am I the only one who continues to obey..."

"As each day passes, your distribution list becomes more bold..."

****
I can only hope to explain why I frown upon this breeding-familiarity-amongst-mailing-list-members.

1) the mailing list only contains "TIER 1" friends, so this means (at the present time) that you are closer to me than "TIER 2" and "TIER 3" (I haven't made a TIER 4 yet, too much hassle moving people from tier to tier) friends which basically means I will pick up the phone/answering machine after a couple of rings when you call. Your frequency of response, prowess in humor & wit & intelligence, acceptable behavior, and minimum level of physical ugliness DETERMINE your temporary TIER 1 ranking and inclusion. Before I go to sleep every night, I take out my notepad and evaluate every TIER 1 member's performance/non-performance and jot down notes/actions to make the appropriate adjustments.

2) the Tier 1 - mailing list is comprised of several groups (so I don't have to type the addresses all the time) - they are:

PCC: College Friends
Detroit: EDS Detroit Days
CoolGuys: California/EDS Days - Guys
CoolGirls: California/EDS Days - Chicks
Adelaide: Adelaide people
MacBank: Sydney guys and chicks

Now, correct me if I'm wrong, but since when did I ever have a big party with all these lovely people from all these different groups in the same room and had introductions for everybody? Okay, Grant (of all people) managed to actually meet nearly everyone from the groups, but HE'S NOT ON THE MAILING LIST NOW, is he? BIG HINT, right there baby!!!! And yeah, all your pics on my website so you guys can check each other out when reading somebody else's reply-all, and fantasize about making love to that ballsy girl or guy who had the gumption to hit the reply-all button - shame on those perverts!!!!!

3) Now, we all remember what happened last week when one of my emails got distributed OUTSIDE MY universe, right???

4) on occasion, I will get outraged by somebody's blatant LIES being propagated through the reply-all mechanism. What's this about this being the closest to chick action in 5 YEARS? I won't even dignify that with an answer. But I will say that yes, at times I will have a lapse of good moral judgment and go out with dumb blondes who wear really tight wonderbras and who like to stand me up, or maybe even go out with big-breasted internet girls who make excuses such as their grandpa died to stand me up. But that's all unbiblical, and I'm not proud of those moments at all.

Now remember, I'm not patronizing or being condescending because as many of you know, I am very humble and don't like to talk down to people, especially the little people. Think of it this way, when you see a 65 mph speedlimit sign on the freeway, what do you think? You'd probably say: "Damn the law!!!" and snort another line of coke from your girlfriend's cleavage. But you see, those laws aren't there to abuse you or even restrict you. Those laws are there to protect you from yourself.

Okay, I've said my bit. Now I'm going to go the gym and become really muscular.

I LOVE YOU ALL.

BRAZILIAN RAIN FOREST

Emails that propose to fix the world's ailments simply infuriate me. What an insult to people's intelligence!

THE ORIGINAL MESSAGE...

From:	Derryn
To:	Chris; Christoper; Dave and Linda; Joe; Marek; Stephen; Stewart; Tristan; Nathan
Date:	Wednesday, June 14, 2000 9:28 PM
Subject:	Brazilian rain forest (worth a shot - Derryn)

Brazilian congress is now voting on a project that will reduce the amazon forest to 50% of its size. The area to be deforested is 4 times the size of Portugal and would be mainly used for agriculture and pastures for live stock...

All the wood is to be sold to international markets in the form of wood chips, by multinational companies...

The truth is that the soil in the amazon forest is useless without the forest itself. Its quality is very acidic and the region is prone to constant floods. At this time more than 160.000 square kilometers deforested with the same purpose, are abandoned and in the process of becoming deserts.

We cannot let this happen. Copy the text into a new email, put your complete name in the list below, and send to everyone you know. (Don't just forward it cos then it will end up with rows of >>>'s)

If you are the 100th person to sign please send a copy to fsaviolo@openlink.com.br

Thank you.

My response...

Date:	Thursday, June 15, 2000 7:56 AM
To:	Derryn; Chris; Christopher; Dave and Linda; Marek; Stephen; Stewart; Tristan; Nathan;
Subject:	Re: Brazilian rain forest (worth a shot - Derryn)

what kind of fascist kneejerk mass manipulation is this????????

first of all, if the western countries would stop making markets for wood products, the wood wouldn't have to be exported, would it???

and if western countries just decreased their intake of steaks and hamburgers and sausages, then people in developing countries wouldn't need to raise pastures for live stock for export instead of propagating instantaneous 1-minute gratification ("yeah, by sending this email I feel good because I saved the rainforest") by email, people should just stop eating hamburgers, buying newspapers, or forget about that 8-seat-dinner table/chairs that people need to get for their capitalist-pig dinner parties so they can impress their bosses and get a salary in the six-figures and get more money to buy more rainforest hardwood furniture.

and that's my take on this

BIRTHDAY IRONY

It was supposed to be the best day of the year...

Date:	Monday, November 13, 2000 11:00 AM
To:	Devin; Dodge; Roberto; Jun; Dan; Derryn; Rowena; Kirsten; Kevin; Joe O.; Bruce; Barry; Tom; Maria; Yvette; Greg; Aldo; Davide; Vahe
Subject:	Birthday Irony!

I must confess that a little cosmic joke was played on me, on that infamous day we all remember as November 10.

As you recall, I enjoy getting my free birthday cake at restaurants on days which aren't really my birthday. All you have to do is go with a mid-size group, sit at the head of a table and make a facetious pouty-face when the pretty waitress comes along, and have some of the chicks at the table support you with a grin or smile or two, and then say: "I'm sad, it's my birthday today... I just turned 30", followed with some "aaawwws". Then you get your free cake at the end of the meal. Of course, you have to be a fearless superhero like I am to be able to pull it off consistently.

Anyway, we had to have the real birthday cake at Black Angus so Charlotte could serve me the birthday cake knowing that she thinks only cheap loser bastards pull off lame stunts like the free birthday cake. So we go in and get the table, and Charlotte is all excited to see us, and I say it's my birthday! She asks for identification, so I give out my driver's license. She scrutinizes it for a long time, obviously to memorize my address details. She even finds us Black Angus coupons so we could get all the meals for US$5.99. I didn't care about the coupons because my lunch was going to be free, as tradition so demanded. Eunice, Maria, Devin and Vahe were there. And Yvette showed up later. The food took a very long time to come out, and I had to leave at 12:55 because we were going to have a company staff meeting at 1:00 pm. And the cake still hadn't come out. Unfortunately, I couldn't wait any longer, so I had to run out taking my birthday cookies and birthday guinness leaving the guys and chicks to explain to Charlotte I couldn't wait any longer. SO I DIDN'T GET MY BIRTHDAY CAKE!!!

Apparently, Charlotte was doing a big preparation in the back, having made several ice cream sundaes and was just about to light my cake when Devin "the Devil" sought her out, and told her that I had left. According to Yvette, Charlotte was very apologetic. So now I feel guilty on top of not getting my free birthday cake. So as you can tell, there really is no point waiting for an entire year to get your free birthday cake, there's no guarantee that you'll get it anyway, so you might as well get your free birthday cake throughout the year!!!

So I thought, well, at least I'll have my birthday family dinner since I can always count on good old Family Dino. I'm driving home when I give them a call 10 mins away from Monrovia and tell them to meet me at Spaghetti Factory in Duarte. Max and Mic say okay and they'll meet me there. I'm just about to exit off the freeway when my mother calls me back and says: "Do you really want to go to Spaghetti Factory? We just had a lot of pizza and we're very full." So my mother argues with me for a minute or so and tells me to just drive home instead. So I think "how odd that they had a big meal before my arrival!". So I get to the house, and I walk in and I see Max in his jogging suit, Mother in her sweatpants, and Mic and the baby Max lying exhausted on the sofa. Obviously, they were going to dress up in their dinner gear anytime now. My mother is pointing to the pile of pizza on the table indicating that they were very full still. This was all very strange. It was odd enough I hadn't gotten any phone calls from them that day, but I just assumed they were just busy with laundry and the baby. So they're just sitting around the sofas watching TV, not saying anything. So I stand up, walk around a little bit to and fro, and then shout: "IT'S MY BIRTHDAY TODAY!!!!!!!!!!!!!!!"

Then there was a silence for a while, and Max, Mother, and Mic were just sitting there with their mouths open. And they said: "we forgot!". Isn't that great.

I celebrate 4 birthdays in a row in Oz, and I always get a birthday call. Now, I'm inside the house and they can't even associate my presence with November 10.

So I just had Papa John's leftover pizza with a couple of cheese sticks. Of course, I made my mother feel guilty by saying: "you know, you only have THREE children..." and then when she said: "okay okay, pick a restaurant!", I answered: "that's okay, I can wait one more year...."

So the point is to be ever vigilant. And now I realize the value of pounding in November 10 into the brains of my dear dear friends, lest such a horrible event occur again in my lifetime.

FUNNY AND SAD STORY

Pride and vanity are a person's downfall...

Date:	Thursday, September 06, 2001 7:17 AM
To:	none *(blind copy)*
Subject:	Funny and Sad Story

Here's a really sad story about how people don't learn from their mistakes and through pride and vanity just make things worse.

So I've put Yvette on 10 weeks silent treatment since Aug 23 (I think until Nov 1 or so) since she refused to buy me the Dockers pants to make up for her Karaoke Party flakiness. Naturally, she hasn't been too happy with that. Then she got mad when she called me up, and I only responded by tapping the receiver with my ballpen. Anyway, she still couldn't accept the fact that I was actually upset with her because she takes advantage of my good nature and thinks she can get away with everything. Then she starts threatening back that she's talking to Devin more (trying to make me jealous), and that if this keeps up, she'll give me silent treatment forever etc.

Anyway, with Bruce's intervention, Yvette says she's given up and says she'll give me the pants, but I should drive to Northridge and pick them up this week. So I take her off the silent treatment and we email each other as usual again.

Yesterday, I went to OAN to pick up my pants. I was running late, so I called her up and said I was going to be late. When I got there, I hugged her and even asked if she lost weight. I even brought her a little photo album to stick all my photos she has in her drawer. So I'm sitting in her cubicle and she gives me this box with a nice blue bow around it. Barry says: "did you get the right size?", and Yvette says: "32 x 30, right?". So I open it up, and in the box were diapers, Gerber's baby food, a pacifier, baby lotion, and candy. Yvette says: "because you're such a baby!!!!". So I look around and ask: "so where are my pants?". And Yvette says: "I told you I wasn't going to get you any pants!". So she's just standing there, all amused with herself. And I'm amused too, because of all the effort she's put in to prolong her silent treatment. So I query her as to the cost of the items, as I might prorate the dollar amount against the value of the Dockers pants. But then my driving up to Northridge and the photo album already negated the cost of the baby stuff.

And what's worse, Yvette used deception and lying to lure me to OAN, only to prove once again that she thinks that this is all just a big joke and that she can get away with it again. How truly depraved and selfish this world has become.

I don't even think silent treatment till November 1 suffices for this level of criminality.

12

FRUITS OF FANTASY

> The life of the creative man is led, directed and controlled by boredom. Avoiding boredom is one of our most important purposes.
>
> *Saul Steinberg*

THOUGHTS ON MARRIAGE

There are more important things to think about than work. I thought I made some valid points.

Date:	Monday, 26 May 1997 11:57
To:	Dale; Bruce; Yvette; Alison; Joe O.; Dodge; Jun; Tom; Debbie; Roberto; Barry
Subject:	Time on my hands

Since coming back for Melbourne, I haven't been able to get back into work mode yet. So I've got some time for some life-question and answers.

Here's a theory that I came up today:

Marriages coming out of dating should be prohibited.

You should only marry one of your friends (provided that they're of the opposite sex, single and HOT!).

Wouldn't this way be better? Think about it. You could fart in front of your friend. Tell them that the dress they're wearing doesn't look good. That they're gaining weight. The possibilities are endless! And you don't need to date! You would just include your friend in the regular social outings. And if your friend borrows money from you, you don't have to be afraid to ask for the money back.So it would kinda work like this...

Joe: Hey, we've been friends for 5 years, let's get married tomorrow!
Female friend who's sexy, smart, rich and single: Sure!

No misconceptions, all honesty...

Joe:	Hey, you're getting kinda fat for those ugly clothes you've been wearing!
Friend-Wife:	No problem, I'll lose the weight and buy new clothes after you give me back the money you owe me. But for now, I'll just fart in front of you.

No need to share...

Joe:	Hey, I just bought a Mercedes E320 for me! You should get a luxury car for yourself also so you don't have to borrow mine.
Friend-Wife:	Okay, I'll buy an LS400 tomorrow!

Sex would be treated as favors, so both of you don't have to be in the mood for it...

Friend-Wife:	Do you think you have time this weekend to have sex with me for four hours? I'll buy you a lunch!
Joe:	Sure, after I finish laundry. And no fast food!

Another brilliant idea from Australia.

SKIT

I don't think I've ever used these lines.

Date:	Sunday, 6 July 1997 11:21
To:	Joe O.; Barry; Dale; Bruce; Yvette; Kevin; Tom; Debbie
Subject:	Another Skit Story

I've always wanted to do this when Yvette calls, but I keep forgetting. This should be acted out as a skit.

Yvette is sitting bored in her cube. She just finished a 12 inch Subway sandwich and the Baskin-Robbins three scoop ice cream has made her sleepy. Before she takes a nap in the conference room, Yvette decides to call Australia.

In Australia, in Joe's apartment the phone rings: Ring! Ring! Ring!

Joe picks up the phone: Hello?
Yvette: Hi! You busy?
Joe: Kinda, lemme just take care of something first. Hold on...

Joe puts the phone down, but it's close enough so Yvette can hear what's going on...

On the phone, Yvette hears Joe talking to somebody.

Joe: Hey Bambi, cover your ass with something, this may take a while!

OR

Joe: Hey Trixie, go out and get some Chinese takeaway will you? Hey, put some clothes on, you dumb chick!

OR

Joe: Hey Trixie, go out and get some Chinese takeaway will you? Hey, put some clothes on, you dumb chick! And take your sister with you!

OR

Joe: Hey Trixie, go out and get some Chinese takeaway will you? Hey, put some clothes on, you dumb chick! And take your sisters, your cousins and your momma with you!

OR

Joe: Mona, I'll have to give you a raincheck. I know you made an appointment two months ago, but this is a long distance call. Look, I'll throw in a freebie. Thanks, see ya!

OR

Joe: Okay sweetie, fun time's over. Daddy needs some private time. Put that back in the fridge, will you? Thanks!

OR

Joe: You've had your four hours of fun, now get out of here!

OR

Joe: You've had your eight hours of fun, now get out of here!

OR

Joe: You've had your hour of fun, put a hundred in the cup on your way out.

OR

Joe: Monica, take these clamps off, will you? I'm on the phone.

OR

Joe: Monica, take these clamps off, will you? I'm on the phone. Ouch! Turn the power off first!

OR

Joe: Dammit Vanity! How many times have I told you, not while I'm talking on the phone!

Back in California, Yvette is wondering who Joe is talking to

Yvette: What's going on? Do you have visitors? Hello?

OR

Yvette: What's going on? Are you talking to yourself again? Hello?

INTERNET STORY

I just made everything up. I tried to make it believable so it would get sent all over the world as internet folklore. But I think it was too long.

Date:	Tuesday, April 06, 1999 4:11 PM
To:	Grant; Davide; Brooke; Greg; Aldo; Nicole; Peter; Simon; Mark; Barry; Bruce; Dodge; Jun; Joe O.; Kirsten; Roberto; Tom; Dale
Subject:	Funny email

Somebody sent me a funny email the other day. You know, the ones that are weird stories about other people, but they seem so real that it could have been true or not. So as I was laughing reading about this fellow who after indulging in an all-you-can-eat pasta and meat sauce fest ended up shitting and vomiting in the restroom, I thought of a story that had happened to me long time ago in my younger days. It certainly wasn't that funny back then, but I guess it is kinda amusing when I think back on it.

I must have been twenty-two or twenty-three, and it was the first time I was away from home. The company had shipped me all the way from Los Angeles, California to the wonderful world of Detroit, Michigan. I didn't know anybody of course, but fortunately, I had hooked up with a pleasant fellow during orientation and decided we should cut expenses and get an apartment somewhere out in the suburbs. It was kinda cool, he was a good church kid so I knew he wouldn't cause any trouble and he'd pay his share of the rent on time. Yeah, those were good times then. It got even better when he started taking me to his church, which I thought was cool, so I could meet all the good-looking chicks in bible study class for young singles. I remember I really had the hots for Denise, she had long black hair, had a really smooth voice and this funny giggle that she kinda ended by sticking her tongue out sheepishly. She was pretty stacked as well. I took every opportunity to hang around Denise when I had the chance. Church was okay too, except the pastor , Brother Billand his wife, Sister Sandy were kinda uptight. Sister Sandy would always look at me suspiciously since I had never asked to join the church officially, even though Ive been attending Sunday school for nearly a year. But hey, my roomie didn't mind, as long as I didn't come to Sunday school reeking of beer, he didn't mind. So it happened that it was Thanksgiving,and since the holidays were too short for my roomie and I to go back to our home states, we just joined the Thanksgiving festivities organized by the church folks. And of course, Denise was going to be there.

The church was just one of those regular buildings that looked like a single triangular roof. You know, the ones that look like a pyramid sticking up from the ground. However, it was a whole lot bigger than it seemed, because on the lower level, just below the ground level, they had a small theatre, a big mess hall, and of course, the kitchen. Denise and I were assigned to do some of the cooking and I guess we volunteered for mashed potatoes and gravy which was easy enough. The kitchen was crowded at first with all the chicks puttering about turkey, doing the stuffing, and making pitchers of ice tea. But you know how it is, once you get the turkey in the oven, its all just waiting time from then. So Im just mashing away at the potatoes, and Denise has just put the gravy on the gas burner on slow heat. Denise and I are just chatting and drinking some pepsi. There's this little kid who knocks on the window just below the kitchen ceiling is (you can see the legs of the kids playing outside from the kitchen), and its Denise's kid brother, Michael. Michael's got this condition that when he gets excited, he has to repeat the last word he's thought all over all over again. Kinda like Tourette's syndrome, but not as bad, I guess. So when Michael knocks to get Denise's attention, its best for Denise to go see Michael. So Denise tells me she's gonna leave for a while and if I could mind the gravy, why sure Denise, I'll do just that!!!! I'm thinking, gee whiz, maybe I am getting somewhere with Denise! So I'm just mashing the potatoes, and I've added some milk to it to make it really creamy and soft. The mashed potatoes look pretty good to me by now, so I decide to give it a taste, and since nobody's looking and everyone's left me in the kitchen, I just stick my finger in the pot and give it a lick. Pretty good! So I stick my finger in to get another blob of mashed potato when who should walk in but Sister Sandy. Sister Sandy sees me with my finger with a blob! of mashed potato on it and she's just going ballistic! Now Sister Sandy isn't that bad looking if she weren't so uptight. Kinda like Kate Jackson from Charlie's Angels, but blond. But I think she uses too much hairspray as her hair always seemed so stiff. But I digress, so she slams the door, comes running towards me, and starts yelling in my face what the heck am I doing sticking my dirty fingers in the mashed potatoes! She goes on and on, yapping and yapping like some angry chihuahua, and all this time Ive got this blob of mashed potato on my finger. Sister Sandy is still blabbing away when Ive had enough, and I thought, what the heck, so I stuck my finger with the mashed potato in her mouth to shut her up. So Im standing there with my finger in Sister Sandy's mouth while the gravy's bubbling on slow heat. Sister Sandy just looks kinda funny and her eyes are just kinda fidgeting, but I guess the mashed potatoes that I made were really good because she starts eating the mashed potato off my finger and starts doing some pretty funky things with my finger with her tongue.

Now, like I said, Sister Sandy isn't exactly unattractive and Denise is always saying how unbiblical it is to have sex before marriage, so I reckon, this ain't too bad. So Sister Sandy is groping in special places by now, and somehow I think, well it is Thanksgiving after all! I guess she just had all that unspent energy that just needed to be channeled elsewhere. So we start getting buck but since its cold we leave our socks on (pretty damn cold in Michigan you know!). And I'm just about to do the horizontal mambo, when Sister Sandy starts to speak in this weird Darth Vader voice, so Ive got to stop and listen to her heavy breathing and Sister Sandy says: "I want to lick your balls in gravy...". Well, this has got me all excited! And besides, what a great story it would bring to my buddies at the office! So that wonderful woman Denise has got this pot of gravy all ready for me, so Im thinking, how convenient! But then the gravy's still hot, so I pour out some gravy into a bowl and let it cool. So Sister Sandy is lying naked on the kitchen counter, and Im squatting on the counter with my balls hanging and waiting for the gravy to cool. The world can't just get any better! Now I don't know about you guys, but squatting is nearly like being in a pooping position, and the pepsi I've been drinking was kinda making me bloated. So I could just feel this fart coming up, but I thought I better hold it in since its not exactly sexy letting out a fart. However, my timing was bad and holding it in just made it worse, because as I was standing on the counter and positioning myself over the cooled gravy to sink my balls into, I let out this fart, I thought it was just a little fart but I guess it was a pretty big fart because I farted so much that the little flames from the gas burner (I was squatting pretty close to the bubbly gravy pot) caught it, and the fart gas kinda caught on fire and it became like a mini flamethrower. Unfortunately, the target of the flamethrower was Sister Sandy's hair and because it had so much hairspray it pretty much caught on fire too. Sister Sandy shrieked like a banshee and she jumped up all screaming and hysterical with her boobies flopping about. Now her yelping frightened me so much that I lost my balance and fell into the bowl of gravy, covering my balls and ass in warm gravy. It kind looked like I had the sudden case of diarrhea but my concern was Sister Sandy who was running around the kitchen with her hair on fire. So I jump down with gravy dripping down my crack, and grab Sister Sandy and take her to the faucet to get some water over her hair. So Ive got Sister Sandy bent over the sink with her head down, while Im holding her from the back with brown gravy dripping down the inside of my legs. It must've looked pretty weird, because that Michael thought who was still looking through the window from the ground level. Now Michael's got this condition that I told you about where he's got to repeat the last word he's thought of when he gets excited, so Michael sees these two naked people in the kitchen, and Im pretty much huddled over Sister Sandy to keep her calm and get the water over her head and Sister Sandy is yelling and screaming, so I guess we did look like something from a porno or something, because Michael starts screaming "FUCK! FUCK! FUCK! FUCK!" Now you don't just that say that thing during Thanksgiving because a lot of the people will notice, most of all your sister, who happens to be Denise. So Denise comes running over and wonders what in the world has got Michael all riled up! So Michael points to us in the kitchen through the window, and by this time Im wiping off some of the gravy off Sister Sandy's groin and legs and Sister Sandy is crying and sobbing and shit. I saw Denise for maybe half a second through the window before she disappeared. But I knew she'd be back, through the kitchen door and bringing in Brother Bill and my roommate. Sure enough, the kitchen door comes crashing down and Brother Bill's eyes are the size of saucers, and my roommate is shouting and pointing fingers at me and Sister Sandy. In the meantime, Sister Sandy is still crying hysterically, her hair's all frizzy and black and smells bad, she's naked except for her socks, and she's still got some gravy on her thighs and legs. Im naked too, except Ive got more gravy, especially on the balls, and some more gravy dripping down from my ass. The kitchen is a mess, there's mashed potatoes everywhere, gravy on the floor, and the turkey's burnt since we werent watching it. I guess it kinda looked as if I went crazy, knocked things all over, raped Sister Sandy, burnt her hair and shit all over the place for good measure.

Needless to say, there was no Thanksgiving dinner that evening, and I got kicked out of church and never invited back. My roommate moved out. Denise sent me hate mail for months. Michael didn't stop saying "FUCK" for a week. Im just glad that Sister Sandy and Brother Bill didn't divorce, apparently "the devil" made her do it, so she was okay again after a couple of weeks. I couldn't laugh back then, but it does seem pretty funny now.

WOULD YOU...

I may still write that book.

Date:	Sunday, June 06, 1999 9:44 PM
To:	Mark; Dodge; Jun; Roberto; Bruce; Tom; Dale; Joe O.; Barry; Aldo; Chris; Davide; Grant; Simon; Peter; Greg; Keith
Subject:	Found some old stuff

I was cleaning up my junk today, and I found an old notebook from my Adelaide days when I used to go to the cafes and write up ideas for my books.

Remember that little game I used to play where you had to do some tough choices (Amanda Vanstone or Madeleine Albright?). I found several pages of them. They kinda made me laugh when I read them again.

Here you go!

They start off with WOULD YOU HAVE...
e.g. would you have sex with Madeleine Albright for 1000 dollars?

Im just using Elle MacPherson (pre-baby) since she's Aussie and she's generally accepted as beautiful, feel free to swap her for any attractive woman of your choice. The object is to see what your threshold is. I mean come on, what good is a little pinky? Oh by the way, before you guys start responding and telling me what they'd do, I can't really deliver Elle or chop off your legs, okay????

Tradeoffs

1 month of sex with Elle and 1 year of blindness

1 month of sex with Elle and 1 year of deafness

1 month of sex with Elle and 1 year of paralysis (no use of arms and legs)

1 month of sex with Elle and 6 months in prison

1 month of sex with Elle and loss of memory from age 1 to 18

1 month of sex with Elle and 3 years living in Bangladesh

1 month of sex with Elle and 1 year living alone in the South Pole

1 month of sex with Elle and have to repeat last 4 years of high school

1 month of sex with Elle and have to repeat college

1 month of sex with Elle and no tv/movies for 2 years

1 night of sex with Elle and lose little pinky

1 week of sex with Elle and lose both pinkies

1 month of sex with Elle and lose both pinkies and both little toes

1 night of sex with any girl of your choice once a year and lose hair forever

1 month of sex with any girl of your choice once a year and lose 1 eye

1 month of sex with any girl of your choice once a year and replace all teeth with dentures

Any girl of your choice all the time and lose both arms

Any girl of your choice all the time and lose both legs

Any girl of your choice all the time and be deaf forever

Big Sacrifice (notice that it's oral sex so some of you might actually opt to do the right thing instead of being depraved, but I doubt it)

1 month of oral sex on Elle and give up eradication of the common cold

1 month of oral sex on Elle and give up the cure for AIDS

1 month of oral sex on Elle and give up the cure for cancer

1 month of oral sex on Elle and drop a couple of nuclear bombs on Somalia

1 month of oral sex on Elle and drop a couple of nuclear bombs on Japan

1 month of oral sex on Elle and drop a couple of nuclear bombs on New York

1 month of oral sex on Elle and the spotted owl becomes extinct

1 month of oral sex on Elle and Los Angeles gets hit with a 3.0 earthquake

1 month of oral sex on Elle and Los Angeles gets hit with a 10.0 earthquake

1 month of oral sex on Elle and blue whale becomes extinct

1 year of oral sex on Elle and secret of cold fusion wont be revealed for another 5 years

Best Friends (this is easy! friends are overrated!)

1 week of sex with Elle and best friend's kids gets chicken pox

Get to feel Elle's breasts and best friend's loses 10% of his assets

1 week of sex with Elle and best friend loses 50% of his assets

1 week of sex with Elle and best friend gets not sex for 1 year

1 month of sex with Elle and best friend is blind for 1 year (only temporarily)

1 month of sex with Elle and best friend cant walk for 1 year

1 year of sex with any girl any day and best friend doesnt have a job for 5 years

1 month of sex with Elle and best friend gets into a car crash (10% chance of being killed)

1 year of sex with Elle and best friend goes to jail for a year (minimum security, best friend guaranteed NOT to be sodomized, so it's not that bad)

Good Sex for Bad Sex (you gotta take the good with the bad! just like life!)

note: interchange Amanda (for Aussies) with Janet/Madeleine (for USers), please. Janet Reno is a legend!!!

1 night with Elle for 1 year with Janet Reno (or Amanda Vanstone)

1 week with Elle for 1 year with Janet Reno and Madeleine Albright

1 month with any girl of your choice, followed by 10 months of oral sex on Janet Reno, followed by 1 month with any girl of your choice

1 year of sex with any girl of your choice, but oral sex on Janet Reno FOREVER

1 month with 4 GIRLS of your choice for one night of gay joy (this isnt necessarily bad)

1 month with 4 GIRLS of your choice for one night of gay joy and youll forget the gay experience the next day (this is a good deal)

1 night with Elle and one night with your best friend's grandmother

1 week with 2 girls of your choice, followed with 1 week with your best friend's grandmother and grandfather and youll forget everything afterwards

1 week with any girl of your choice every year for 1 night of great gay anal sex every year (no selective amnesia here!!!)

Do it for Money?

1 night with Janet Reno for 100 bucks.

1 night of oral sex on Janet Reno for 1000 bucks.

1 year of oral sex on Amanda Vanstone for $1,000,000.

1 year of gay sex for $1,000,000? (this is aint bad!)

1 year of gay sex for $1,000,000 and youll forget everything

1 year of oral sex on Madeleine Albright, but 20 years later you get 1 BILLION BUCKS!!!

1 week of oral sex on Madeleine Albright and you get a chance to bet 1 million bucks on black or red on roulette.

1 night of sex with your best friends grandmother for 1 million dollars which she later tells you is her retirement money

1 week of sex with animals of your choice (I suppose collies look like Steffi Graf) for 1 million bucks and nobody knows about it.

1 night of sex with animals of your choice for 1 million bucks but one of your friends took a picture of you.

Dreams may come true...

1 year of oral sex on Madeleine Albright for a top of the line Mercedes

1 week of oral sex on Madeleine Albright for a pool table

1 week of oral sex on Madeleine Albright for a big screen tv

1 week of oral sex on Madeleine Albright for season's tickets to any sporting event

1 month of oral sex on Madeleine Albright for 1 years worth of eating free at your favorite restaurants

1 month of oral sex on Madeleine Albright for a swimming pool

1 year of oral sex on Madeleine Albright for 5 years all-expenses paid round-the-world trips/travel

1 year of oral sex on Madeleine Albright for free beer for the rest of your life

1 year of oral sex on Madeleine Albright for free pornos for the rest of your life

1 year of oral sex on Madeleine Albright for free CDs for the rest of your life

You cant lose!!!

Sex with Elle in a VW beetle or sex with Madeleine Albright in a Mercedes (you get to keep the car)

Sex with Elle or sex with Madeleine Albright AND $10,000

Sex with Elle or sex with Madeleine Albright AND $100,000

Sex with Elle or sex with Madeleine Albright AND $1,000,000

One night with Elle and get herpes OR 1 night with Madeleine Albright and get a 30% raise the next day (this is tough)

One night with Elle and 1 million bucks OR 1 night with Madeleine Albright and 2 million bucks

One night with Elle and one goodlooking gay guy OR 1 night with Madeleine Albright and your bestlooking female coworker

Sex with three girls of your choice for one night OR sex with three girls for three weeks (1 girl/week) but there's a 50% chance that the girls wont show up.

Sex with an ugly girl every night, OR sex with a pretty girl every six months

Sex with a bitchy, ill-tempered chick with a hot face and body every night OR sex with an avg girl but can tell jokes, cook like a chef, and likes your friends (she isnt fat).

Dubious Choices

Sex with Elle with 1 breast missing OR sex with Winona Ryder with no legs

Sex with Elle with both breasts missing OR only oral sex from Winona Ryder

Sex with Elle with no legs OR sex with Winona Ryder with no arms

Sex with Elle with your mom watching OR sex with Winona Ryder after she had sex with your dad (this isnt too bad)

Sex with Roseanne for 1 month OR Janet Reno for 1 week (no-brainer here)

Fat Oprah for 1 month OR Janet Reno for 1 week

Whoopi Goldberg OR fat Oprah (oral sex on both)

Sex with Martina Navratilova for 1 month OR Janet Reno for 1 day

Personal Choices

Rich and short penis OR poor and long penis

Goodlooking and long penis OR ugly and short penis but guaranteed to have sex with any girl of any choice once a year

porno actor making 50K/year OR business owner making 200K/year

beautiful children + ugly wife OR ugly children and beautiful wife

sexy girl with dog who craps all over the place OR avg girl who has toilet-trained dog, gets slippers, and scares away burglars

sexy girl with uncontrollable farts OR sexy girl with bad breath

master of martial arts OR porno star (tough choice for guys)

porno star OR have xray vision

porno star OR have ability to see one day into the future

thank you, thank you very much!

A FABLE

I like to make up fables. I didn't get any good responses. Yvette's solution was for a wizard to give back Omar's fingers using "magic". And of course, I got the usual sexually suggestive fantasy from Tom.

Date:	Friday, September 03, 1999 11:12 AM
To:	Yvette; Tom; Rowena; Joe O.; Helen; Barry; Dale; Bruce; Alicia; Aldo
Subject:	Ending This Story

Help me out figuring out the ending or moral to this ancient tale of wisdom which I just made up.

The Tale of Omar the Merchant

It was the seventh year of reign for the Caliph of Baghdad. To celebrate the seven years of prosperity and peace, the Caliph decided to hold a parade in honor of his works. And so it was that on the seventh day of the seventh month of the seventh year, a most magnificent fleet of soldiers, carriages, and floats commemorating the Caliph's great deeds, swept down the palm-lined Grand Avenue of Baghdad.

Thousands clamored and cheered to the colors and sounds that rumbled noisily past them. But not everyone was so impressed.

Omar the Merchant stood glum-faced in front of his store, and ranted angrily that business was bad because people were not able to cross the street to get to his store because of the parade. And also the many onlookers were blocking his fine display of carpets and selection of silverware. Omar the Merchant had worked hard in his life, and it had taken him many years to finally have his store on the Grand Avenue, and it angered him that the Caliph would deprive him of a day in business. And so Omar turned to his wife Mara, and said: "The Caliph has not known a day's worth of hard work in his life! Who is he to make parades in honor of himself, while the rest of us suffer to make a living for ourselves!!!! Strip the Caliph of his clothes, he is nothing more than a fat pig. Why, I could wrap up one of Ali's pig with any of my carpets, put a copper pot on the pig's head, and nobody could tell the difference between the pig and Caliph!"

But fate was not smiling on Omar the Merchant that day. For at the very moment Omar insulted the Caliph, the Caliph rode by in his golden carriage and heard the very words spoken by Omar. The Caliph was enraged and ordered his soldiers to take Omar back to the palace. Mara pleaded with the soldiers not to take her husband, and wept when they took him away.

The next day at the palace, the Caliph had Omar brought to him. Omar had spent the night in the foulest dungeon, and knew that a quick death would be his most merciful punishment. Omar also knew that the Caliph was a cunning man and prone to unusual cruelty.

The Caliph merely said: "For your insult against the Caliph of Baghdad, you have brought the punishment of death upon yourself." Omar sighed when he heard this and expected nothing less. But the Caliph continued: "But since your crime happened on a day of celebration, I will allow that goodwill to affect your sentence. You may choose between death by sword, or 10 years in my dungeon..."

At the words of being spared certain death, Omar immediately replied: "I choose 10 years!!!!!".

But the Caliph had not finished yet with and continued "...10 years in my dungeon but for every year, one of your closest friends will be put to death."

And so in his haste, Omar had condemned 10 of his closest friends to death.

The first year had passed, and on the anniversary of his first year, the Caliph had sent down a guard to tell him that Ali the Butcher would be chosen to die for the first year of his sentence. Omar wailed and cried: "I have known Ali for twenty years, in hard times he has always been there to help me, and I was there to help him. But for my own selfishness, I have sent Ali and my friends to death!!!" Omar turned to the guard and said: "Friend, give me your knife."

But the guard refused for the Caliph had decreed that Omar must suffer the ten years in prison, and all means possible to take his own life had been removed. And Omar said: "I vow that for every friend that has to die, I desire to have a finger removed." And the guard took pity on Omar's pain and with his knife, cut off one of Omar's fingers.

And so it went on for the next 9 years. On the anniversary of his imprisonment, the guard would give him the name of his friend chosen for death, and Omar would extend his hand, and the guard would cut off one of his fingers.

On the final year, the guard came down and told him that this was the day he was to be set free, but also that the 10th victim had been chosen, and it would be

Mara, his wife. And Omar was beyond himself with grief, for Mara was truly his friend of all friends. For the last 10 years, she had lovingly sent him letters, and although forbidden to see him, he knew that she still loved him as much as the day they had met. And he loved her equally as well. Omar extended his hand, and so his last finger was removed. With that, the prison door opened, and Omar was free to leave the prison which had been his home for 10 lonely years.

The guard led him to the palace gates, and opened them for him.

Omar walked out into freedom and sunlight, and who did he see waiting for him? But his nine friends and his wife Mara.

Omar could not believe his eyes, and winked and blinked to make sure that he truly was seeing his friends and his in the flesh. As they all surrounded him and welcomed him back to the living, the guard walked up to him and said: "Know that I brought to the Caliph's attention your vow, and the Caliph decreed that for every finger you sacrifice, a friend shall be spared. Had you not kept your word, there would surely be no one here to greet you."
****
I just thought that the ten fingers for ten years was a neat idea. But the morality of the tale is a bit confusing. He can't even shake their hands for goodness sakes!!!!!

THESPIAN

I love word games...

Date:	Tuesday, October 26, 1999 4:03 PM
To:	Dale; Joe O.; Greg; Aldo
Subject:	THESPIAN

I'm just having a wordy day today! Look at all the fun words and sentences you can make out of "thespian"...

t h e s p i a n

apeshit'n	"'are you apeshit'n me???" or ape n' shit "'geeze, he was going ape and shit!'
penis hat	"I'd like a twelve-pack of penis-hats, please"

pantiesh	"take off your pantiesh, honey", spoken like Sean Connery, I guess
she-paint	"got any more of that she-paint, boys?"
A pen, shit	"I wanted a pencil, you gave me a pen, shit!'"
he snap it	"pencil broke, he snap it"
heat pins	"it's cold, I need some heat pins"

SECTION IV

A MAN FOR ALL SEASONS

The world is my country,
all mankind are my brethren,
and to do good is my religion.
Thomas Paine – Rights of Man

13

THE TRAVELER

> My favorite thing is to go where I've never been.
>
> *Diane Arbus*

AYERS ROCK

An epic travel story.

Date:	Saturday, May 08, 1999 8:07 AM
To:	Rowena; Kevin; Kirsten; Alex; Dodge; Jun; Roberto; Nicole; Aldo; Davide; Grant; Grant; Greg; Mark; Peter; Simon; Bruce; Tom; Dale; Joe O.; Barry
Subject:	Mr. Dino's Trip

There's probably some rehash with this, since I already sent off some prior emails. It is kinda long, but don't worry, you don't have to read it if it's too long. I won't cry.

Mr. Dino's Trip to Central Australia

I kept a journal for most of the days of my trip. Here it is in all its painfully detailed entirety.

April 28, 1999 - Leaving Sydney

Checked in the Greyhound bus terminal at around 1:00 pm (bus leaves at 3:00 pm) and went to lunch in Chinatown. Ordered my favorite, steamed pork in dark mystery sauce in a hotpot. Not bad. Then played pokies to kill some time before heading back to the terminal and getting in the bus. As luck would have it, I had two seats to myself for the trip to Alice Springs. That was fortunate because 2 days on the bus being squeezed in with a total stranger with funny body odors would be quite unpleasant. It somehow took forever to get out of the greater Sydney, so I took out a book and tried to read. But soon a competition raged between a Vietnamese woman and a Punjabi man on who could talk the loudest in the bus. And I was sitting somewhere in the middle of the two. I comforted myself with the inevitability that one of them would tire soon. Well, at least one of them did. Arrived in Canberra sometime in the night to have dinner for 30 mins. The café was serving a host of mystery meats, white mystery meat, brown mystery meat, and red mystery meat. I chose the brown mystery meat (deliciously described as beef stroganoff). Canberra was extremely cold! Why they ever chose to put the nation's capital in Canberra is a tough question indeed.

Sleeping on the bus was a tough challenge as many of us would find out in numerous experiments on the best possible sleeping position. For me, being a person of lithe and graceful stature, I guess the best position was to extend the feet straight under the handlebars of the forward seat, recline my seat as far as I can get it, cover my head and shoulders with my leather jacket and stick my hands under my shirt on my belly to retain as much body heat as possible. This seemed to work the best. I must say that it would have been handy to have a girlfriend to curl up to, or at least have a nice warm blanket. Whatever is cheaper.

However, sleep was indeed a precious commodity to come by on the bus, and I constantly switched from dream-state to wake-state. During these periods of temporary lucidity, I thought of some interesting verbal techniques I could use for the future. I realized that it is much more interesting to describe a person with two adjectives separated by a "yet". Here are some examples:

Natasha-Stott Despoja: Pristine yet delightful

Amanda Vanstone (Madeleine Albright look-alike): Repulsive yet harmless.

Keanu Reeves: Chick magnet yet homo.

Kind silly, I know. But you gotta fill in the hours, and I had about 48 hours to go.

We were travelling at night, so there wasn't much to see. But it was pretty flat, with a lot of orchards and farms. I reckon Australia needs some more mountains.

April 29, 1999 - Arrived in Adelaide

Finally arrived in Adelaide. Everything still looked the same. In fact, everything was still so familiar that I felt like I could go back to my apartment on Rundle and Union, take a shower, walk to EDS and it would have been perfectly normal. Now, I always have a shower every day, so I decided to try the showers at the bus terminal, and they were perfectly fine. Then I wandered off to pay an unannounced visit to my former EDS colleagues on North Terrace. What a fancy building! I looked like a grimy tourist in my blue jeans and worn shirt and knapsack. But a quick call from reception got me an EDS visitor's pass (which I kept and added to my ever growing collection of visitor passes (I must have visitor keys and ids to get me in all kinds of buildings in Adelaide, Melbourne and Sydney). Nitin, good fella from my old project came up to get me, and the project team were all pretty happy to see me. In fact, they were all still there, Greg, Chris, Keith, Nitin (and Mark was off vacationing somewhere). Nitin even brought up my old code on his monitor to show me all the enhancements he's had to do on it. I didn't want to stay too long as I wanted them to keep on working so they could be productive and get my EDS stock up to its proper value, which in my estimate is $65-$70 per share, and a stock split soon after, but alas, it's wasting away at a terrible $50-$53 per share. Wandered off to Rundle Mall and had a quick meal at the food court, everything is slightly cheaper in Adelaide, like a dollar off for a meal. While eating my chicken wings, I noticed two young fellows bump into each other and a big pushing and shoving match ensued between the two. I had forgotten that Adelaide seems to have its fair share of young hellions. Speaking of trouble, I walked over to Hindley St. (the red light district of Adelaide), and found myself an internet café to check on my email. Figured out how to do get my home email from hotmail using POP, and I was able to receive quite a number of emails to my delight! In fact, I even got email from someone I fancied (and it's not Rowena), so that was cool. Too bad she doesn't fancy me. I bet, it's because I'm fat. I can't help it if I have a weight problem!!!! Before I left on my trip, I had set myself up with several internet trading accounts, and I checked out my latest positions. Microsoft took a dive, and I still hadn't gotten Compaq at $23. Oh well. Plenty more of days to go.

By the time I reached Port Augusta, I realized how expensive going by bus can be. It's actually cheaper to fly instead of taking the bus. It's $429 for a round trip to Alice Springs by plane, and $440 for a round trip by bus, but you have to book 3 weeks in advance. Also, you end up buying all kinds of food and drinks on every bus stop, so it really adds up. I was also getting worried that I hadn't pooped in two days. The little nugget I pressured out in Adelaide didn't really count. Damn this low fiber diet!!! However, I was feeling more and more relaxed and my insatiable desire to rush things and always be busy was subsiding (you know, idle hands are the devil's tinsnips). I guess, the freedom of the vast Australian outback does that to you.

April 30, 1999 - Finally got to Alice Springs

Just arrived in Cooper Pedy just before sunrise. Something tells me to buy thermal underwear in Alice Springs. It's bloody freezing! Still having difficulty to fall asleep so I resorted to the technique of fantasizing about my favorite girls to get me to that dream-state. Another thing I realized is if you can't shower just yet, and you're feeling kind dirty, just brush your teeth and wash your face. It made me feel heaps better. In Adelaide, we picked up this crazy fella who had the uncanny ability to hold up the bus at every stop. It was amazing. This guy had a comment on everything. Sometimes, you'll think that some people are idiots from the way they talk, but if you really listen carefully, they're really not that stupid. But they're still annoying nonetheless. This same fella was constantly asking this German girl what she thought of Hitler: "You from Germany? What do you think of Hitler?" I guess it is an ice breaker. Listening to that man go off on his monologue, I thought of that so-ever important question: "what is the measure of a man (or a woman)?" Is it the sum of his experience, or the potential of his gifts? I reckon, monetary success has got to fit in there somehow too. As you can tell, I had to get off the bus soon, because if I didn't, I would surely go nuts thinking about the intricacies of human nature.

Looking out the bus window, one could see the wide expanse of the Australian landscape. It is not at all dry and desert; in fact, it is kind lush and thriving. The vegetation is pretty low (shrubs, bushes, grass, small acacias), but it is everywhere. As far as I could tell, this country could use some more people.

We watched "The Net" starring Sandra Bullock on the bus. 10 minutes into the movie, I just had enough of that cyber nonsense. Just made me laugh that they were showing these programmers as attractive people, give me a break, other than me and my close friends who are programmers, let's face it, programmers look like dorks. Got to Erlunda and I realized that there is something that you can't see from the inside of the bus. The flies. They were everywhere. And they wanted to get into every orifice of your body. In your eyes, ears, nose, and mouth. I really wonder how the aborigines can stand those flies.

Finally got to Alice Springs in the early afternoon. Checked into the hostel, and I saw two topless chicks at the pool. Euro chicks from the look of it. Thank goodness for Euro chicks and their desire to get a tan. It wasn't really that hot either, but it was pretty bright. Later on I found out that the two Euro chicks were in my camping group, Anne (nice Swedish girl), and Xena (crazy Danish girl). My room was okay, it was a single (had two beds) but I didn't have to share with anybody, and I had to use the common toilet and shower facilities, but they were fairly clean. Later on in the afternoon, I took a walk to the city center, not bad, a little small Alice Springs is, but then again, they only have 20,000 people. Had dinner at KFC, oddly enough, the aborigines were probably the primary customers at KFC, I thought that KFC would be really bad for them due to their lack of tolerance of high-cholesterol. But I guess, it would be unfair to ban them from KFC. But they do have self-imposed bans on buying/serving alcohol to aborigines.

May 1, 1999 - First Day of the Tour - Ayers Rock

Woke up at 5:00 pm to take a shower. Pretty cold!!! Had a quick breakfast of toast and tea, spilled my tea on my jeans. So that was a good sign to have a big brown stain on my thigh. The tour bus picked up and we were greeted by Darren, a pleasant young chap. Throughout the trip, Darren only wore shorts, no matter what the temperature was. Before the trip, Grant was telling me that I'd be pooping in a hole in the ground and taking showers from a water bag hung up on a tree. Well, for the price I was paying for this 3 day camping trip, I really wasn't expecting much. But imagine my surprise when we got to the Ayers Rock camp site, and they had magnificent toilet and shower facilities. You could eat off the toilets, it was that clean! No problems with water pressure, and they even had phones and laundry facilities. We had new tents, sleeping bags, and a mess hall that had a fridge and electricity. It was really well thought out! Brilliant! Had quick sandwiches for lunch, and we headed off for Ayers Rock. By the way, it took us four hours to get to Ayers Rock from Alice Springs. The distances are incredible in this part of the country.

As we were approaching Ayers Rock, Darren, our guide reminded us that the aborigines preferred that we not climb the rock for two reasons: one, its unsafe, and two, it's a bit disrespectful to be climbing this spiritual place. Even the aborigines don't climb the rock themselves. Now, as you all know, I have this mental problem that once I get something in my head, I can't stop until I've done it. So I was intent on getting up that rock. Nay, I was hell-bent on getting up there. And besides, with all due respect, I certainly didn't have any plans to desecrate the Uluru (the local name for Ayers Rock).

Now, Ayers Rock is exactly what it is, it's about 400 meters of rock protruding up from the earth. Funny thing is, we knew there was going to be a chain that would guide us up on the rock. I thought it was just going to be a little rinky-dink chain to show you where you were supposed to go. But this chain starts 80 meters up from the base. The idea being is, if you can't get up the first 80 meters on your own, you probably shouldn't be going up the rock in the first place. Needless to say, I just had to laugh at that little test! Please, spare me these little challenges! So I rushed up the rock in my recklessness, and I soon realized that this was no mere test. This was tough. We started off as 17 who wanted to climb the rock, but only 10 managed to get up to thė chain (we were 22 in the tour group). When I got to the chain, I saw how heavy and thick the steel chains were. These were chains you could attach an anchor to, or pull tractors. The chains were so brightly polished so you could see that people were using them well. I would soon realize the value of that chain.

I climbed up the side of Uluru, grasping onto that chain. I realized that my steps were getting slower and smaller. I was really getting tired, and lugging two bottles of water around my waist wasn't helping either. It was pretty steep, I'd say it was around 55-65 degrees incline for most of the ways, and you couldn't really do too much of turning around and enjoying the scenery because it would startle you how high up you were (from the smallness of the vehicles and the people at the base). The Swedes who were ahead of me were moving like machines. Anne and her boyfriend were pretty tough Scandinavians. Halfway up the chain, I couldn't climb anymore, and I wrapped myself around a metal post and had to rest. I motioned to the English and Norwegian girls to just walk past me, because no way was I moving. Nick, old guy who was my tent-mate passed me at this time also. At this stage, I was looking down to the base and saw how steep the rock was. And I really thought, "this is really stupid. I could really kill myself". Have you ever done something, and 10 minutes later, you really regretted and realized how stupid that decision was? Well, I gotta admit, that doesn't happen to me very often, but at this time, I knew this was one of those moments. But fortunately, guys don't have common sense, but they do have a lot of pride, and as the 4 young chicks and that old guy had bypassed me, I thought: "if they can do it, so can I!". And I pulled myself and kept on going. Still clinging on to that beloved chain. I finally got to the end of the chain, but I was just half-way up to the summit. The chain was gone but now it was just white lines painted on the red rock to guide us the to the top. This wasn't easy. At some stages, you had to run down to gain momentum so you could get up to the next ridge. I must say, it was very physical. If you could have seen me tackle those rocks, you would've been very proud of me. I finally got to the top. There is this bronze marker on the top, and I touched it, and that was that. I made it to the top. The four chicks and Nick were still there, so we took pics of each other. The feeling to be alive was just marvelous. I was expecting some profound revelation when I reached the top, but let me tell you, just to be alive on God's green earth, or rather God's red earth, that was profound enough. I took some pics of Katarina, the well-endowed Norwegian girl. Katarina and Liva were the pretty Norwegians, but they were kind frosty. Oh well, from the pictures, you'd never notice. Now climbing down was equally dangerous, just imagine, walking down a slide. So we clung on to that chain again. Nick taught me a good trick to walk down the steep rock. Just walk zig-zag down. Brilliant! You can learn from old people after all.

We finally got down to the safety of solid earth. What a relief!!! But the funny thing is, all of us who had climbed the rock all felt the same way. We all had the same fears, doubts and the love of the chain. In fact, we couldn't stop talking about that chain. Pretty weird. I guess we were all scared, nobody just said it at the time. I have to admit, there is no time or desire to disrespect Uluru. But honestly folks, I would not advise you to climb the rock. I just did it, because I'm crazy. But you can be smart and use your common sense and not climb it. We later went to a picture taking spot to take a picture of Uluru at sunset, but I left my camera in the bus, so I don't have any pics of me standing in front of Uluru. That's okay, I just had some wine and crackers (courtesy of the tour).

We went back to camp, had dinner and a campfire and just chatted about the day. My legs were aching from the climb. The Norwegians and English girls ate like horses. I was quite amazed to see Katarina and Liva gorge themselves on so much food, and they were just normal sized girls. The English girls were equally ravenous but they were kinda fat and plump. The German girl, Simone, referred to the 4 as the Spice Girls. When I had taken a shower, this strange German fellow asked me where I was from, so I answered, and said "yourself?", and he gives me a sarcastic look and says: "I'm just asking" and doesn't answer. What a dork. Must be a computer programmer to lack such social skills. Thomas was his name. For some strange reason, Thomas was always at our campfire even though he belonged to another group. I think he took a liking to one of the fat English girls. I don't know why, there was a fine Scottish or Irish lass in his group with a lovely mane of brown hair (unfortunately, her legs were equally hirsute). Back to the English girls, they were always complaining that people couldn't get their names straight Vicky and Katie. But both of them were English, fat and had diarrhea of the mouth (those two chicks just couldn't stop talking!!!!), so of course, it was hard to tell them apart.

Mike, Nick's older brother, warned me that Nick was a terrible snorer. But it was okay that night, as I had no problems getting to sleep.

May 2, 1999 - Second Day - The Olgas

As promised by Darren, we were woken up at 5:00 am to get ready for the Olgas (it's another rock formation that is marked by the numerous domed rock structures). It was pretty hard to get out of the sleeping bag because it was so cold (around zero celsius), and also we were all wrapped in this sleeping sheet that we were given in addition to our sleeping bag). No way was I going to take a shower in that cold.

Instead I just dressed as fast as I could and grabbed some toast and sat in front of the campfire and watched Katarina eat quantities of bread that would put Roseanne to shame. I wonder where all that food goes to? But at least Katarina was very attractive. Oh the wonderful things God blesses us with sometimes.

We got to the Olgas just before sunrise. We were all wrapped up in sweaters and jackets but as we started hiking it soon got fairly warm. Now you have to imagine, we are in the middle of nowhere, there's red rock, sand, and dry vegetation everywhere and we're wrapped up like eskimos. It's common I suppose of all desert climates. Problem is, we're all loaded up with water bottles so as it got warmer, the sweater and jacket were just more things to carry. You know how I always say, red rock this, red sand this, everything's red? Well, that's just due to the oxidization of the rocks, but if you dug deep into the Olgas or Uluru, it's actually grey. We hiked through the Olgas, but it wasn't as strenuous, and it was a good time to chat with some of my fellow travelers. And yes yes, I am able to carry on a decent non-internet conversation in which I don't abuse anybody or play mind-games with them. Come on, I can be charming when I want to be!

Finally finished the Olgas, so we went back to the campground to pack up and head off to the Kings Canyon campsite. On the way, we stopped off at a rest station and I lost my watch. The same Citizen watch my dear mother bought for me. Oh well, I've had it for 2.5 years, and besides, Ayers Rock gave me my life back, and I gave it back my watch. Fair trade I suppose. On the way to the campsite, Darren stopped by the edge of the road and asked us to pick up some firewood. Now, I don't know if you can visualize it, but in the bush, there is no shortage of wood and dead trees. It is just thriving. To be sure, they are not big trees, but there are trees and bush and shrubs everywhere. It was fairly easy getting big branches and logs from the bush and giving it to Darren to tie on top of the baggage trailer. Mike practically dragged this entire tree but we couldn't tie it down, so we tried breaking it up in two. But we just couldn't. The Italian guy tried jumping on it to break it, but it didn't break. I cut myself in my left hand but I didn't cry.

We got to our new campsite which was basically a cattle station. It wasn't as sophisticated as our first campsite and the hot showers were powered by a woodburning stove. Still hot enough though!! Darren made damper (traditional outback bread) and prepared big black kettles of food to be placed on the charcoal. It somehow worked, and it tasted great! We had a good time just chatting around the fire and getting to know each other. Of course, I didn't let out Donald Duck or Nepotutu, as I didn't want to shock them. Actually, it kind slipped out the previous night when Darren asked if we knew how he was going to wake us up at 5:00 am in the morning. So I piped up: "with a cattle prod?". So they thought that was kind weird. I guess I should've just said "gentle anal-probing?". But later on, they got the hang of me. It just takes a while to get used to my sense of humor, that's all. Sleeping in the tent was a different story this night. Nick unleashed the full fury of his snoring. In fact he woke me up and the English girls in the next tent. The Danish girls were pretty gutsy and slept under the stars in their swags. Oh yeah, I finally know how the Southern Cross star formation looks like. But I still can't figure out due south from it.

May 3, 1999 - Last Day - Kings Canyon

This was our last day of the tour, and we headed off to see Kings Canyon. I must say that Kings Canyon was a whole lot more exciting than the Olgas. More to see (and more to climb). Darren would always point out to us what all the places and plant meant to the aborigines so it was quite interesting hear all the stories about aboriginal laws and legends. The stories are really laws for they all have some form of meaning or moral, they call it Tjukurpa (which means laws). Darren was pointing out an interesting plant to us, it was called the Ippi-Ippi plant. Ippi means breast, so it was actually breast-breast. The reason being was that the plant has the milky substance which was used to dress wounds. Unfortunately, you couldn't rub the ippi-ippi milk into your eyes as it created this caustic coating which would in effect render you blind. Just through thousands of trial and error, the aborigines were able to figure out all the properties of the plant life and how to use them to survive in this harsh environment. While we were hiking, I actually saw this one girl with a huge gash in her thigh, her tour guide simply took her to an ippi-ippi plant and they applied the milky substance to her wound , and that was that!

Our hike was 3.5 hours long, but it was well worth it. We came upon this rock ledge overlooking the cliff. It was kinda like those road runner cartoons where the coyote stands on the ledge and it breaks off, that's what this ledge was all about. I had Nick snap me a pic while I was on the ledge. The two Norwegian girls were absolutely fearless, they got on the ledge but Liva crawled up the ledge so she could have a nice model shot of her self on her elbows, and Katarina dangled her legs over the ledge. We had to cringe when they did that. It was unfortunate that many of the folks had fear of heights and edges, so a lot of them couldn't even get up to some of the places.

We later went to the Garden of Eden, this sort of oasis in the heart of Kings Canyon. There was a pool of water but it was a little cold to be swimming in. But this one guy from another group strips down to his swimmers and jumps in.

As he is swimming, he yells out to his group to take a picture of him using his camera. But everyone's just laughing at him, and he's freezing his ass off. I don't think anybody took a picture of him.

After King's Canyon, we went back to the camp site, and packed up, and headed back to Alice Springs.

The group was going to meet in Bojangles for dinner in Alice, but I had some business to take care of, do some laundry because I was running out of underwear, and my jeans were all grimy. And I promised Dodge that I would try and get him casino chips whenever I'm in a city which has a casino. So I dressed up using my limited wardrobe after I had done the laundry, and took a taxi to Lasseter's. That was a pretty small casino. I reckon, everything could fit in the Coral Room of Star City. They also had strange rules in Lasseter's. But it didn't matter, because I kicked ass and won the casino chips (had to be doubles!!) that Dodge wanted and left for Bojangles. Got to Bojangles and most of them were there. So we had some wine, and I chatted with the Swedes and Danes and Poms. The Northern Euros are quite reserved but they'll thaw eventually. I really liked that Anne girl. Too bad she's already taken. Just something wholesome about them. Anyways, Xena was trying to make the move on Darren, and I was kinda sure they'd be boinking at the end of the night. Nick and I were talking about life in general, and he picked the right guy to chit-chat about the meaning of life, because when it came down to the guts of what's important in life, we both agreed that the most important thing a person could have is: choice. And if some of you know me, then you also know why it's important for me to have choice. It was kind cool that a total stranger come upon "choice" on his own, thousands and thousands miles away in another country and a different age group as well. I guess people aren't that different after all.

Emily, our part-aboriginal hostess was chatting me up, and I really thought I'd have a good chance of getting a taste of the local wildlife that night. I made Emily buy me a beer, and she gave me a good expression to use "THAT'S BLOODY HUGE!!!". I don't exactly know how to use it that line, but I'm sure I can work it in somehow. Anyway, the party tapered off, and Xena, Darren, Emily, Nick and I moved on to the next night club at Malenka's. Xena and Darren are in the back, talking deep stuff. Then my plans to get bush tucker are messed up when Emily says she can't stay because she's a local and she's not allowed in Malenka's. I didn't quite figure that one out. Local being aboriginal or local being Alice Springs local? Anyways, I wasn't fussed. Nick and I played pool which ended by me knocking the eightball prematurely in the pocket. Then we went home! Separate hotels of course, because I'm not homo. Although, there's nothing wrong with being gay!!! After all, we're all God's children.

May 4, 1999 - Trying to leave Alice Springs

Shouldn't have had that bottle of red wine, because I woke up and had to puke out dinner. Woke up late in the morning, took a shower and wandered off into the city to go to the post office and see if I could find the museum of Central Australia. Unfortunately they had moved the museum and I didn't want to walk anymore and my bus was leaving at around 3:00 pm, so I headed back to the hostel to get my gear and took the shuttle to the Greyhound terminal. Unfortunately, when I tried to check in they told me that I had reserved a seat on a non-existent bus. So I couldn't leave until the next day. I raised a little stink, and the best thing they could do was give me a room in Malenka's for free to sleep overnight. Which was fair enough. I probably needed the sleep anyway. So I just cruised around the city some more, and bought me a crappy SWAT watch (not SWATCH, but SWAT) to keep time since I lost my watch. Then I just relaxed for the day and took naps.

May 5, 1999 - Left Alice Springs

Finally got on the 10:15 am bus to Adelaide. The bus was rather full, and we had kids and babies on the bus, so it kinda smelled a little. I also had a person sitting next to me so it was kinda cramped. Funnily enough, he was on the same bus from Adelaide to Alice Springs, so we got to talking, and we even talked about climbing Ayers Rock. That Ayers Rock climb is a good bond. I thought I was weird, but this guy quit his job and sold his 2 BR unit to travel all over Australia (he's Aussie). I just quit my job and sold my BHP stock, but this guy was going to do some serious travelling. The bus trip was long and painful, and we just tried to sleep through it.

But before leaving for Adelaide, I managed to get in touch with Brooke, fellow Sydneysider, who was working in Adelaide for a couple of days. So Brooke is kind enough to meet me the next morning so I can crash at her hotel room while she's busy working in the next building. EXCELLENT!!! Thank goodness for Brooke!

May 6, 1999 - Arrived in Adelaide

Got to Adelaide around 6:00 am and waited for Brooke at the Radisson at around 8:00 am. Brooke came by and gave me her card, so I took a shower and cleaned up, and decided to cruise the city before meeting the guys for dinner later on in the evening. It was quite productive! I had my film developed, got a haircut, went to the Central Market to get my pull-apart bread and sausage, and watched a movie whilst eating the bread and sausage, I even checked out my stock positions, and I was able to buy Compaq at 23 dollars/share. Unfortunately it was now 22 ½. It was just like old times in Adelaide. Then I went to the casino to win some chips for my dear friend Dodge in California. I kicked ass, and got his chips for free, then I went back to the hotel room to take a nap. Then it was time for me to make a move, so I dropped Brooke's card at reception and I checked in my bags at the Greyhound terminal. Then I walked to Café Buongiorno, my old hangout and met Keith, Greg and Davide. I don't know what happened to the rest of the guys, but it was good to see these fellas! I made Davide pay for my share of the pizza since he felt guilty for not coming through for me like Brooke.

We went over the pictures that I had taken, and just chatted and crapped on about stuff. Pretty good. Saw Brooke again later on with some other EDSers, chatted and then took a taxi to the terminal to get on the bus to Sydney. Long day, I tell you.

May 7, 1999 - Back in Sydney

Long bus trip, but I made it back safe and sound. Pulled out heaps of mail. Logged on to the internet to pay off my bills. Took a nice long shower, and I thought: "this was one of the best trips I ever had!"

What's next? Queensland in June? Or Tasmania?

BLUE MOUNTAINS

I still don't see where the "Blue" in Blue Mountains come from.

Date:	Sunday, May 16, 1999 2:43 AM
To:	Kareena; Bruce; Tom; Dale; Joe O.; Barry; Simon; Peter; Nicole; Mark; Greg; Grant; Davide; Aldo; Brooke; Roberto; Jun; Dodge; Kirsten; Sandra; Rowena; Karen
Subject:	Ho Hum Blue Mountains & Koreans

So I went to the Blue Mountains outside Sydney this Sunday with Oz Experience's 1 Day Tour. The flyer they had described all these fascinating and exciting things we were going to do in the Blue Mountains, but I was horribly disappointed. The tour consisted of taking us to vistas to take photographs of waterfalls, stone structures and other famous sites, but we hardly did any bushwalking or any serious hiking. There was good stuff to see like the waterfalls but we didnt even come close! I was really upset that we didnt even get to climb the Three Sisters. I mean, we're already there! Let's just climb the thing!

We did do a forty minute hike down Katoomba falls and took the steepest railway up back. But come on, forty minutes is just warm-up for me!! Im used to hours and hours of excruciating, sweaty and fearsome hikes and mostly uphill too. Plus the trail wasnt a trail at all, they had wooden steps, and steel bridges and stairways. I want my feet to be one with nature, baby!!!! None of these man-made stuff! I even brought my hiking boots this time (because I climbed the Rock with tennis shoes and that was a big mistake), but they werent needed at all. It was mostly just picture taking and shouting some echoes, that's all. If I had wanted to see some pretty sights and do cheap thrills, I might as well have just stayed at home and watched a porno and opened a jar of peanut butter. But I digress.

But on the way up, we did take this little train thing up the steepest railway (it mustve been 80 degrees at some point) which was okay, but it didnt make me cry or give me any fear, so it wasnt really that great. But there was this girl next to me who was paralyzed with fear, she couldnt get out of her seat and her fingers were clenched to the bar in front of her. Come on sister! We've got this wire mesh roof above our heads, we've got a conductor up in the back with some form of emergency brakes, and there's a rubber bumper at the end of the cliff to stop a crash (granted, it probably wouldnt do any good with a load of 100 people and steel crashing down at 32 ft/s2), so there was a lot of safety involved. It wasnt like we were grabbing onto a chain and watching every false step (you guys know what Im referring to).

We had 3 Koreans with us and it was weird because they werent dressed right. One of them had a suit on and all three wore leather dress shoes (they didnt hold up very well when we were hiking in the mud). But they seemed okay in the beginning. Until we got to Featherdale Wildlife Park.

They had all these kangaroos and wallabies jumping around freely in the park (so you could walk up to them, pet them, feed them etc.) Once the Koreans saw the kangaroos, they just went apeshit. One of them runs up to one really timid kangaroo and starts stroking its back. Maybe a little bit too hard, because the kangaroo started hopping away. So what do you do if the kangaroo starts hopping away (and youre Korean)? You grab its tail!!!! So the Korean guy starts pulling on the tail, and now everybody's looking at him. But the kangaroo manages to escape and the Korean just goes ballistic and starts chasing after him (this guy is around early 40s, looks old). The kangaroo escapes to an off-limits area, and the guy sneaks in under the bar and continues to harass the kangaroo. Finally one of the other Koreans grabs him and points him to other kangaroos, so he goes off and pulls the tails on the other kangaroos. So we're all shaking our heads and getting upset with the Koreans (that's how wars get started!!! with all these cultural misunderstandings!), so one of us are getting ready to say something but it turned out it wasnt necessary. Because the Korean Kangaroo Abuser found a Koala. There was this little chubby Koala walking on the ground, so the Korean sees it and starts yelling and shouting to get the camera ready. The Korean grabs the Koala and starts lifting it up. He mustve thought it was like a harmless teddy bear or something. I dont know if most of you know have really taken a close look at Koalas but they have very ferocious claws. More like talons really. I started shaking my head and told the Korean, "you shouldnt do that..." but it was too late. The Koala grabbed on the guys chest with his four sets of sharpened black claws, and thats all she wrote! The expression on the Korean's face was just priceless. The look of horror and pain was just magnificent to behold. The expression was similar to a guy getting kicked in the nuts, or what we used to do in Detroit, a bunch of guys ganging up one unsuspecting guy and giving him a titty-twist (or several). I thought the guy was gonna piss in his pants right there, 'cause he kinda bent over and let go of Mr. Koala, who just scampered away. The Korean stopped picking up and touching animals after that. I was just laughing my head off in my own cruel yet special way. Thank heaven for life's little pleasures.

After that, we got on the bus and returned to Sydney.

I will have to return to Katoomba and climb the Three Sisters on my own. Forget Oz Experience, that was a bit of a rip-off, they couldve done it so much better instead of stopping off at all these vistas. I'll just wait for some of you USAers to come out and we can climb it, right Dale?

QUEENSLAND

My quest to visit all Australian States and Territories.

Date:	Monday, November 01, 1999 1:11 PM
To:	Dodge; Jun; Roberto; Brooke; Helen; Rowena; Dan; Aldo; Davide; Derryn; Greg; Keith; Simon; Kirsten; Bruce; Dale; Barry; Joe O.; Tom; Maria; Yvette
Subject:	Back from Queensland

Dear Dear Friends,

Saturday...

Well, I'm back at work - reviewing all the stuff I have to do for the day. Last night I got back from Queensland. It was pretty good. I had thought Brisbane, Surfer's and the Gold Coast (especially the latter two) would be more spectacular, but it was just okay. I think I'll have to go up the coast a little more next time. But I also went there to see my dear dear friend Keith and wife Angie who live in Carindale.

They picked me up at the airport Saturday afternoon, and we drove off to the Gold Coast to see the beaches and Conrad's Jupiter casino. My trustworthy Olympus camera broke during one of Derryn's "let's-not-catch-any-fishies-today" fishing trips, so we had to stop off at a photo store to buy one of those disposable cameras - so I'll have to see how these pictures pan out. Walked around Surfer's, took some snaps of the beach (we didn't go on the beach, nobody wanted to get sand in their shoes - we were dressed up because we were going to the casino and dinner later), and had ice cream using one of the many coupons in Keith's Entertainment book (yeah, they have them here in Oz too).

We made reservations at the Ana hotel at Hattie's for 7:30 pm, so this gave us time to kill at Jupiter's where I could win casino chips for my dear dear friend Dodge in N California. The casino/hotel looked very nice - the casino was on two levels, the lower play was on the top level though which was odd. But I sat on the blackjack table and KICKED ASS for 10 minutes, enough to get a set of casino chips (but I forgot to get doubles because the dealer and pit boss chickies were kinda cute and distracting, and I was explaining to Keith and Angie the intricacies of this so very sweet game). Apparently Keith and Angie don't really know much about the casino so we messed around the pokies a little before saying bye bye to Jupiter's.

It was off to Hattie's, a rather fancy restaurant in the hotel. For myself and Keith, we ordered the SEAFOOD PLATTER for two. When Angie's main meal came out, I thought "gee whiz, that looks rather small, I wonder if the seafood platter would be big enough...". But when the platter came out... SWEET MOTHER OF MERCY!!!! This was gonna give the 42 ribs I had in Tony Roma's a run for its money. It was on a platter 2 - 3 feet long, stacked with prawns, mussels, oysters, crayfish, and giant moreton bay bugs on fresh fruit. I had to take a picture of it before we started on it. Then we took another picture whilst eating it. It was very difficult to finish. I gave up and we still had 1/4 to go, but Keith just kept on going and going, so I felt guilty and helped. Bruno, our waiter from Switzerland, conversed with me in German, but Lulu (also Swiss or German) with her teutonic features was by far the more attractive choice. Then we went back to Keith's house.

Sunday...

We went to Mt Coot-tha to get the view of Sydney, and then barbecued at the park. We made a magnificent fire in the barbecue which Keith lovingly stoked with that deep hypnotic gaze men get when around fires. Women always wonder why guys love fire so much. Again, that is a very simple explanation. Women can give birth and therefore life. Men can't so they're jealous, so they do the opposite - kill and destroy. And fire is one of the great destructive forces. You know, yin and yang.

We were going to go hiking around the park, and we were in the car already to drive to the trail, but then I got a lactose-intolerance attack in the car (must be from the ice coffee whilst at the cafe on Mt. Coot-tha), and I told Keith to take me to the nearest toilet as possible. But the park toilet was kinda dark (in fact it was so dark that Keith peed on my foot while were standing there), so Angie said we should try the toilets in the nearby botanical gardens. Apparently, long time ago they too had the shits and needed to find a proper toilet. So we drove there and I found the toilet. It was clean but the door wouldn't lock, of course. So naturally, while I was giving thanks to God's grace on the can, some Korean or Japanese dude opens up my door - DAMN THESE FOREIGNERS!!!! "Don't be knocking when the toilet's rocking", that's what I always say! Anyway, I had flushed out most of that foul poison from my body, so we strolled around the gardens and took pics. Heck, we were already there. Supposedly, on one of the pics, Angie said I had a really angelic look on my face and should send it to my mother. I guess, I looked so at peace because of the big dump that I had just taken. I'll have to check out that picture when it comes out. Then we went back to Keith's house and watched "Payback" with Mel Gibson on video. I must remind myself to get an outfit for fall and winter that looks like Mel Gibson's outfit in the film. Good styling, I think.

Monday...

Said farewell to Keith and Angie and took the bus to Brisbane. Dropped off my bag in a locker, and strolled the streets of Brisbane. For some reason, I was drawn to this building called the Treasury Casino. I was doing well, but I got greedy and started playing 3 - 4 boxes. And I lost pretty quick. But this time I got casino chip doubles for my dear dear friend Dodge. Then I walked over the bridge to the Southbank (and checked out the museum, I think this museum needs some more exhibits), and the stuff around that area. I would say that in 3 years time, the Southbank will be really nice. They even have a little beach there (artificial, complete with lifeguards and sand). Would be a good place to take a girl there on a date, I reckon. But heck, what do I know about that???? Was getting tired now from all this walking so I bought postcards and sent them off to the US and abroad. Then took a taxi to the airport and I got a lecture from this Asian guy who knew how to fix all the problems of Australia. I just said, "just bring in 1 million Chinese immigrants from Taiwan and Hong Kong, that'll fix the economy straight away".

And that was about it, I was back in my apt at 6:00 pm. TASMANIA IS NEXT, BABY!!!!!

TASMANIA

More casinos to visit!

Date:	Sunday, November 28, 1999 10:19 PM
To:	Dodge; Jun; Roberto; Brooke; Helen; Karen; Rowena; Simon; Greg; Derryn; Davide; Aldo; Dan; Kirsten; Bruce; Dale; Barry; Joe O.; Tom; Yvette; Maria
Subject:	Tasmania

Dear Dear Friends,

Well, I've made it back from beautiful Tasmania. It was quite surprising what I found over there But anyways, let's start the painfully long story.

Flew out from Sydney Friday morning and arrived in Launceston at around 9:00 am. Picked up my rental car and quite apprehensive about that Chinese fortune teller's warning about not driving more than 300K and of course, my erratic driving on the left side of the road. Not to worry, I only had 2 near-head-on collisions, one being the result of making a u-turn on an entry road to the highway, and I drove into the right lane in oncoming traffic much to their delight! And the other trying to overtake a vehicle on one of those two lane roads. Luckily, I get a shooting pain in my neck causing an instant headache whenever I'm in danger situations, so that helped my alertness somewhat.

Unfortunately, the headache lingers on for 30 mins or so after the danger has passed.

I checked in the hotel in Launceston, a quaint manor type of accommodation. And drove straight to Cradle Park, west of Launceston. It's not easy to get to places in Tasmania and you gotta go through little towns (towns are everywhere!!!) and take these little roads. Hertz warned me not to go on unsealed roads (gravel & dirt roads) as I would be liable for $1200 if I damaged the car, but when I got to Cradle Park, I had no choice to take a 7K unsealed road to the hiking area for Dove Lake. Needless to say, I picked up a lot of rock and gravel on that road which caused quite some noise in the undercarriage of the car.

I can't really describe Tasmania. All I can say is, when the first Europeans must've seen Tasmania (apparently they didn't though) they must've thought "YAY! WE HIT THE JACKPOT!". The greenery, rolling hills, vast meadows, lush forests remind you of some Bavarian countryside or even the natural settings of let's say Kentucky or Oregon. Absolutely gorgeous!!!! Of course, the trees are all different being of the acacias and eucalyptus type trees and not the big firs, pines and redwoods. Cows and sheep everywhere! But I thought I had gotten lost because after 3 hours of driving from Launceston, and I came upon this stretch that reminded me of some kinda nuclear holocaust. Large dead ashen trees strewn for miles on end. Timber cutting? Forest fires? So I thought crap, this doesn't look like a natural reserve. But then just around the corner, there it was Cradle Park. I drove in, and I didn't expect to find anything because outside the park it looked like a big cigarette ash tray. But as I drove closer to Dove Lake and started adding the little pebbles to my transmission Cradle Mountain rose in the distance (I think the name comes from the fact that it looks like a cradle). BEAUTIFUL!!! And just at the valley below the Cradle was a huge lake named Dove Lake. It was a lake and mountain area that kinda reminded you of movies where some feral mountain men hunters would kidnap your girlfriend for either cannibalism or procreation, and you had to take a bow and arrow and kill all the hillbillies whilst covered in mud and deer's blood. I don't know, but that's what sprang to mind. I hiked around Dove Lake and took plenty of pictures. Because I'm a machine, I was able to hike with little physical effort. But I must admit, that bloody tripod was getting pretty heavy climbing up the hill. What's weird is that a lot of the forests are rain forests. Which you think would be improbable since Tasmania is pretty south. And here I raise another point, Tasmania kinda reminds me of a quaint European country with the trappings of English gentry. But if you really really really think about it, the location of Tasmania, where Europe/England is in comparison to Tasmania, you just have to wonder WHAT THE HECK ARE ALL THESE WHITE PEOPLE DOING SO FAR SOUTH!!!! But I think they did a fine job, nonetheless. I drove back to Launceston, had one of my near head-on collisions trying to look for the casino, and then kicked some ass in the Launceston Country Club Casino to win chips for my dear dear friend, Dodge. The casino itself looked like a big country estate mansion, very few tables, more pokies and slots. And they even had $2 tables! Ha ha. Naturally, a big city boy like me had to show these simple country folk how to play blackjack. After winning the chips and dinner, I went back to the motel.

The next morning was a tour of Launceston. I parked in the city, but I got trapped by the annual x-mas parade! And I couldn't leave until the parade was over. So I visited the museum, and checked out a stuffed Tasmanian Tiger (possibly the worst taxidermist job I've ever seen), saw the monkeys in the park (they have these bunch of crazy monkeys entertaining the tourists), and hiked around the Cataract Gorge (more beautiful nature). I even took a chairlift across the gorge to get back to the city. Since I was stuck in the city I indulged in the local food (jacketed potatoes and ollie poftes, or something like that - DELICIOUS!) at the fair. After the parade had cleared up, I took a terribly long drive to Bicheno to eastern part of Tasmania. THREE HOURS+. Finally, I got to Bicheno, and after checking in, I immediately drove to Freycinet Park, where I did some more hiking and took more pictures of the beautiful scenery and abundant nature. The hike was pretty tough though, as it was really uphill and the tripod and the water were getting pretty heavy. By this time, my tripod was falling apart. Ah faithful tripod from my Grand Canyon days... I got pretty hungry when I got back to Bicheno, and there are only 750 people in town, so you can imagine how limited my selection of restaurants would be. But I was recommended NEPTUNE'S to have seafood. So I got the seafood platter (of course) with crayfish, oysters, prawns and scallops (crayfish is lobster here but not with the big claws). DELICIOUS! I even had fresh berries and cream, with tea. All for under 60 bucks aussie. Naturally, I dined alone, but since I don't have any feelings, it doesn't really matter now does it?

The next day I drove to Hobart, and all I can say is, don't go to Hobart on a Sunday. The city is just quite dead on Sundays. I walked around the city, Kelly's footsteps to Battery Point (the oldest part of Hobart), Salmanaca etc. Hobart itself is quite spectacular but a bit more developed and newer than Launceston. And with more water. Plus Hobart's got this big mountain in the background. I walked from the city to the Wrest Point Casino, which is easily one of the most attractive casinos in Australia. And because it has waterfront settings, I don't think any of the Las Vegas casinos can match that. You can buy food with the money you've won, and eat just outside near the sea. Gorgeous!!!! So I kicked ass again to win chips for my dear dear friend Dodge, and got into verbal fights with stupid Asian people at the blackjack table. Since Dino don't take crap when he's anchor, that was bound to happen. I told the old Malaysian/Indonesian/Singaporean/Chinese guy: "Hey, why don't you play at the $10 table where you can be all alone and play by yourself and nobody to bother you". That kept that old little man quiet and angry under his breath for the rest of the night. Since I was victorious at the casino, I indulged in all-you-can-eat buffet, and I indulged in the salmon, moreton bay bugs, mussels and fine dessert selection. A bit steep at 30 bucks, but hey, you're only in Hobart once.

And that was about it. The next day I drove to the airport, expected to get charged for wrecking the car (making ugly noises now) by Hertz, but luckily I only got charged with gas. So that was lucky. As far as I'm concerned, that chinese fortune teller got it all wrong!!!! Weird pagan Chinese fortune-telling hocus pocus scores a ZERO!

Got to Sydney, had somebody kicking the back of my seat constantly on the plane, so when I turned around to do some action I saw she wasn't all right in the head and her mom was there taking care of her so I'm glad I didn't yell at her, got ripped off by taxi driver, picked up keys to my new place, and new place has great harbor views. Now back in the office to pick up my luggage and take it back to my new apt. Postcards already sent abroad, and pictures to be developed soon. I LOVE YOU ALL.

EUROPE

Back to the Vaterland.

Date:	Sunday, January 02, 2000 5:45 PM
To:	Karen; Dodge; Jun; Roberto; Derryn; Dan; Davide; Greg; Simon; Aldo; Rowena; Helen; Brooke; Kirsten; Bruce; Dale; Barry; Joe O.; Tom; Yvette; Maria
Subject:	Munich/London

Dear Dear Friends,

Well I finally made it back from my Munich/London trip. Needless to say, I have written an epic email which you may want to read at a more convenient time. However, I kinda begin the story with CHICK action and end it with CHICK action, but then again, we all know how all Joe Dino CHICK action stories end...

Bangkok

On Dec 23, I left Sydney for London/Munich but had to pass by through Bangkok. Unfortunately, we were delayed for 2 hours. At this time, a wild-eyed, short-haired, skinny German girl sat next to me. I noticed she was a bit odd because each time I'd look out the window (she had the window seat), she'd turn and smile at me nervously. We did a little chit-chat but she didn't seem like talking or so I thought. Sometime during the flight, she disappeared. However, the steward came up to me when serving dinner and started questioning me if there was anything wrong with the German girl. Apparently the German girl had been telling him her entire life story. We were about to land when the German girl appeared again, but she was nearly in tears since we had arrived in Heathrow so late and she might miss her connection. But in addition to that, she also wanted to get some "psychological help" before flying on to Germany. Cuckoo!!!! She wasn't that HOT anyway.

Missed my Flight

We landed in Terminal 4, and I had to catch a connecting flight in Terminal 1 in Heathrow, but I only had 5 minutes to do so. So I ran like mad, asked the security guard if I could jump queue, and raced to the gate. Alas, I had missed the flight by a couple of minutes. So they gave me L10 worth of food vouchers to spend in Heathrow, and booked me on a flight to Munich 6 hours later.

Munich

Finally flew in to Munich (baggage arrived intact as well), and Mic, Joachim and baby Max were there to pick me up. We drove straight to Esslingen (a town outside Stuttgart) to spend xmas with Joachim's parents. Of course, being part-Aryan, I flattered the Grossmutti and Grosspapa by talking to them in German (kinda rusty, but it was okay). Apparently, they do this exchange gift thing after dinner on the 24th, but I was well-prepared having brought in presents for everyone. I brought the little baby boy, a big stuffed kangaroo, and little beanie animals (but all being Australian animals - echidnya, kookaburra, platypus etc.). I gave Joachim an Upside-Down map (I love that gift!!!), the Grossmutti a glass Koala and Kangaroo (notice the Australian theme here), and the Grosspapa a boomerang (the Granpa has muscular dystrophy and is confined to a wheelchair so he can't throw the boomerang but he can always hang it up on the wall). And Mic, I gave a $5 flashlight (hey, me being there is gift enough - okay okay, I gave her money later on). Oh yeah, there was snow outside, so it was a white x-mas.

Conversing with Grossmutti

I took plenty of pics of me and baby Max (same name as my brother, we just like to recycle name, in fact, if I get a baby boy, God willing, I'll call him Max too!!!!). An amusing incident happened when I was alone with Joachim's mother. She was telling me how in the 80s when her husband could still walk, they were still able to travel. But now, due to her husband's condition, they can't. She kinda hinted it was ironic how now they have the means and time to travel, but physically it can't be done. So I decided to contribute my own profound thoughts about this subject. I told her the story about an acquaintance who left work one day, went to the hospital, and was dead 1 week later due to cancer. Of course, my moral of the story was "do the things you want to do, you don't know how much time you have". In hindsight, and considering Grossmutti's age and Grosspapa's precarious condition, it may not have been a very cheery story, but hey, at least I was able to make conversation in German!!!!

Munich

On the 26th we said farewell to Grossmutti and Grosspapa, and drove off to Munich. Mic and Joachim had a very nice apartment, and I took more pics of baby Max. That night we had dinner at Block House (a steak restaurant which Family Dino used to go to whilst we were living in Germany in the old days). I didn't do any sight-seeing as I just wanted to spend quality family-time, but we did indulge in Leberkase and Weisswurst, and watched crazy German talk-shows (the most emotionally cruel talk-shows in the world, I reckon - made me cringe).

London

Said farewell to Mic, Joachim and baby Max, and flew to London. I wasn't even there for five minutes (I hadn't even opened my big mouth yet), when the security guard came by and demanded to check my passport . I guess I looked like a cold-blooded killer or terrorist. But I just gave him the Asian smile, and showed him the passport and all went well. There's now an express train to Paddington from Heathrow, so it only took 15 mins to get to Paddington (my hotel is only 2 mins away walking). As I sat in the train and saw the bleak dark cloudy skies (it was fairly cold - but not as cold as Munich), I thought to myself "Lord almighty - why do people live here??????". As far as I'm concerned, they should've kept the convicts in England and sent all the non-convicts to Australia. That makes more sense now. But I digress.

The Hotel

I was staying at the Hotel Castleton for a very reasonable 58 pounds a night, and I didn't expect much for that price. The room was really tiny, and it had a little ensuite (shower and toilet) which was new, so I was pleased with that. You know what's odd? I noticed that in Munich and London, a lot of these showers don't have that mount to hang up that showerhead. So you gotta hold the showerhead and aim it for whatever body part you want to clean. That's all fair and well, but if you need to do two-handed shower operations like I do (shaving is one example, you gotta pull the skin with one hand while shaving with the other), it's a bit of a pain.

British Museum

I didn't want to waste anymore time, so I went to the British Museum to check out all the artifacts, statues and monuments the British stole and plundered from their colonies and enemies. I'm a history and museum nut, so the whole place was just amazing!!! The Elgin Marbles, Rosetta Stone etc. all the classics were there!!!! But the funny thing is, the whole museum is an odd mish-mash and the rooms don't really make any sense - stuff is just scattered everywhere. But I guess it's because they're breaking it out in time periods and geography. It was also here that I was stopped by a security guard for taking a pamphlet and not putting 50p in the money box (I thought it was voluntary). I then went to the National Gallery, and saw some great artwork by the Masters (this is mostly non-British stuff), and then it was on to the National Portrait Gallery just around the corner. All the museums are very conveniently located, have great toilets (I didn't take a dump in any of them though) which you don't have to pay for - it's 20p if you want to use train station or public toilet anywhere else, and have nice gift shops.

Tower of London

The next day I woke up early and headed for the Tower and Tower Bridge. I got there when it just opened so the crowds weren't crazy yet. I took one of those tours by the Beefeaters, and it was pretty funny, I recommend it. Did you know that Humpty Dumpty is based on Richard III? That's what I learned from the Beefeater. Saw plenty of armor and the crown jewels. In fact, I spent an outrageous 3 hours around the Tower (it's not just a tower, but an entire castle with stuff in it). I then walked to Parliament, passed 10 Dowling St, and tried to get in Parliament with the thousands of other people on the street. Parliament was closed for some reason, or I couldn't find the entrance. So I walked across the street and checked out Westminster Abbey. I didn't realize how fantastic Westminster Abbey is!!!! That place is just amazing. It's like a gigantic yardsale of stone coffins, headstones and statues. Really weird, yet inspiring. I had passed St Paul's Cathedral (another magnificent structure) but I refused to pay entry to enter God's house (it was like 7 pounds to get in!!!). But then I had to pay to get into Westminster Abbey as well!!! Oh yeah, I also passed Cleopatra's Needle, it's not that big. Then I walked a little more and visited the Tate Gallery which keeps all the British art, like Blake, Hogarth, Sargent etc. I was mightily impressed by the quality of the exhibition. Some of the paintings are quite memorable. I especially liked Lady MacBeth by Sargent as she's holding up a crown. Each time I go to a museum, gallery or site, I buy postcards from the shop, but I also bought some generic ones to send off to my dear dear friends. By this time I had formed the opinion that Londoners are a rude bunch, so I was quite surprised when I was buying 13 postcards from this street vendor that she actually tried to be friendly and told me she couldn't let me go with 13 as an unlucky number and I should take one for free. How nice! Speaking of opinions, I only saw two pretty girls in London, and they were both Australian. Just kidding!!!!! But here's something that's not a joke, every male pommie is named James. I don't know why, but that's the most popular name there. You can yell out James, and you'll have most of the guys turning around. Not that there's anything wrong with that...

Madame Tussaud's

On the 30th (I'm now running out of time since the 31st and the 1st are coming up), I went Madame Tussaud's wax museum. It was okay, and the figures were really life like, but personally, I think they should have had an x-rated section since they're such masters in emulating the human face and body. Not that I would ever go to any unbiblical display, but I think it would bring in more people. Speaking of people, the line was practically half-a-kilometer. So many people, and it was raining!!! I can't imagine how it would be in summer. I passed by 221 Baker St (Sherlock Holmes!), that was crap. Then went to Buckingham Palance and took pictures. After that I went across the Thames to check out Imperial War Museum, that's quite a good museum, if you're into war. Then I was really tired since I've been going like a machine, and went back to the hotel to relax. I had a pleasant surprise when Bettina, an old primary school classmate, called me up to say hi. We hadn't talked in nearly 20 years, and it was only a couple of months ago that we got in touch by email. She's German (once again, GERMAN!!!!) but lives and works in London, so she sounds pommy. We chatted for a while and agreed I'd leave her a message on New Year's day and try to hook up before I leave for Sydney.

Dickens Inn and a Yard of Beer

I forgot, my dear dear friend Joe O. told me to check out the Dickens Inn and try to swig down a yard of beer. Apparently if I get it all down in one go, I get the yard for free!!! So whilst I was still in Sydney, I was asking tips from my workmates on how best to approach this (of course, I'm not gonna be able to do this, but at least I wanted to look good trying!!!). Apparently, Bob Hawke, a former Aussie prime minister used to be a champion yard drinker and there was a technique in getting it down by swirling the yard glass and creating a downward force to slam the liquid down your throat. So I get to the Dickens Inn (it's near the Tower), and ask if they do yards. The chick just looks at me blankly and says no (again, they're not very helpful these brits), so I tell her the story about how I'm supposed to do the yard and we should take a picture of it. She just says "no no no, we don't do yards, I can give you 4 pints...". Okay, obviously this means that a yard is NOT equal to 4 pints. As most of you know, my personal world is a nice little geometrical fantasyland where everything is black and white, right and wrong, and there's nothing in-between. Hey, anything else is hypocrisy, but that's just me. So my brain was unable to reconcile 4 pints with one yard, so I aborted the mission since I was unable to fulfil the original mission. So I took pics instead.

New Year's Eve

I had plenty of time to kill before New Year's Eve so I tried going to another art gallery, the Wallace Collection but it was closed. So I walked to Kensington, to check out Princess Di's palace. Now, when I say "walk", I don't mean a little stroll. London is huge!!!!! It's absolutely big, you can walk everywhere but it's gonna take some time. I took a pic of Kensington, but I made a mistake on sitting too close to the grass, and my pants picked up a lot of mud (it was raining again) on my backside, so it looked like I had crapped through my pants (I was wearing my whitish-beige pants too). Then I went back to the hotel to do laundry and wait for a good time to start walking towards the Thames so I could get a good view of the fireworks. It was horrible. There were hundreds of thousands of people. Thousands and thousands cramming into each other. There was no crowd control either, I got to Westminster bridge and if people had gotten a little bit more angry, there would've been a stampede and people would've been crushed (the older people didn't fare too well, as they got injured, mostly their legs). So I decided to try the south bank instead. It was really cold so I took shelter near a big office building. Other people had the same idea, and this Colombian couple sat next to me and we started talking about the Brits, cocaine and Colombia. They even gave me some of their tequila or something like that. Too bad, I wasn't planning to do anything unbiblical. Then the fireworks started (the river of fire failed miserably), and the sky was lit up like mad. We were so close to the fireworks that crap and embers were falling down on our heads. Then I remembered that I wasn't really into fireworks, and wondered what the big hoopla was all about. So it was all over, and we all tried to catch a train but all the stations were overloaded, so I got lost and walked for 2 hours in the rain until I got back to the hotel.

Stood Up

Before I checked out of the hotel, I called Bettina and left a message for her to meet me at Leicester Square at 4:30 pm. The funny thing was, her answering machine was playing "Dancing Queen" by ABBA. Finally, someone who agrees that ABBA is the greatest musical group ever (in the northern hemisphere, the Bee Gees being tops in the southern hemisphere). I had more time to kill, so I went to Leicester Square and a bird pooped on my shoe. Then I went to Trafalgar Square where they were having a big parade and party. I climbed up Nelson's monument (where the lions are) to take pics, and I got mud all over me, and a bird pooped on my bag. Then I went back to Leicester Square and waited for Bettina, but I didn't see her or missed her or whatever. But I didn't cry or anything since I'm used to being stood up. But I did think it was pretty funny. I guess I can tell a favorite Bettina story of mine now. I think it was in 5th or 6th grade, and I was a bit rowdy, and Bettina wasn't anyone you could be rowdy with, she was one of those tall, athletic, German valkyrie type CHICKS that really gave me a lot of damage. Needless to say, I feared her. But anyway, she had me cornered me up against the wall. Her arms were against the wall, with my head between them, and it was obvious she was going to inflict some serious pain to my lithe and fragile frame. My brilliant mind was racing to think up of an escape, so when she was looking at me face to face, I suddenly kissed her on the lips. This momentarily stunned her which let down her guard and I was able to sneak under her arms and run away like crazy. She never caught up with me, but if she did... well, I would probably be programming with one hand now. As you can tell, my penchant for sex and violence was being nurtured already then. Of course, none of you will ever mention this to Bettina should she ever become a regular on the mailing list. Then I went to the airport and waited for my flight. Some old guy (over 40) was playing the arcade game Daytona USA, and I challenged him, and I KICKED HIS ASS!!!!! Speaking of ass-kicking, there were quite a few casinos in London, but they were all closed so I wasn't able to get casino chips for my dear dear friend Dodge.

Sydney

It took 22 hours to get back to Sydney. My neighbors were Anton and Katarina, an elderly German couple, and I practiced my German on them too. MORE GERMANS!!!!! Checked into the hotel since I don't have an apt again (not until tomorrow).

Final Thoughts

I think London is a fantastic city, and I could live and work there if it had decent weather and the people are friendlier. But there's just so many things to do and see.

Postcards are sent, and pics to be developed soon. I LOVE YOU ALL!!!!!!!

CIVILIZED COUNTRY

The lack of shit gaskets still upsets me to this day.

Date:	Friday, October 22, 1999 3:22 PM
To:	Dodge; Jun; Roberto; Brooke; Alicia; Helen; Karen; Rowena; Simon; Greg; Derryn; Davide; Dan; Aldo; Keith; Kevin; Kirsten; Maria; Yvette; Bruce; Dale; Barry; Joe O.; Tom
Subject:	Civilized country????

Sometimes I think "gee, Australia is such a modern country!" with all their mobile phones, coinless payphones, electronic banking and billpaying, public transport etc. But you know what? All that modern crap doesn't really matter when you've been getting the shits like I've been for the last week. Why in the world don't the restrooms here have toilet seat gaskets? You know, the little round paper things you put on the seats? But noooooooooooooo, instead I have to pull off the 3-5 paper towels, arrange them neatly on the seat and hope they don't slide off by the time I put my butt on the seat. And mind you, most of the time I don't have time for such niceties, as most guys know, if a guy's got to go bad, the pants are already off by the time we open the door. So there I am, sighing and heaving, cold-sweating bullets, getting the shakes, pain and fire in the belly WHILST rearranging the paper towels in a geometrically acceptable formation.

I'm sorry, but when you're walking to work at 4:00 am on a Saturday morning in the rain with the poo-poo monster trying to explode out of your ass, then turning off all the alarms on the floor, and then having to be the Martha Stewart of improvised toilet seat gasket replacements, I am just bound to write my humble opinion about this. Other than this, Australia is indeed a fine and beautiful country.

By the way, other than the horrible injustice and abuse taking place in the restrooms of North Sydney, this week wasn't too bad personally. I took advantage of the big stock market drop in Australia (very rarely do get this right but I got 2/3 hits on this one), got my tax refund, got my new eyeglasses (the optometrist looked at my frames and said "you can do better" so I picked a half-frame Armani which was really expensive but it looked really intriguing, but he knocked it back and said: "too big for your face" (who cares! just take my money, fool!), then he picked this half-frame (Blumarine) which is quite unique looking and was the cheapest of the three (a little copper Polo was the other) I had selected, anyway, I like it).

And just when I thought I had run out of candidates to answer "who makes the clown laugh?", another contestant enters the fray! These little unexpected twists are just so very interesting. But then again, when I put milk in my coffee and see the face of St. Agnes of the Blessed Marzipan in the milk swirl, I find that interesting as well.

14

The Motoring Enthusiast

A man in a car to is like a nut in a shell.
Anonymous

CAR BUYING

I didn't feel too bad when I left the car lot.

Date:	Wednesday, April 05, 2000 7:27 PM
To:	Roberto; Jun; Dodge; Charles; Craig; Kirsten; Bruce; Barry; Joe O.; Dale; Tom; Yvette; Maria; Eunice; Helen; Aldo; Brooke; Davide; Greg; Simon
Subject:	Car Buying Experience

Dear Dear Friends,

Some people are emailing me if I'm sick or if I'm still alive because I haven't sent out any mass emails for an incredible 2 1/2 weeks. But I just didn't feel like writing, that's all. However, the same folks said that I make them laugh with my stories (that's all I am really, just a silly clown - but who makes the clown laugh, huh? who makes clown laugh?!! especially on a down-market trend where I bought Palm for $106 and now it's hovering at $40). So I was gonna write up my car-buying experience at least since that's semi-interesting and semi-amusing.

Warm-Up

So I moved house on Mar 26 (with Barry, a dear dear friend), and after hanging up all my clothes and throwing the futon mattress on the floor, I was all ready to go car shopping. Earlier in the week, I was tempted to go for a used car at the used car superstore CarMax (basically, all the cars are on the lot with sticker prices and no haggling, so you don't have to worry about dealing). I also considered ordering a used car from imotors.com - you just give the specs you want and they'll deliver the car to you after 2 - 3 weeks or so with satisfaction guaranteed. But I didn't have time for that. Then of course, I went through all the car dealers and checked out their stock, but as usual everything was overpriced. I passed by a Toyota dealer and asked how much a 96 Corolla was, the salesman said: $13K. I told him I saw the same car in CarMax for $8K. Then the salesman said he could sell me a 99 Corolla for $13K, how about that?? isn't that a better deal? I could tell it wasn't going to be easy. Naturally, if I bought a new car then it wouldn't be too much of a problem but I hadn't decided yet on what new car to get, and after coming from Australia, I'm even less inclined to go for material possessions (earthly waste, what I call it). So until my birthday arrives this year, I decided I would settle on a little putt-putt car to get me going for the next couple of months. Besides, I wasn't in the mood for car payments yet.

Going for a Ride

So Bruce, Devin came by and picked Barry and me up. We headed to KarPlus (yep, spelled with a K) which is basically a big dusty lot with lots of repossessed cars. I must say, there were really a lot of cheap cars, mostly American that seemed pretty decent - $5K for a 96 Ford Taurus, $7-$8K for a Ford Mustang etc. but I wanted to go Japanese so I kept on walking around with JORGE, the latino salesman. So then I saw a purple/magenta Nissan 200SX that looked okay from the outside but the color was just way too fruity for a manly man like me. Then I saw a black Nissan 200SX at the end of the lot. It had a busted right blinker, some door dints, and from what I could tell, two tires were ripped. But the sticker was only $6999 (gotta add tax/rego later), so I said, let's give it a test ride anyway. So I took it for a spin around the block, and turned on the aircon full blast, it was working but I noticed the idle was pretty low, so I remembered that. Well, it did the block and the engine felt fine, so I went back in and did the negotiating.

The finance guy said $8K out the door. I said $7K out the door. We settled on $7300 (so technically, I won).

Then he asked how I was going to pay for it, I said "put it on the credit card". Then he started crying and said that there's a 3% credit car surcharge (that's $220). I told him that's his problem. Then he went back to his boss and came back and said how about if I pay $175. I said no. Then he asked if I could pay half of $175. I said no. He kept on crying so finally I got tired and pulled out a $50 and just gave him the cash. But I said I wanted two good tires and replace the right blinker. Deal! In the meantime Bruce ran in and punched me in the shoulder because he had been waiting outside for a while, and Jorge didn't tell the guys I was dealing. So I punched him back. But then he punched me again. And then I tried to punch him again but I slipped and banged my knee on the desk. So Bruce won. We won't be punching each other anymore.

Replacing the Broken Bits

So after putting it on the credit card, I drove off to the tire place to get the tires. And the little boy who was replacing it, started replacing all four, but I had only negotiated for two, but the little boy showed me that the other tires were bad too, so I said "go ahead, change them all!". So he changed them all, but as I was taking off before they could bill me for two additional tires, a big Mexican man stopped me and said “WAIT!!! you took 4 TIRES!!!" so he made me call the dealer and I told the dealer all the tires were bad, and the dealer says "okay, but that's all we'll do for you!" meaning he wasn't going to do anything with the right blinker, fine with me. Tires cost more anyway. So after that, we dropped the car off somewhere and ate lobster in Santa Monica.

The next day, the battery died, so I replaced the battery - $50. And then I took it in for service just to make sure it gets the basic things done - so I paid $200 for an oil change, tune-up, electrical charging check, and battery cable replacement. oh yeah, by this time we noticed that the engine check light was on all the time.

This week I was tired of the low idling and the airconditioning sometimes kills the engine at low idle so I brought it in, and they said I had to replace the intake valve which would fix the low idle, aircon and engine check light - that cost another $250. And that's all the money I spent on top of the $7300, so now my total is $7800 out the door, which is still far far far less if I had bought an $8K off the lot (because that would bump it up to around $8.8K out the door).

So now the car runs great. I think I'll fix a little windshield chip today, and I noticed also that when I load up the car with gravitationally-challenged people the car creaks. But the mechanic told me not to worry about it. That's fine, I suppose. Besides, I'm sure it will last until November. And I replaced the right blinker with a part I ordered from Nissan Car Wreckers in Sacramento (that's a great place, they have all the parts).

However, I've forgotten how expensive it is (waste of money) to have a car - my car insurance is going to cost $1K/year (it was going to be $2K/year with my original insurer), and of course, gas prices are up this year. Well, at least I'm not making any monthly payments on it. Plus all this driving is replacing all my walking which was how I able to maintain my fluctuating weight. But since I have all my weightlifting equipment in my room now, it will be just a race of getting muscle or getting fat.

And that's about it - that's how the car hunting went.

THE SUFFERING OF HEROES

Where is the justice?

Date:	Friday, June 29, 2001 7:47 AM
To:	Dodge; Roberto; Aldo; Chris; Vahe; Davide; Dan; Karen; Rowena; Debra; Barry; Eunice; Yvette; Joe O.; Derryn; Jun; Bruce
Subject:	The Suffering of Heroes

Because Im a superhero car mechanic (or at least I think I am), I decided to fix up the bitch-magnet-mobile in preparation for its eventual sale. Two things needed attention. The driver's sun visor, and the button on the automatic transmission shifter popped out.

I go to Miller Nissan on Van Nuys and order the sun visor. But we're looking at the schematics for the shifter, and Im asking the parts guy how to replace the button. The parts guy says it's probably easier to replace the entire assembly (the knob/handle thingy). So I look at it, and I say: "are you sure I can do it?". The guy says: "Sure!!! just take the two screws off, replace it, and attach the wires". So I order it. All for 70 bucks.

I pick up the parts yesterday (the guy still tells me its a piece of cake), and get to work on the shifter. I try the button first before dismantling the assembly, and sure enough the button doesn't fit my shifter. But it does fit the new shifter. So I think, okay, that's why I have to replace the entire thing. This part replaces whatever my part is. And then I notice that shifter goes well beyond below the console, so I have to take the console off first (where you put your coins and ballpens). So I unscrew the console and try to take it out. It goes up half-way, but I can't quite get the console off the shifter and the handbrake. I figure all I need is a little bit of superhero power of which I have plenty of. So I start pulling up on it, and give it a fraction of my power cosmic, and the console comes roaring off the shifter and handbrake straight into the Great One's face.

Luckily, my lower lip managed to stop the console from breaking any of my teeth. So my lower lip has just exploded into bits of flesh and blood, and I run inside the house to put some ice in it. Hey, no guts no glory, that's what I say. So it hurts a little bit, but not enough to make me cry. After staunching the flow of blood, I go out to the car again, and this time Im excited because I got the console off. I remove the little thing protecting the shifter (the one that says P, R, N, D, 2 etc). And when I take it off, I see 1 billion little wires snaking themselves from the assembly to under the hood! No way can I figure that one out!

So Im furious. My car is a mess, with screws and assemblies all over the place. Im bleeding to death. And I cant do it myself. I call up Nissan and give the Parts Dept a piece of my mind (Im still holding an ice cube wrapped in a towel to my lip). I explain the events to the parts guy, and he tells me he's very sorry that I broke the part and that he'll give me a discount on the broken part. I tell him: "what do you mean broken part??? the only thing broken is my lip!!!!". Then he has the gall to tell me that service will cut me a special deal and install the assembly for $130 instead of $160. I say: "why??? I already took the damn thing off!!!!" For some reason, the issue of the button came up again, and he tells me if we can just work with the button, and I tell him that the button they gave me doesnt fit anyway. Then the parts guy looks at my invoice and tells me they gave me the wrong part. I tell him I'll be right over.

I get over there, and I restrain myself from jumping over the counter and delivering deathblows to all the employees who have their names stitched on the polo shirts. Finally he gives me the button, and sure enough, it looks exactly like my old button. So I return the assembly (button was only 5 bucks) and get credit for $50. I go back home and try to figure out how to get the damn button in. Barry arrives. Thank goodness because Barry has the strength of 20 elephants. And we try to jam the button in the shifter together. Still won't work. I now realize that Im all frenzied up and need to approach this with a clear mind. So I calm down and think of pleasant thoughts, like my new BMW or cutie-pootie Amy. I visualize the inside of the shifter and the shape of the button, and come to the conclusion we were on the right track by jamming it in, but we have to jam it in slightly diagonally. I position the button, and then press it in with just a tiny bit of superhero force. Click. And it worked.

Then I spent another 30 minutes finding all the screws, putting on the console, and attaching the sun visor. And my lip had stopped bleeding.

Thank you sweet baby jesus.

MY LIFE IS COMPLETE

It's amazing what money can do for you.

Date:	Monday, July 02, 2001 7:38 AM
To:	Grant; Dodge; Roberto; Alison; Aldo; Chris; Vahe; Nancye; Brooke; Davide; Dan; Karen; Rowena; Debra; Barry; Eunice; Maria; Yvette; Joe O.; Derryn; Jun; Bruce
Subject:	My Life is Complete

The dealer called and said my car was ready Sunday. So thankfully Varand, Yvette's husband, volunteered to drive me down to Hermosa Beach to pick up my steel blue, auto, gray leather and prem package BMW 325i which had just come off the boat.

When we got to the dealership I thought I would have some ugliness erupt last minute because Alfred, my salesman, said BMW would match my lender's financing rate of 7.19% APR, but I told him he had promised me 6.75% on Friday. Alfred just said, "oh really? no problem!". And that was the only issue that cropped up.

I did the thing with the finance manager who tried to sell me theft protection, car alarm, extended maintenance etc. I took none of it. For some reason my loan payments seemed smaller than expected even with the 6.75% APR, and I couldn't quite figure it out. Later on when I got home, I realized that my out-the-door price was 200 bucks lower than the out-door-price I was quoted, so I got the car for $34,800. If I had known that, I would've written the checks for less 200 bucks. But there were so many numbers, and I was too excited to be thinking straight.

Oddly enough, floor mats dont come with the vehicle, instead a piece of cardboard was in lieu of the floor mats. That had to go. Alfred gave me the basic rundown on how to operate the vehicle. It's a very nice ergonomical layout. Not too many gauges and buttons to remember. But still enough features to make me dizzy. I have to figure out how to turn the rain sensor off. The other good tip he gave me was that I didn't have to fill up the tank with premium gas, but I could do with the mid-grade. Great! Also, only do maintenance when the car tells you to do it (the little computer tells you when). Then it was off on the freeway!

It felt great! I really like the V6 (I definitely didn't need to buy the 330i with the bigger engine), and I love the passing power and handling. I'm not even allowed to go over 110mph because of the break-in period, but it went fast enough. I also liked the braking, it just goes mmmmmmmmmmmmm when you press the brakes, and you dont weave around.

Got home to Woodland Hills, and allowed family Z. a test drive. Later on went back to Monrovia to show the car to brother and mother, but mother was the only one there. She's not into cars but I could tell she liked it because she was using the arm-rests. So we went to West Covina to have Filipino halo-halo (a sweet ice drink), and to show off the car to other Filipinos who drive BMWs and Mercedes.

Then it was back to Woodland Hills. Barry had come back, and he drove around in it too. He was hesitant first to get in the car, but after finding out that Yvette had driven it already, he just jumped in and programmed the powerseats for his seating style.

It was night-time already and the only thing I could do was watch the BMW video that came with the car, but I still couldn't figure out how to turn the rain sensor off.

When I first got the car on the freeway, I thought to myself: "why didn't I do this sooner?". I was so happy in my shallowness that I nearly cried.

You see, money can buy happiness.

This Sunday, I may take a drive down Topanga Canyon and see how close I can get to the side of the road before plummeting 200 feet down the canyon.

FLOOR MATS

You bet I wasn't thinking straight. I ended up buying the floor mats for $135 from a dealer.

Date:	Tuesday, July 03, 2001 7:38 AM
To:	Aldo; Vahe; Davide; Dan; Rowena; Barry; Maria; Yvette; Bruce; Margaret
Subject:	Floor Mats

So I wasn't thinking properly, and didn't add the floor mats to the amount financed. I wasn't going to get it because I was over budget by 25 bucks (US$35K was my limit), but it turned out that the car was 34.8 out the door, so I did have room for the floor mats, but I was just too giddy in anticipation of the vehicle to be thinking straight.

Anyway, too many people have been test driving and checking out the car, so I really needed floor mats before they scuff up and dirty the carpeting.

So I bought a set for $20 from Target. Gray. When I tried to fit them in, it was kinda small on the passenger's side, and it didn't fit in the driver's side. So I took scissors and cut the driver's side into shape. But it kinda looked ugly, so I called up a dealer and they were $155 a set. So I thought, oh forget it. Then I went to Pollo Loco to have dinner but I took the Nissan just in case some Pollo Loco diners touched my car with their greasy fingers. I heard from someone that Costco had really nice floor mats so I went there, and they did have beautiful floor mats for the same price. The carpet was so much better than Target's. So I got those and put those in. The passenger's side looked great. But I still had to cut the driver's side. But I cut it too much. So then I took another piece and cut it to the shape to put it back together again. So I have 1 big piece and 1 tiny piece. But then on the edges, the threads started fraying. And I couldn't deal with that. So I took some glue and tried to glue the threads, but that didn't work and the threads didn't hold.

It was getting dark and I was all sweaty and dirty from cutting, and crawling in the car. Then I thought of using candles! I took some candles, lit them, and used the hot candle wax to hold together the threads. That worked great! Except I got candle wax all over the floor mats which left this whitish streak in the gray carpet. I tried to pull it out and break it up, but I only spread the white wax more. So I took a comb, and combed it out. That only took 15 minutes.

After 2 hours and $40, I was done. As I was breathing heavily on the sofa holding a glass of water, I thought to myself "geeze, I spent 2 hours fixing something which is located under my right foot which nobody will ever see".

So maybe today, I will go to a dealership and buy those floormats because it sounds so silly now to be driving such an expensive car with 4 Costco floormats, with one of them split in two separate parts, and the threads held together with candle wax.

DISASTER!

I'm living with it. At least until I bring it in to the dealer for its first service. Then they can fix that metallic clang.

Date:	Tuesday, August 07, 2001 8:16 AM
To:	none *(blind copy)*
Subject:	Disaster!

So remember how I started parking in the "wide" parking spaces in the parking structure? The theory goes that if you park in the "compact" parking spaces, you're more likely to get a ding because the cars are parked closer together.

I was leaving work, and got to my car when I saw that this mammoth pickup truck (literally the largest motorized vehicle in the structure) had parked butt-end first in the spot next to me (so our driver side doors were next to each other). It was so big, it's front was sticking out into the road 5-6 feet, and it was so wide I had to squeeze in to get into my car. I thought "crap, he must've dinged me", but I checked it out before I left and I couldn't find any dings, so I was relieved.

Then I drove back home and parked the car in the driveway. As I was lovingly wiping off the day's dust and dirt off the car, I noticed a slight visual aberration on one of the rear doors. But I could only see it at a certain angle and when the sun shone on it a specific way. Sure enough, there was a little ding. I didn't notice it at first because the paint didn't break. So I have my first ding, so now I can move on to bigger dings.

As I was contemplating revenge against the monster pickup truck and blaming hairy mountain people who wear NASCAR t-shirts, I realized that my ding was on my passenger side. So it couldn't have been the monster truck. It was the bastard to the right who disrespected me. Unfortunately, I did not notice the specifics of the other vehicle.

Then I noticed that the rear passenger-side door makes a slight metallic clang (katunk) when opening. the other three doors make a subdued unlatching sound (kathung). so of course, I opened and closed the offending door about 200 times trying to figure out what the problem was.

After 1 hour, I determined that by putting on rubber tape on the metallic U I was able to prevent the metallic U and the latch from striking each other that makes that clang. but it looks a bit ugly, so I took the tape off. I thought about taking it back to the dealer to see if they have a better way of fixing it, but I don't want them opening up the door panels and unscrewing stuff. I'm probably the only one who notices that sound anyway.

I say the metallic clang just adds character to the vehicle.

15

The Noble Worker

> They say hard work never hurt anybody, but I figure why take the chance.
>
> *Ronald Reagan*

PLEDGE

Electronic Data Systems was the company that Ross Perot founded. The company used to brainwash loyalty and long hours into their new recruits. I guess it worked with me because I stayed with them for seven long years. What a dork.

Date:	8/20/93
To:	Vtd-team Group
Subject:	EDS Pledge

Whenever you need a little pick-me-up or are feeling down, just recite the EDS Pledge, but have a tissue ready just in case you start crying from happiness or pride.

EDS Pledge

Your colors white and blue,
EDS, I pledge myself to you.

No need for a husband or a wife,
When EDS is my mate for life.

Whenever I touch my monitor or cpu,
EDS, I think of you.

Plano, Detroit or Russelsheim,
EDS, count on me, anywhere and anytime.

Your colors white and blue,
EDS, I love you.

MYSTERY QUESTION

I used to come in the office at 6:00 am to do early morning support. Being left to my own devices, I used to think up of interesting questions for my work mates by the time they got in 2 hours later. I did give them a hint and said the answer starts with a "B". Some people said "balance" and "blondes".

ORIGINAL QUESTION...

Date:	10/17/94
To:	Albert, Alison, Barry, Bruce, Dale, Debbie, Gary, Maria, Tom, Vinh, Yvette
Subject:	Mystery Dumb Question of the Day

To give you guys more incentive on this:

The person who guesses this, gets a Sizzler lunch (doesn't matter how much) next week. But you have to answer before 9:00 am!

What is something we all look for, and then when we find it, we all immediately throw it away?

Clue: But some people will "admire" this something for a short while, especially after a long exhaustive search, before inevitably throwing it away.

ANSWER...

Date:	10/17/94
To:	Albert, Alison, Barry, Bruce, Dale, Debbie, Gary, Maria, Tom, Vinh, Yvette
Subject:	Answer

What is something we all look for, and then when we find it, we all immediately throw it away?

Clue: But some people will "admire" this something for a short while, especially after a long exhaustive search, before inevitably throwing it away.

Answer: Boogers

HUNGRY THIEVES

The audacity!!! I still eat Chi-Chi's meatball sandwiches to this day.

Date:	2/23/96
To:	It-team Group
Subject:	Refrigerator

This may seem like a petty (yet humorous) story but it's not the first time this has happened:

Last night I was driving home on the 405 and right before the Roscoe exit I remembered I had left my Chi-Chi's meatball sandwich, plus several buns in our fridge. Remembering how much I LOVE meatball sandwiches, I dangerously crossed several lanes (in rush hour traffic, mind you) to get to the Roscoe exit and turned around for OAN.

Imagine my chagrin (and amusement) when I opened the fridge door and discovered that my meatball sandwich and the buns had miraculously disappeared!

Now, I'm not asking for the meatball sandwich back, but please consider checking the contents of lunch bags/containers and verifying that it does belong to you before checking them out. And if you do have a hankering for something in the fridge, just ask if you can have it.

Thanks!

BROTHERS IN ARMS

My worst nightmare – working with computer nerds...

Date:	Friday, October 15, 1999 11:21 AM
To:	Brooke; Alicia; Helen; Karen; Rowena; Dodge; Jun; Roberto; Simon; Greg; Derryn; Davide; Dan; Aldo; Keith; Kevin; Kirsten; Bruce; Dale; Barry; Joe O.; Tom; Maria; Yvette
Subject:	Hello From Sydney

Dear Dear Friends,

It's been a while since I did a mass email but that's only because I have been quite busy at work, and my hours (5 am to 2-3 pm) are not conducive to adventuring-type scenarios. In fact I started work at 11:00 pm tonight, and I'll just keep on going like the machine that I am (I work Tues-Sat).

Let's start with magnificent work! Tonight is the 4th time I've been moved around in the office. For a while, I was even out of the office, in the adjacent conference room but Sybase found out we were drilling holes into the wall and kicked us promptly out. The personalities and characters at work are mind-boggling. Like Grant said last week: "This is your worst nightmare, isn't it?". I think the second day I was here, I was surrounded by two programmers who crapped on about which was better, Java or C++. Next time the nerds do that, I'm just gonna say: "HEY! IF YOU'RE SO SMART, WHO MAKES THE CLOWN LAUGH??? COME ON, WHO MAKES THE CLOWN LAUGH, YA FREAKING BRANIACS!"

There seems to be a little bit of thieving/pilfering going on around here, as I just got an email threatening immediate termination to those caught doing such things. And we're only around 8 people at any given time. Brothers in arms, but criminals with our backs turned. I also soooo enjoy listening to folks here tell me which girls they've been boinking. It's quite the professional environment here.

I was a little disappointed by the incredible poor showing of my DEAR DEAR FRIENDS in Sydney. I was stood up 3 TIMES in the last 2 weeks. You know your names, you naughty Sydneysiders! Thank goodness for Brooke (must be an EDS thing) who can always keep her lunch plans. But being of magnanimous generosity, I still gave them my beloved casino buckets and half-dollars I got in Vegas. I'm nearly out of buckets. I may have to start giving them one each instead of a set of five since I HAVE SO MAAAAAAANNNY dear dear friends.

I'm heading up to Queensland in two weeks to meet up with another dear dear friend of mine. And I have to book my trip to Tasmania soon afterwards. I like doing these kinds of trips, gives me a chance to learn more about this great country and increase my knowledge so I can spread more lies about Oz to unwitting Americans. I learned about Hoop Snakes the other night. That'll fit in nicely with castrating Drop Bears.

Hey, have you noticed that I hardly mention Grant at all? Well, that's because he hasn't been to work for 2 weeks! But still getting paid! What kind of great deal is that!!!!!! And therein lies the conundrum!

Bye bye

XMAS PARTY

I kinda saw the humor in the xmas gift.

Date:	Friday, December 10, 1999 12:29 PM
To:	Bruce, Dale; Barry; Joe O.; Tom; Yvette; Maria
Subject:	xmas party

Yesterday was our company xmas party. We had it on the beach, and some guys brought a motorboat and a jetski. But it was overcast and cloudy. We also had Secret Santa exchange gift. I gave Warren (mr. chatterbox) a vegetarian cookbook because he's always saying that if you eat McDonald's everyday you'd die in a year. But guess what I got? A McDonald's Happy Meal. I thought that was pretty cheap since the gift limit was $15, and the Happy Meal only cost 3 bucks. But the guy who gave it to me was one of the owners of the company and he was just crapping himself laughing about the gift. I guess he gave it to me because he always sees me with McDs coffee in the morning.

Everybody was getting pretty annoying, and I wasn't drinking (because I had foolishly inebriated myself the prior night - all I could remember was someone slapping a 20 in my hand and saying: "take a taxi, man, take a taxi...", so my patience with the little people was getting thin. Luckily, all the Asians were getting antsy, so I hitched a ride with a Chinese couple and the Korean guy who is allergic to alcohol, wears a cowboy hat and has a ponytail.

We said goodbye (I was saying: "buh-bye, all the Asian people are leaving!!! It's nearly 9:00 pm, it's an ethnic thing!"). There was a young English girl there (20 yr old, I think), and she reminded me of the English girls that I had met in Ayers Rock. Kinda chubby, talkative, and had all kinda 'cute' mannerisms. I hope they're not all like that in England.

Beautiful sunny day now in Sydney.

INIQUITY BEFORE XMAS

It's tough being fired before xmas, thank goodness it wasn't me.

Date:	Tuesday, December 21, 1999 2:14 PM
To:	Helen; Brooke; Davide; Greg; Simon; Aldo; Yvette; Maria; Bruce; Dale; Barry; Joe O.; Tom; Kirsten; Dodge; Jun; Roberto
Subject:	Iniquity before xmas

Fired before xmas

I love using that word!!! But although I don't have any feelings, I couldn't help being struck by the irony that happened last Friday. So after going home and having dinner, I went back to N Sydney to meet up with the boys to have a drink at the "Rag and Famish" (we just call it "the Fag"). I got in, and I notice that Sung (the Korean guy with the cowboy hat and ponytail) is drinking beer. Goodness! And he's allergic to alcohol and gets sick for days on end if he has alcohol. He says: "Today is my last day". He got sacked! 1 week before xmas, and 2 weeks before his 3 month probation was to end. Apparently, he didn't do anything wrong but the company budget is a bit strapped since they had a falling out with their namesake company in the USA (yeah, the company I'm supposed to be heading back to). People get sacked here and there, so that's not a big deal. But it turned out that his wife was coming over next week from Korea (he hadn't seen her in a year or so). Because I have the sensitivity of an ice cube, I asked him if he was going to tell his wife, and he said "no". How sad is that! But since I'm emotionless, the most I could do was buy him a beer and pat him on the back. And there I am, complaining that the British pound exchange rate sucks, and I'm crapping on about how the casino spanks me silly. And people are getting fired in front of me. I suppose wanton malice does exist. So yesterday, I bought lunch for Todd and Craig at yumcha to make up for the bad karma from last week. Now the world is in perfect harmony again.

Typing in Paychecks

But that's not all!!! So I'm mr earlybird at work, but yesterday the HR guy was already in since he had been working on payroll the entire night. He looks like crap, he's in his shorts, tshirts and his tennis shoes are all over the floor. He rocks to me, and says: "I don't want to fuck up the paychecks, can you enter in the numbers for me?". So I say: "SURE!!!!!". Sure enough, he reads me off the paycheck deposit amounts for the employees, and I select the person's name, and enter in their numbers! So guess what, now I know what most everybody earns in the office! Ha ha! What kind of company allows their employees to know what other employees make???? This is mad! Hamsters are being run by gerbils. That's what I think.

Plenty more stuff like Grant going mad, going AWOL and his new diet, but he's silly so I don't want to talk about him. Well, tonight is my last night at my current apartment (I guess that's why you guys are holding off on the barrage of xmas cards since you guys don't have my permanent address, right????), before I move out tomorrow and fly out tomorrow afternoon to Europe for a frigid 10 days. Anybody want anything from Munich or London?

Have a very nice xmas and a happy new year!

And since it's the merry season, let's all remember that any man fast enough can grab a tiger by its balls, but only a hero will keep on squeezing.

RUNNING THE OFFICE FROM THE GIRL'S TOILET

Just another day at the office!

Date:	Sunday, November 21, 1999 4:55 PM
To:	Karen; Yvette; Maria; Bruce; Dale; Barry; Joe O.; Tom; Kirsten; Dan; Aldo; Davide; Derryn; Greg; Simon; Rowena; Helen; Brooke; Alicia; Dodge; Jun; Roberto
Subject:	Running the Office from the Girl's Toilet

Dear Dear Friends,

Saturday's are the days I dread the most. Reason being, I go into work at 5 - 6 am in the morning, and 99% percent of the time, these fuckers at work changed something Friday afternoon and in all likelihood my analog line is disabled, and various components of my PC are missing and lying somewhere else in the office. But this Saturday was going to be special.

First thing I do is disable the alarm. Then I gotta call the security company so the alarm isn't reactivated in 10 minutes. However, I notice that the phones are all dead. That's odd!!! And then I realized it's all pretty quiet and dark. The servers and PCs are all dead. There's no power!!! By this time the alarms have been reactivated and they're going off like mad. So I deactivate it and search the floors for some phones. Nope. So I gotta go out of the building and look for a payphone. Finally I get in touch with Josh, and he says he'll take care of it because all the prod systems are down. So I go back to the building, turn off all the alarms. And five mins later this guy comes in and tells me that the power's been cut to the entire building. I tell him we need the systems up. So he tells me that the only power he can give me is an outlet in the girl's toilet. So we run this 20 meter extension cable from the girl's toilet into the office, and we power around 10 computers, UPSs, monitors AND the phone system off this one line. What a joke!!!! And to top it off, I had production moves to do. I hate that place.

Finally, I had enough of that place and left in the afternoon to visit the casino. The casino pulled down my shorts, spanked me silly and made me cry like a little girl 4 hours later. However, they gave me a free meal.

On Sunday, I went to the airport to say bye-bye to Dan & family who were going back to Indonesia for an undetermined amount of time. So there were a bunch of friends and family wishing Dan well, and there was some crying as well. But since I don't have any feelings in that little piece of black coal where my heart is supposed to be, I didn't cry. I don't think you should make them feel more insecure or sad as it is so I just say "Don't worry Dan!! Everything will be okay!". So I just tried to make them feel better by talking about how it's too bad we have to wait until people are dead before we can cremate them, or poisoning the water for people over 40.

Then I had yumcha with Derryn and Jane, and I mediated between the two on Derryn's desire to buy a boat and Jane's desire to get a cat. Surely a happy compromise can be found. On the one hand, a boat is expensive and won't get used much. On the other hand, you get cat hair on your suits, and cats are often involved in witchcraft (you know, cats are aspects of witches). Plus they get hairballs all over the place. And if a cat was as big as a human, they'd eat you. Yumcha was okay, but I swear, the dishes are getting greasier and greasier!

Only 4 more days till Tasmania.

FIRED!

Personal and work life have all melted together in my apartment.

Date:	Friday, February 04, 2000 2:39 PM
To:	Sandra; Oscar; Pam; Nitin; Nicole; Nancye; Mark; Linda; Beth; Chris; Keith; Jenn; Eunice; Julie; Belen; Manuela; Bettina; Helen; Greg; Davide; Brooke; Aldo; Simon; Maria; Yvette; Tom; Joe O.; Barry; Dale; Bruce; Kirsten; Derryn; Dan; Rowena; Roberto; Dodge; Jun; Alison
Subject:	Update

Dear Dear Friends (yes, the irregular friends are included today),

So I just wanted to let you know that I'm up and running again after having been booted from the office 1 week ago. They also decided to separate me that day instead of accepting my two-weeks notice. That's fine, that's another 2 weeks severance pay. But of course, they're refusing to pay me out. Please don't worry about my finances, and don't send me money like you all did last time when I quit before. It was appreciated though.

Unfortunately, they confiscated my hardware & all work documentation, so the company in the US had to ship me everything to my apt. Yesterday, I hooked everything up and my apt looks like a warzone with cables, computers, printers, power cords all over the place. I guess working from home is a whole lot more comfortable than working at the office. However, my worst nightmare of being surrounded by computers, technology etc. has come true. I hate computers!!!!!! It wasn't that flash at the office anyway, considering I used to run powercords from the girls' toilet to power the computers in the office. And besides, I got a stupid McDonalds Happy Meal for my xmas exchange-gift, so that just shows you the caliber of people I used to work for.

For those Aussies who love me, my mobile# is 0401 166 954, if you're on Optus, you should call after 7:00 pm then it's free and we can talk about magic ponies, holy crystals and casinos until the wee hours of the night. We also have a pool and a view of the Harbour, so if youre a Sydneysider and want to go swimming feel free to drop by. I had to get the mobile# (I hate mobiles, everybody knows where you are), so I could talk to New York and be on the computer online at the same time. I'm thinking of putting the handsfree-set on, but I would just look such a pretentious dork (even though I am alone sitting in my jammies and wearing my pointy crown) that I just can't bring myself to do so. Thank you sweet baby Jesus for providing me with some humility.

I was hell-bent on suing the company to recover my pay, and termination payout, and I had already enquired about lawyers (they call them solicitors here), and I reckon it was gonna cost me 1000 bucks for paperwork and 6000 bucks to go to court. Some of my dear dear friends also gave me their legal connections so I was all ready to KICK SOME ASS. But for some reason, I woke up the next day and I was somewhat blessed with a more serene mood (thank you HOLY SPIRIT!!!) and I told myself "you know what, I don't feel like suing them this week", and lo and behold, I had a very fortuitous day that day which included financial gain and an interesting story that would really not surprise many of you knowing the sick sick sick world that I live in. GDI Oz still didn't pay me, but there's no rush to get into litigation but yet I have some money for the casino, go figure!. And in addition to that, I somehow have changed my awful awful ways and cruel (yet witty, I may add) attitude towards kilogrammatically-challenged people. I will never make fun of fat people again. Oh how the Lord works in miraculous ways.

Oh yeah, thanks for all the xmas cards and presents and packages I received for xmas last year. That was great, I got so much that I thought my place would become a regular fire hazard with all the envelopes, cards and wrapping paper just all over the place.

To all those I haven't emailed/talked to for a while, I hope you're all doing well. I'm still stuck in Sydney, but I reckon, the end days are coming so I would say March I'd be trying to move back to Los Angeles.

I LOVE YOU ALL!!!!

SECTION V

THE NAKED DAY

Real life seems to have no plots.
Ivy Compton-Burnett

16

Moments & Fragments

To be a good diarist, one must have a little snouty, sneaky mind.

Harold Nicolson

COMMANDER PEPE

I hadn't written to my friends in California since I got to Australia in November. I guess Yvette was concerned and had emailed me asking how I was doing. Thank goodness I had Commander Pepe to help me out. Yvette and friends thought I had lost my mind after this email.

Date:	Friday, 6 December 1996 13:50
To:	Yvette
Subject:	RE: New note

Dear Mrs. Yvette Z.,

Joe is unavailable right now, as he is busy getting ready to give his deposit to the realtor for his apartment. Joe may have already introduced me to you, I am Commander Pepe, Joe's best friend in Australia.

Yes, Joe thinks your stories about Scott are very funny. I think maybe Joe regrets giving his hire recommendation for Scott as obviously there may be some brain damage surfacing now. But that doesn't really matter now, does it?

I do not personally know Bill, but I know Joe thinks he is a very smart guy. Good for him! Joe says. Does this mean Joe O. will have to work even harder now?

Joe wants me to tell you about his apartment. It's in the city, maybe a 25 minute walk to the office. It is a one bedroom place, but Joe doubts he is even going to use the bedroom because he has no furniture, and of course, I live in Joe's briefcase.

Joe has to get a fridge, a tv and maybe a fan. He'll probably just rent them, so when he moves he doesn't have to take them with him. However, Joe is planning to buy some sleeping bags and maybe an iron and an ironing board, but that's probably not necessary as he will probably take his clothes to the cleaners to be cleaned (no washer and dryer either). And it doesn't have air-con, which may be dangerous in the summertime as it can get pretty hot here. But the location is excellent, it is on one of the main restaurant streets in Adelaide, and it is super-close to the markets and the cinemas. The great thing is, Joe won't need a car either. Taxis are pretty cheap, and since Joe doesn't really buy a lot of material things, he'll probably be able to save some money.

Joe congratulates you on your pregnancy. Hopefully it will be a boy. By the way, Joe wonders why you're calling him a "babe".

Anyway, tomorrow will be Saturday for Joe, and he'll probably be moving some of his stuff into his apartment.

Joe sends his regards, and he expects some funny replies from his friends in the States.
Sincerely,

Commander Pepe

SLEEPING ARRANGEMENTS

My lack of proper sleeping equipment greatly bothered the Australians. Mark always thought this conversation should have been a comedy skit.

Date:	Wednesday, 29 January 1997 10:10
To:	Alison; Bruce; Yvette; Dodge; Barry; Jun; Kevin; Kirsten; Tom; Max; Joe O.; Vinh; Kevin; Roberto; Debbie; Dale
Subject:	Australia Day Weekend

Hello! The latest news from Oz!

It was Australia Day this Sunday, so it was a long weekend (Monday was off). On Friday, I was invited to dinner with a group of people attending Phase II/ Technical Training. We ate at Stanley's, a famous seafood place, on this street famous for restaurants (it's just one long street full of restaurants). It was pretty good (I had fish and prawns), but do you guys remember when you were 23 - 25, and went to Phase II/Technical Training (for those of you non-EDSers, just pretend you know what I'm talking about)?

Remember how you thought how clever, witty and spontaneous you were? Well, they were kinda like that, these young ones were. There was this guy from New Zealand (red-bearded guy) who just kept on talking and talking about nonsense. And there were the usual stories about people drinking themselves silly, and having hangovers coming to class. These kids. Then we had a silly conversation about my living arrangements. My project leader was there (his fiance teaches the class), and he made mention that I slept on the floor. The conversation kinda went like this:

Nicole: Joe, Mark told me a really funny story that you slept on the floor in the living room.

Joe: That's right, I sleep on a sleeping bag.

Fat Girl Sitting Across: Why don't you buy a bed or a mattress?

Joe: Because I don't want to have move a lot of things.

New Zealander: That's not a bad idea, I'd sleep on the floor.

FGSA: Why do you sleep in the living room?

Joe: Because the TV's in the living room.

Mark: But tell them what you have in the bedroom...

Joe: I've got the fridge in the bedroom.

FGSA: Why do you have fridge in the bedroom?

Joe: Because it makes too much noise in the kitchen.

FGSA: And?

Joe: Because my living room is open to the kitchen and I sleep in the living room and I can't sleep if the fridge is too noisy.

I guess it does sound weird when you really think about it.

Saturday was laundry, market and movie day. Watched "Fierce Creatures". Awful movie. Not even video quality.

Sunday was Australia Day. Went to the zoo, but the day was so hot that all the animals were taking shelter from the heat, or sleeping. I think I only saw half the animals. Then they were passing out free cake at the South Australian museum so I walked on over there, and got myself a mouthful of sugar and jam (sweetest cake ever). Thank goodness I had a bottle of water. Then the movies were $5 because of the holiday, so I watched another movie, "Long Kiss Goodnight", that was okay.

Monday was SuperBowl day, but I watched ANOTHER movie, unfortunately, the city of Adelaide finally caught on about the $5 deal, so I figured I'd watch a really old movie that came out several months ago "DragonHeart" assuming everybody else had seen it. WRONG! It was so unbelievably crowded. But I had the Akubra hat on, so it didn't really matter.

Tuesday was back to work. One of the guys was having some problem writing up a complex SQL statement. So he went around asking for some help. The SEs looked at it, and said, you need some temp tables, some views, having clause etc. Then some of them even tried to write the SQL for him but it didn't work. I figured it could be done with a simpler solution, so I built a couple of tables, and tried it out. No temp tables, no views, no group bys, just a simple inner select. The guy was pretty amazed at the solution. As he verified the results, I was in the process of doing my traditional raising of my fists in the air, shouting

"Victory" or "Brilliant!", but I remembered my past history of making all the other people feel insecure, so I put my hands in my pockets and bit my tongue, but it was pretty hard holding back, I tell you!

Talk to you later!

SHIT STORY

I should've moved to another apartment complex, but the stories kept coming in.

Date:	Thursday, 3 July 1997 15:45
To:	Alison; Bruce; Yvette; Dodge; Barry; Jun; Kevin; Kirsten; Tom; Lynn; Max; Joe O.; Vinh; Kevin; Roberto; Debbie; Dale
Subject:	Another Shit Story

Hello!

Again, people have been nagging me that I haven't been providing regular updates to them. Since I exist purely for other people's amusement, I am glad to provide you all with last week's adventure (by the way, I've been working weekends, so I haven't been able to get out much).

Last Sunday at 9:00 am I was leaving the apartment building to go to work. Just when I had opened the apartment building door, a sudden stench hit my nose. Luckily, as the odor staggered me, my vision accidentally floated to 2 - 3 inches below my tennis shoe, and I saw the biggest pile of crap I have ever seen. It was a neatly compacted pile of fresh shit that was about six inch square and maybe 4 inches high. Now, you have to envision the apartment building entrance which has a recessed doorway. It would be quite difficult for a dog to reverse it's butt (like a car backing out) into the doorway. Furthermore, there were quite a number of cigarette butts scattered all over the doorway, which indicated to me, a group of smokers had congregated in front of the doorway. Probably, one of them decided to take a dump while his buddies (must be guys who did this) made a human shield to protect him from the cold weather and prying eyes.

I sidestepped the poop and went to work. I stayed as long as I could at work in hopes that my neighbors would clean up the crap before I got home. After 5 hours, I thought, surely one of my neighbors may have cleaned up. I was wrong. As sure as those phantom crappers will burn in hell, the pile of crap was waiting for me when I got to the apartment. Enraged at the utter disregard of hygienic standards of my neighbors, I bounded several flights of stairs to the fire hose (just a regular hose) located on every floor. Turned on the water, and hosed the crap into the street. It took 10 minutes to get rid of all the crap. I couldn't do it any faster or with a stronger water pressure as the crap would fly up into my face if I applied more pressure. After performing the deed, I ran like a screaming banshee to my apartment and took a long shower. And that was my traumatic Sunday.

Today, I was offered a potential position of technical team leader on a new project (over 5 - 6 SEs), in a group of 15. But I politely declined. I could provide details, but it's not as interesting as the crap story.

Bye bye!

FIRST FOOTY GAME

The Adelaide Crows won the championship two years in a row. And I was part of it.

Date:	Sunday, 14 September 1997 16:18
To:	Alison; Bruce; Yvette; Dodge; Barry; Jun; Kevin; Kirsten; Tom; Lynn; Joe O.; Vinh; Kevin; Roberto; Debbie; Dale
Subject:	First Footy Game

So I finally got to go to an Australian Rules Football game.

Adelaide, had made it to the prelim semi-finals, so this was going to be a hot game in the city. But on TV, they were reporting that a lot of the Adelaide Football Club members were upset that they had to pay 32 dollars per ticket, so a lot of them were going to give up their reserved tickets. So I asked my manager who had some membership passes to lend me his, so I could go. Well, he didn't have them with him at the time, so he actually dropped by the next morning on a Saturday to drop them off at my place (that's what I like when the bosses come running to me, and give me stuff!). So armed with the membership passes I went to the reservation ticketing agency and got a ticket.

The game was on at 7:15 so I waited for the special footy bus in the city at 5:15. But the 5:15 bus never came, so it was the 5:35 instead. Before that, a bum had asked me for 50 cents, I denied him, and after recovering from the shock that he wasn't getting any, he yelled "FUCK OFF!". Later I saw him being talked by two old women, one of them holding his hand and probably asking him to join a church or something. That's nice. And then shortly after that, a hippie couple and a dog started crossing the street while it was still red for them, bringing buses and cars to a halt. The hippie man started yelling at the buses and the cars, waving his red and white balloons at them (yup, balloons). As he passed us (the footy queue), he offered us a helium whiff from his balloons. So finally the bus came, and the bus ride was a long painful ride. Man, I miss my car. We finally got there.

And after five minutes, I finally found the members entrance. The member's area was packed of hundreds of fans, you guessed it, DRINKING BEER. It was just like a big bar. Some fans had three big cups of beer each. Beer beer beer everywhere. It had been raining previously, so the benches were wet, luckily I had a bought a towel, to protect my butt. Then the game started, it was the Adelaide Crows vs the Geelong Cats. Geelong being the favorite. It was more fun listening to the fans than the actual game because it was kinda like a game on how to use the most curse words in one sentence without repeating oneself. I packed some Whoppers with me, so I ate one, but the smell of fresh chips proved alluring so I got up and bought some fries (yes, fries are called chips, and chips are called crisps).

I needed some ketchup with the fries, so I grabbed the nearest red squeeze bottle. and poured it on the fries. Surprise surprise. The red bottle LOGICALLY contained vinegar. Australians like vinegar with their fries. Well, it didn't taste that bad. I stayed for the first half, each quarter being 30 minutes. So I figured 1 hour of footy was enough. So I grabbed a taxi, and headed back to the city. During the trip, my Greek taxi driver asked me if I was Canadian. Canadian? What the hell? And we talked sports, in particular soccer for most of the trip. Yup, these taxi drivers, they like to chit-chat. I noticed that the Ethnics (that's what they call non-Anglo Australians), kinda pride themselves as being separate, so when it comes to sporting events, teams are primarily Greek, Croatian, Armenian etc. And then after the game, they all beat each other up because of 100 years ago when King Zogog of Barbaria took all the goats of someone's uncle, and they all remember it. Kinda funny, but sad.

And yes, the Adelaide Crows won. And they're now in the semi-finals against the Western Bulldogs! The four teams in the semis are North Melbourne, St. Kilda, Western Bulldogs and Adelaide. The first three teams being teams from Melbourne. Go Crows go!

ACTION

Just another potpourri of activities going nowhere...

Date:	Tuesday, 23 March 1999 11:54 AM
To:	Barry; Bruce; Dodge; Joe O.; Jun; Kirsten; Roberto; Tom; Dale; Davide; Brooke; Greg; Aldo; Nicole; Simon; Mark
Subject:	Action

Hello dear dear friends,

Sorry I havent been sending out my emails but Ive been bit busy lately. So what have I been up to last week, lets just bullet them since Im a little rushed to elaborate and write it in my usual prosaic style. No particular order.

1) continued trying to hit on blues singer at Ryan's but always getting interrupted by women I dont sleep with anyway - amazingly enough, I dont think the blues singer is interested in the great one

2) on the same night, managed to get invited to a casual dinner with the biz folks, and got at least $100 worth of drinks and food from that group. I SCORED!!!!! plus the biz boss said I could come back to MacBank anytime.

3) been triviaing with Alicia and talking casino with Kareena. Kareena wont go to casino until after Thailand (yeah right), and Kareena also lied about being able to get me into the high rollers area. Stunned the two chicks and a couple of biz folks with my GIMME TEN questions (I still think that has potential).

4) still messing around on the net with holy crystals and all, in fact Lilacs_and_Licorice who hated me wanted to engage in some christian cybersex talk, but I told her (could be a guy!) that that was unbiblical.

5) Brooke to show me mercy sometime this week and have drinks with me in public. Already told my biz friends to come down and check her out. Im sure Brooke doesnt mind.

6) Talked so much casino with Kareena that I got all excited and won $200 at the pokies (slots) at the bar in front of the bank. So I thought that this was a sign from heaven and Ive been asked to double it. So I went to Star and they promptly relieved me of it, plus $100 of my own money. THOSE BASTARDS!!!!!!!!!!

7) Helen and Aldo came down and we had steamed fish in chinatown. Not bad. Showed Helen the city (on the monorail too), and as luck would have it, some of my colleagues saw me on the street walking with Helen, and they probably thought "hmmm, Joe isnt a loser after all, THAT STUD!!!!".

8) Have horrible pain running from the top of my right eye to my jaw. Must be getting old cause as soon as I take sinutab, it doesnt hurt as much. Thankfully, the humidity is ending.

9) Still not sure whether or not to take the train or fly to Alice Springs, but all the pretty girls said to fly, so thats what Ill do.

Okay bye bye

HAILSTORM

Oxford St. was a mess the day after. Cars and store windows all smashed up.

Date:	Wednesday, April 14, 1999 3:07 PM
To:	Kirsten; Roberto; Dodge; Jun; Simon; Peter; Nicole; Mark; Greg; Grant; Aldo; Bruce; Tom; Dale; Joe O.; Barry
Subject:	safe

Just wanted to let you know that the hailstones that were the size of golf balls and cricket balls that fell on Sydney last night didnt kill me. Im okay. Thank you all for the kind emails that were sent regarding my well-being.

Man, those hailstones were BIG! I could hardly hear myself, it was that loud. Normally, I'd run out and try to catch the hail with my mouth (you know, hail is just like snow, just a little bigger and rounder), but I dont think I could fit a cricket ball in my mouth .

FLOWER CHICKS, THE QUEEN, FORTUNE TELLER, AND THE PROPHET

Busy week.

Date:	Monday, November 08, 1999 2:20 PM
To:	Dodge; Jun; Roberto; Brooke; Helen; Rowena; Dan; Aldo; Davide; Derryn; Greg; Simon; Kirsten; Bruce; Dale; Barry; Joe O.; Tom; Yvette; Maria
Subject:	Flower Chicks, the Queen, Fortune Teller, and the Prophet

Dear Dear Friends,

What an interesting weekend it has been! Kinda long again, but you guys are used to it. By the way, my old email address has been dead for a week. And this email address is just temporary.

So apologies to those I haven't been responding to because I probably never got those emails if you sent it to the old email address.

Flower Chicks

It all started Friday when I went into town to check out cameras for my Tasmania trip. The selection was poor and the prices were exorbitant, so I decided against it. Instead I rang up my dear dear friend Rowena to see if she wanted to come out for coffee (to prevent the barrage of crude emails similar to the Commonwealth Bank girl incident, I will just say that yes, Rowie is pretty, thin, blond and engaged but I don't have any unbiblical desires towards her - NOT THAT I'M GAY AND DON'T LIKE WOMEN!) Anyway, Rowena tongue-lashed me for the gall of calling her up that day, and standing her up the prior day (I was supposed to have coffee with her on Thursday but I never rang up or emailed - email down - to cancel or confirm - TYPICAL MALE BASTARD!!!!). So I guess that was a no then. But Rowena said Dan was in the office, and Dan always comes out to play. So I met up with Dan at the pub and had some rum and cokes. So feeling whimsy, I decided to go to the florist and get a flower for Rowena to make up for my total lack of manners. I was looking for something innocuous yet clever and cute (just like me!!!), so I asked if they had one of those little thin glass cylinders to put a flower in. What luck, they had one more of those test tubes (as they call it). The rum must've been pretty strong because my accent must've been out of control and going all over the place, as the flower chicks kept on pestering me where I was from, and what my accent was. They didn't seem to want to accept that it was a Filipino accent, and their eyes lit up when I said I had lived in the US for a while. The meaty flower chick finally got out a purple/lavender flower and stuck it in the test tube. And I said (in a terribly inflated voice): THAT LOOKS SPLENDID!!! The two chicks were a bit startled at my outburst and the meaty chick said: "My my, that's such a big word." To which I grinned and said "Are you saying it's such a big word from such a little man????" And the two other flower chicks on either side of the meaty chick started giggling. I can't quite remember the entire conversation since that was my third drink already and it was getting fuzzy, but needless to say I WAS HORRIBLY SHAMELESS for the entire ordeal. I think I even said: "THAT FLOWER LOOKS SO GOOD, I COULD EAT IT!!!". To which of course, all 3 flower chicks squealed in delight. Too bad, the three chicks' combined income wouldn't come close to 70 percent of my income. And then I sent Dan off back to the office to deliver the little flower.

The Queen

Saturday was the referendum, and we had to vote if we wanted to keep the monarchy as the head of state (and have parliament pick a president instead). Now, not to be too political. But I always thought that it would be nice if they had a real Australian flag, and I'm not much of a proponent of divine right as such presumptuousness is an affront to God (I better stop here...) So after work, I went to the city, checked to see if I was on the roll, and yes I was. I said Yes to the republic and I also said Yes to the Preamble (I didn't think it was that bad!). The mood for the republic seemed pretty positive, and I thought for sure New South Wales would at least vote for the republic. But alas, only one Australian state voted for the republic (Victoria) falling short of the required 4/6 states to carry the republic. Population wise, it was 45% for the republic to 55% against the republic. How odd, huh? So we all woke up Sunday and the Queen was still the head of state. I don't get it, the Queen isn't even HOT!!! Maybe 50 years ago, but not now!

Fortune Teller

I decided to have all-you-can-eat Korean BBQ in Chinatown for lunch on Sunday, and then meet up with Dan and family for dessert. I kinda thought that the Korean waitress was kinda cute, but she had totally let herself go. Her hair was all messed up and she was wearing those big black boxy/blocky eyeglasses from the 50s. Why do people wear those things! Anyway, I ate enough pork and beef to last a couple of days. This isn't going to help me with my weight problem, that's for sure. So we're just walking around, and Dan sees these pictures of this old man holding palms of people. And there's also this big giant Feng Shui divining metal plate hanging in the window. So I say: "Come on Dan, let's try it out!". So we go in, and we ask how much it costs to have our palms read. And he hands us this menu (just like a chinese restaurant menu), and it's got all these items and prices ranging from 1 yr forecast for 60 bucks to entire life forecast for 300 bucks! So hey, what's 60 bucks??!! So I sit there but before he starts, Dan says: "You also do the past?", and the old guy says "yes, because nobody believes me if I don't do the past". So he traces the outline of my right hand on a piece of paper, and then takes my left hand and copies over the markings of my left palm to the traced outline. He looks at my left hand and says "you spend a lot of money, you have extra ring on your middle finger, buy ring to cover that and you'll stop spending!" WOW!!! What a genius! I knew I have a generous soul, but I never realized I could become more thrifty by just simply getting a ring on my middle finger. This is kinda how it went:

Old Man: Life not easy for you and family. Life still hard for you and family, but right now is getting better.

Old Man: from 1 to 7 years old, you have hard life. nobody help your mother and father with you.

Joe: yeah okay (kinda true - but then again, that's not too uncommon!)

Old Man: until 20 - you don't have good time in school, you can't become doctor or lawyer

Joe: yeah (kinda true since I was always moving schools but I had some good runs!)

Old Man: from 20 to 29, you don't save and make a lot of money

Joe: yeah (I think he was wrong on this one)

Old Man: 29 to now, it's getting better, you make more money

Joe: yeah (okay, that's true but most people at this age should be making more money).

Old Man: This year, no good year for you. Don't drive more than 300 kms, don't fly more than 1000 kms, don't spend money, and people talk bad about you.

Joe: okay (what about my Tasmania trip? and flying back to LA? and people are always talking trash about me behind my back, big deal!!!).

Old Man: Next year, much better. You have good relationships...

Joe: With whom???!!!

Old Man: With everybody!!!

Old Man: Next year, you make good income. If you want, you start own business and it will be successful. You no good working for other people or company. You better with own business. You move east, to the eastern suburbs. People help you financially. You watch out for stomach problems next year.

Joe: Okay (sounds fair, but who ever likes working for corporate fascists? As for going east, I guess California is east of Australia. People help me financially, that I gotta see. AND I ALWAYS HAVE STOMACH PROBLEMS).

Old Man: Your relationships... <grabs my hand>... up and down! <does wave with his hand>

Joe: Okay (big surprise there!!! woohoo!)

Old Man: in 2002 you have dangerous period for 10 days (he draws black triangle on my palm), warning! You come see me then.

And that was that! So when I got home, I rang up my mother and told her to send me my gold serpent ring. But apparently it was only 14K, and the Great One needs something a little bit more expensive than that. Isn't that funny, now I have to get a really expensive ring so I'll stop spending money. I was thinking of getting one of those long thing gold clasps that those Chinese emperors used to wear with ornate Chinese characters inscribed on it. I think that would look dashing.

The Prophet of Kirribilli

It was Sunday night, and I was lying bed thinking about what kind of beautiful gold ring would be worthy to reside on my middle finger, and just when I was about to ask super-powers from the dear Lord, I was disturbed by this loud voice talking about sheep, flocks etc. I thought it was some kinda sheep farmer losing out on a business deal. So I go to my window to tell him to shut the fuck up, but I see that it's a guy in the phone booth crying on the phone, and he's waving his fists about like an angry man. Again it's best for me to transcribe the highlights of said phone conversation.

Prophet (crying): I have never been made welcome for the last 16 years!

Prophet: Why can't people see that I am the prophet that Jeremiah has prophesied????

Prophet: It says in the bible that a country will decide on choosing a new leader, and that's Australia! we just had a referendum, the prophecies are being fulfilled! We are the Jews! I am a Jew.

Prophet: I met my wife the other day. She is a heretical prostitute. We are going to marry but she doesn't know it yet. Do you know when? It will be the day of the two prophets.

Prophet: She channels Native American spirits, and she says I'm a genius. And I should go forth and have my book published - The Fallen. Only 1000 heretical prostitutes have read the book. But if more read it, it will become a world best-seller.

Prophet: I have the drive of a serial killer, but I use that strength for good.

Prophet: You have to have hate to do these things.

Unfortunately, it wasn't really very cohesive so it really doesn't make any sense. But I sat entranced for 1 hour listening to this man rant and rave (and in tears!!!). How hard it is to quell an angry and lonely heart. I like that line though "heretical prostitute".

And finally...

Whales

Last week was the Melbourne Cup, and this guy who always like to show-off (not me this time) was blabbing about he picked the winning horse and how he could've made money off of it (he's always talking coulda/woulda/shoulda) BUT HE DIDN'T EVEN BET. And finally I got tired of him and I said: "IF LITTLE FISHIES COULD TALK, THEY WOULD TALK LIKE WHALES". That shut him up. Why am I so mean and cruel? I don't know, I just don't know... I'm sure the good Lord frowns whenever I do that.

ERIN GRAY

Meeting Erin Gray, another highlight in my life...

Date:	Sunday, June 11, 2000 7:12 PM
To:	Nancye; Devin; Aldo; Brooke; Davide; Greg; Simon; Helen; Yvette; Maria; Eunice; Tom; Joe O.; Dale; Barry; Bruce; Kirsten; Kevin; Grant; Karen; Rowena; Derryn; Dan; Dodge; Roberto; Jun
Subject:	I SCORED!!!!

Dear Dear Friends,

Clearly, my busy and eclectic schedule has not been detrimental to my regular disbursements of emails, but it seems that recent mass emails have been more "concept" and "event' emails versus the journal type which gives a so much more accurate description of the Great One's activities.

As the title suggests, I am quite thrilled with this Sunday's escapades but let's begin with Friday...

Friday-Saturday

Friday was a bit of a financial disaster as EDS stock crashed by 26%, which was a pity as I had been raking in the profits (albeit on a small scale) with my $59-$70 game of trading in/trading out and profiting with a 10% margin. So I just bought more of EDS stock at $44 and hopes it sinks to the $30s on Monday so I can buy some more. My lawyers in Australia who supposedly are trying to recover my superannuation (401K equivalent) and severance pay have finally shown their true colors as they are now just billing me for every conceivable interaction, and they sent me a horrendous bill (itemized of course!!!!) with "a please pay asap"; however, the results of their endeavors have yet to materialize. So that's another pinch in the wallet. I guess, I'll just give them a call on Monday and drop them so they can stop bleeding me. I really wonder what these lawyers are good for. Surely they must all be thin-lipped people to be so utterly evil and devoid of morals and ethics. But that's okay, that's another profession that's hellbound anyway.

So I wasn't too happy on Friday, but I amused myself with writing up some emails and thinking up of more scenes for my "Raising Hell" screenplay (that's the title suggestion that won, by the way. I came up with it. So there.) And besides, it's just money. And we all know that we can't take our wealth to heaven anyway.

Friday evenings and Saturday were spent with the Dino family, and I attended my cousin's college graduation in Cal Poly Pomona. There were 1,100+ graduating, so we had to wait until all their names were called. That only took 2 hours. Plus it took another 45 minutes to get out of the parking lot.

My reprints and enlargements of my favorite photos were finished and I could pick them up on Sunday, so that was good. And my mother gave me some special dishes and fruit to take back to Woodland Hills.

Sunday - Erin Gray / Chumash Pow-Wow / Target Altercation

It was comic book convention day! So I drove back home to dump my clean laundry, get my favorite comic book convention carrying bag, and jump into my comic book convention outfit (shorts and sandals). I drove to Los Angeles, to the Shrine Auditorium (where the Oscars are held), and is just outside USC.

So I'm walking around with my little blue EDS tot bag, and I happen to see this older dark-haired woman manning a table. At first I thought it was going to be Julie Strain, the breast-baring vamp of B-movies since she was going to be appearing for autographs. As I approached her, I noticed how pretty she was, and I thought: "SWEET BABY JESUS!!! IT'S NO OTHER THAN ERIN GRAY, FROM BUCK ROGERS OF THE 25TH CENTURY AND SILVER SPOONS!!!!".

Time had been kind to Erin, as the wrinkles and lines on her late 40s/early 50s face only made me realize that granny-sex may not be so unappealing after all. She was still fairly thin, and she was never dominant in the chest area, but she still had the Erin Gray sweet-looking gal look from the 80s. So I stood in line with the rest of the freaks (there were only 2 or 3 others who recognized her), and I chose the attached picture for her to sign. I was a bit flustered being face to face with one of the most attractive women on the planet, so I didn't have all my raging wit in gear. But then I thought, surely I could do better than the guy before who said he was in love with her because of her sparkly lipstick. So as she gave me my signed picture (which now hangs neatly next to a framed newspaper picture of Sydney city), I managed to squeeze in this conversation...

Joe: Thanks! I'll show this to all my friends! So what are you doing now? Are you still doing TV & movies?

Erin: Yes, I have 4 movies. One is with Burt Reynolds, "The Last Producer", and "Social Misfits" and “Women's Story". I'm also working on a "Killer Instinct"

(I don't really know if it's "Killer Instinct" but something like that.)

Joe: "Killer Instinct"!!!! Do you get killed in that movie?????

Erin breaks out laughing and starts shaking her head. Can't stop laughing. Obviously, she got the word-play, and the inference that fading stars are usually killed off in their cameo roles. A little joke between us, as we both know she isn't hot material anymore, but I'm too much of a fan to embarrass her. I'm sure she appreciates that.

Joe: I guess I have to watch the movie to find out, huh?

Erin: I won't give the plot away (still laughing).

And that was about it. She told me to check out her website www.eringray.com, and we said bye-bye. ERIN, I LOVE YOUUUUUUUUU!!!!!!!!

On the way out, I passed by the table of the black guy who played "Boomer" from Battlestar Galactica in the 80s, poor guy, nobody recognized him.

I kinda felt sorry for Erin, she must have fallen on hard times to be selling autographs at the comic book convention. But the point was, I made Erin laugh!!!! I made Colonel Wilma Deering giggle!!!! How fantastic is that!!!!!!!!????? I equate making Erin laugh to having sex with 3 average looking girls, or winning $500 bucks on lottery scratchers. I mean, come on!!!! This doesn't happen very often.

Then I drove back home, put some rice in the rice cooker, and drove off to the Chumash Pow-Wow fest some 5 miles away. My Gurkha knife which Dale had brought from Nepal was in need of a new handle and my workmate Tom Garvin had recommended I seek out the knives craftsmen who attend the Chumash Pow-Wow events. So I found this one guy (looked more like a cowboy than a Chumash Indian) who had these sets of fantastic knives (bowies etc.) with great handles made out of antler. So we started to talking and I brought out my knife (it was truly the most cunning and bloodthirsty knife within 1 mile) which was all crusty and fire-burnt from the last camping event. And we settled on a price and plan to have the handle replaced. Great!!!! I'll have my knife back in 3 weeks.

Then I went to Target to get my reprints and enlargements (what a great price!!! I got a couple of large enlargements and plenty of reprints, all for 20 bucks plus). And I got into a yelling match with this old fella customer service guy who raised his voice against me. I'm sorry, it's the Lord's Day, it's only 20 bucks worth and I don't have time to be yelled at by some old rusty cracker who's probably pissed because his ex-wife is on his tail for alimony backpayments. So I gave him my intellectual condescension, and reported him to the store manager.

Then I went back home, took a swim while Barry was painting all the patio furniture, and ate lunch afterwards. Then I got a frame for Erin, hung her up, read some comic books, and watched the Lakers/Pacers Game 3.

What a great day!!!!!!!!

I LOVE YOU ALLLLLLL!!!!!!!

MOVIE REVIEW OF "WHAT LIES BENEATH"

I probably received 40 – 60 reply-alls to this email. The girls were especially vocal. Some even threatened not to bring their hot CHICK friends to the Karaoke Party.

Date:	Wednesday, February 07, 2001 10:45 AM
To:	Richi; Nancye; Vinh; Vahe; Margaret; Debra; Eunice; Kirsten; Kevin; Tom; Barry; Bruce; Maria; Yvette; Jun; Roberto; Dodge; Karen; Rowena; Dan; Helen; Greg; Davide; Aldo; Belen
Subject:	Movie Review of "What Lies Beneath"

I usually don't do movie reviews as people may not have seen the movie yet, and I tend to give the plot away. But last night, I watched the Harrison Ford and Michelle Pfeiffer movie "What Lies Beneath" suspense thriller, and I thought to myself: "gee whiz, all men should watch this movie". And let me tell you why.

The story revolves around Claire, a wife and mother, and Norman, her doting, good-looking, caring, brilliant scientist husband (a man most of us men would easily identify with). Claire had a near-fatal car accident a year ago which made her edgy and neurotic, and they also moved to Norman's father's old house on the lake. Their daughter Caitlin (Claire's daughter from her first husband) also left home to go college, so Claire is a bit tense. Brilliant Norman is working on a big research project which is near completion.

Then Claire starts being haunted by this girl Madison. It turns out Norman had an affair with Madison, a sexy graduate student. When Madison threatens to disrupt the beautiful family and career Norman had built, Norman had to kill her to save his marriage and his job. But Madison starts possessing Claire and causes all kinds of problems. Finally Claire figures everything out, and wants Norman to tell the police so they can get Madison's body from the river. Norman pleads and pleads with Claire to forgive him so they can start all over again, but Claire wants Madison to be dug up. Then Norman, in his desperation, realizes Claire is going to ruin him and tries to kill Claire. Eventually they both end up underwater in the river in their truck, and Madison's ghost grabs Norman, and he drowns/dies while Claire swims to safety.

The reason I say all men should watch this is the simple moral of this movie: chicks cause trouble, especially pretty chicks.

It all started with that vixen Madison who seduces brilliant and hard-working Norman. Norman was probably spending a lot of time at his research work, away from home, not getting the attention he should be getting from his wife Claire. Then Madison steps in to fulfill her fantasy of having an illicit affair with an older and more experienced man. When Norman realizes he has made a mistake, and tries to cut Madison off, Madison goes all crazy like they all do when guys break up with them first instead of the other way round, and wants to destroy everything, including Claire. Norman protects Claire by getting rid of Madison. So Norman is thinking "yeah, I did good and fixed everything". But Claire, because she is intuitive and curious, figures everything out and confronts Norman with it. Instead of helping Norman, Claire decides to turn Norman in to the police!!!!! After all the things Norman had done for her!!!!!!!!! What an ingrate!!!!!! Good grief, he said he was sorry. But nooooooo, sorry is never enough. And Claire has to give it to Norman where it really hurts. So what's Norman supposed to do? Now he has to get rid of the second chick! But then at then end, the two chicks (one is even dead!!!!) gang up on him and kill him.

I cried for Norman. Now I know how it feels when doves cry.

17

Our Precious Health

Every invalid is a physician.
Irish Proverb

DOCTOR'S APPOINTMENT

I didn't want to die of nut cancer.

Date:	Thursday, April 19, 2001 10:16 AM
To:	Debra; Vahe; Joe O.; Jun; Roberto; Dodge; Rowena; Daniel; Tom; Barry; Bruce; Maria; Yvette; Davide; Aldo; Kirsten; Kevin; Dale
Subject:	Doctor's Appointment

So I've been having this pain/discomfort in my upper left leg/thigh, groin and left testicle for the last 6 weeks.

Naturally, since I can do my own medical research through the internet, I've become pretty much paranoid that it's a hernia, testicular cancer or prostate cancer. Because of the symptoms, I've pretty much ruled out hernia (as it would be excruciatingly painful), and prostate cancer (I'm too young, and there'd be a lot of urinary disorders). So I figured it's testicular cancer, and the doctor would have to take one of my nuts away. Of course, that would make me very very sad if that were to happen, so the fear of testicular cancer probably kept me from doing a doctor's appointment, and besides, I thought, "if I wait long enough, the pain will just go away."

But the pain lingered on for 6 weeks, and I was thinking, "gee whiz, if it was some muscle pull, shouldn't it have gone away by now?". And then on the weekend, my nuts were kinda hurting, but that probably only because I had been giving myself Self-Testicular-Exams (as prescribed on the internet) for 5 consecutive days, and I probably overdid it. So I finally made an appointment to go the UCLA Medical Center for an exam. They made me fast for 16 hours.

When the pretty Asian girl in the white robe walked in the examining room, I thought: "oh no, don't tell me a female doctor is substituting for Dr. Daryl Lum!". I can't have my nuts examined by someone so pretty! Thankfully, she just took my weight, my pulse and blood pressure. She was surprised that my blood pressure seemed pretty high, and asked if I was nervous. I should've said: "Nervous? Only around you, baby". But of course, you only think of these clever things one day after. Joanne was a cutie-pootie.

Then the good doctor came in. I astounded him with the vast medical research I had already accumulated prior to the visit, and described my concerns regarding testicular and prostate cancer (having ruled out the hernia). So we went down to business and he examined my groin and nuts. He made me cough a lot of times. Of course, he didn't find anything. No swelling, no masses. Nothing. He sure fondled my nuts a lot. I was hoping he wouldn't want to kiss me since many a times people get carried away by the moment, but he was pretty professional about it. We skipped the rectal exam for prostate cancer since I don't fall into that high-risk category, but he did make me give a urine sample to check for any apparent problems.

So he must've thought I was a paranoid hypochondriac, and made Joanne take some blood samples to check on any abnormalities. Joanne said I was brave because I didn't cry like some of her patients do when she sticks needles into them. What a cutie-pootie.

Now I have to wait for the lab results for the blood and urine, and call in next week.

BLOOD TEST RESULTS

From the depths of defeat to the heights of victory.

Date:	Friday, July 27, 2001 8:14 AM
To:	Aldo; Davide; Karen; Rowena; Barry; Eunice; Maria; Yvette; Joe O.; Bruce; Dale
Subject:	Blood Test Results

Remember how the during my "nut cancer" phase, I had some blood work done and the doctor told me that my cholesterol was 211, and it was too high? (over 200 is bad).

Anyway, the doctor made me come in last week to do more blood work to break up the cholesterol and see how much is good cholesterol, and how much is bad cholesterol.

Basically out of that 211, he was going to break up into HDL (good cholesterol), LDL (bad cholesterol). So he said that based on 211, my bad cholesterol should be lower than 160 in order for us not to worry too much (ideally it should be be 130), and my good cholesterol should be 35 or greater.

So yesterday he calls me back and gives me the results.

My good cholesterol is a whopping 66 (normal 35)!!!! So that explains why my blood had so much cholesterol.

And my bad cholesterol was 128 (way below the danger line of 160, and even lower than the ideal 130)

So because I have twice the amount of good normal cholesterol than normal people, I have concluded that my genetic superiority (I see no other explanation) gives me license to eat all the greasy, fatty and rich foods without fearing any health consequences.

Bring on the roast pig, baby!!!!! BRING IT ON!!!!!

18

Farewell to Fools

I tell you the past is a bucket of ashes.
Carl Sandburg - Prarie

One always begins to forgive a place as soon as it's left behind.
Charles Dickens

Goodbye California

My last day at the Van Nuys account. I'm off to Australia for the next 3 years or so. I think I had just seen the Island of Dr. Moreau in the cinema.

Date:	10/31/96
To:	Everyone Group / JABBA, Everyone Group / R2D2, Everyone Group THE-FORCE
Subject:	Bye Bye

A little story first...

The Island of Dr. Dino

There was a twinge of sadness as I watched my disciples find their places on the cold, earthen floor. This would probably be the last time I would see many of my loyal ones. They sat patiently across from me, their legs crossed in strained anticipation of my parting words.

I raised my hand and said: "I will be leaving soon my faithful ones, but before I depart, I will answer your most pressing questions".

One of the neophytes bravely spoke up: "Master, before you leave, do you think you could remove the electro-shock implant grafted to my rib-cage?".

And the room erupted in laughter, for all we knew that Oscar still had a long way to go before graduating from the SED program.

Thus ends the strange story of Dr. Dino, whose inhuman experiments on SEDs and SEs alike, have earned him his terrifying place in SE history.

And so the time has finally come to say thank-yous and goodbyes...

I've had had the good fortune of working with most of you in the last three years, and I'm very impressed and happy with the great working relationship I've had with my customers and the IT team. I don't ever recall an unpleasant or unprofessional encounter with any of my customers, and aside from the occasional death-threat on the freeway, life has been very good to me at OAN. I've worked at OAN for about 3 1/2 years (nearly half of my EDS career), and although I certainly had my share of entertainment in Detroit, I must confess that OAN has brought me the most smiles and laughs. Heck, sometimes I show up for work just for the amusement factor! With fond memories I shall remember matching wits with the yeggman who often tipped victory into his corner by threatening me with bodily harm less I accede. Or how about those evenings at the 94th with Bruce and Barry - picking up CHICKS? And especially proud am I of Yvette, who just a mere three years ago blindly did whatever I told her to at work, and finally three years later, after robbing me of all my wisdom, sure talks back a lot now. Remember Vinh scheming to get me dates? For all those people and stories I haven't mentioned, take comfort in the most disturbing fact that I have a really, really long memory, and you and your antics will one day be published in a future book.

I've made some good friends at OAN, and if wealth was based on the number of friends one has, I'd be a rich man. Unfortunately, to burst the idyllic, and utopian bubble of many, I believe wealth is based on the number of EDS stock shares one owns. Just kidding, it's not the number of shares that matters, but the value of each share. But I digress, let us return to this so-called friends concept. Although a lot of you know me as an easy-going fellow with having few compunctions of sharing some bizarre personal story, I'm really quite a reserved person who keeps a lot of the "good stuff" to himself, and one of the things I do not do often enough is to thank all the people who've helped me personally and professionally at OAN. I wish I had enough room to list all the friends I've come to appreciate, but that would be a long task indeed. There is one person I would like to publicly thank, and that person is Vinh. I thank Vinh, not only for her support and help in my transition to Australia, but also for the years of friendship she has given.

Of course, I am sad to say goodbye to all of you, but I am happy to start a new adventure. I admit that there is a slight feeling of apprehension and unsettlement of going to another country, and a different job. But considering my prodigious command of vocabulary, affable yet cunning personality, devilish good looks, and incredibly accurate guessing, I should be in pretty good shape to bluff my way through any challenge they might present.

Sometimes people ask me if I think I'm doing the right thing, and all I can say is that even if there is no guarantee that the future will be that brighter day, it is that faith in a better tomorrow that gives us courage to find our place in the sun.

Goodbye and Good Luck!

GOODBYE EDS

Finally, an era ends. Goodbye Adelaide, South Australia. Hello Sydney, New South Wales.

Date:	Thursday, November 13, 1997 2:43 PM
To:	Dodge; Jun; Roberto; Alison; Vinh; Tom; Joe O.; Debbie; Dale; Bruce; Barry; Yvette; Kevin; Kirsten; Lynn
Subject:	Last Day

Howdy Boys and Girls,

As you know, today is my last day with EDS. What an interesting ride it has been for the last 7 1/2 years. Yep, starting from that day in 1990 in Northridge, Great Western account when the hiring manager looked at me and said: "Here's your salary, and you're going to Detroit, do you accept?" What a fateful decision it was. But I'm glad I did it; otherwise I wouldn't have met a lot of you fellas and gals (especially that Janet F., mmmmmm, just kidding). But you know, we've got things to do, places to go, and people to meet, so bye-bye it is.

Anyway, I'm off to Manila tomorrow and coming back to Sydney on Dec. 13 and hopefully find an apartment/studio. Hey, I may be even around for the 2000 Olympics! Oh yeah, I won't be back in the US this x-mas. But that's okay, save those presents you bought for me. As always, I will continue to supply MY FRIENDS with the ongoing adventures and profound insights on life.

Bye bye!

GOODBYE FASCIST BANK

This wasn't a bad goodbye email. I was applauded for it's humor. I quit my Sydney job to go camping in the outback and 4 months later I was in California.

Date:	Friday, 9 April 1999 10:31 AM
To:	ISD EQL Equities Lending; CBG BS EQL All
Subject:	Before I leave...

Dear All,

Well, I still have the lunch and afternoon to do, but just in case I get a case of sun stroke at lunch time since its such a magnificent day in Sydney today , I'd just like to say its been great working with you fellows for the last year or so. I'm sure when I'm climbing Ayers Rock, or when I'm dehydrating slowly sprawled out in some forsaken piece of red desert, I'll be thinking of you all and those special MacBank moments.

Some highlights I'd like to point out (mostly non-work related of course)

1) winning money off Damian and Peter on who was going to win the AFL Grand Final (go Crows go!). The best thing about that was that I know absolutely nothing about Aussie Rules. Yet somehow I felt my win was just like taking candy from a baby. Go figure!

2) enhancing Grant's gambling problem by introducing him to the joys of blackjack (and making him memorize all the book rules, he was a little apprehensive first on hitting on 16s, but he soon snapped out of that quick - you would too, when an 80 year old lady from Hong Kong starts calling you bad names).

3) somehow got included in the trivia team to represent MacBank at UNSW, and we won! I reckon, those IQ tests MacBank tortures everyone with, finally paid off. Bad thing about that event was that some people thought I ripped off one of

the Grace Bros gift certificates, but I know it was the tall big guy with the gap in his teeth that did it.

4) causing endless confusion on level 20 by looking too similar to Dan T. because we both have black hair and wear glasses. But that's understandable, I always mix up Edwina and Rowena. Thank goodness Rowena has blond hair to differentiate her.

5) enjoyed playing the "pretty gooooooood" game with the level 20 folks. For some reason, they like to get me to say "pretty goooooood" which evokes much laughter. I dont know, but I get kinda tired of hearing myself say that.

6) I will miss Gerard's most detailed production support calls - "Hey Joe, Fulcrum's busted". It's even better when listening to it on voicemail.

7) best pub story I heard was from Peter C. about his buddies stealing and stuffing port glasses in the front of their jeans, that had me in tears - I'm sure he can be persuaded to retell it. Of course, Andrew A.'s "lighthearted" story from the EQL conference last year may give that story a run for its money.

8) taught Dan T. blackjack and started his gambling problem - the pinnacle came when Dan walked away from a table with chips falling out of his pants pockets, we were all very proud of Dan that night

9) consistently thankful to Rowena for telling me which girls are too tall for me; unfortunately, there's a trade embargo on midgets in Australia, so I guess I won't be dating for a while.

10) plenty more moments I'm sure, but I can't quite remember since I had a big night last night

And that's about it. Hope to catch up with you guys later on in life, careerwise, casino or just plain old getting plastered at Ryan's.

Cheers

Joe

GOODBYE CALIFORNIA

My three month gig in California ended. Back to beautiful Sydney!

Date:	Wednesday, September 29, 1999 3:15 PM
To:	Dodge; Jun; Roberto; Rowena; Nicole; Karen; Helen; Alicia; Brooke; Aldo; Dan; Davide; Derryn; Greg; Mark; Peter; Simon; Kevin; Kirsten; Bruce; Dale; Barry; Joe O.; Tom; Maria; Yvette
Subject:	Back to Sydney

Dear Dear Friends!

Well, today's my last day at work here in California. And tomorrow I will be flying to Sydney and arriving sometime Friday night. You can still email me at any of my email addresses (including this one). What's even better I have a FURNISHED (damn these material possessions!) studio apartment for 6 - 8 weeks whilst I'm in beautiful Sydney (supposedly I'll be reimbursed for it), so any of you can come visit me and enjoy the spectacular sights of Sydney (I know the bald-headed guy who's getting married this week was thinking about free honeymoon accommodations, congratulations to Tom by the way!). It's great weather in Sydney, so I've heard.

I usually put something profound or witty in the bye bye emails, but other than taking a nice big unexpected dump this morning because of those hot pepperoncinis they give out at Tommy's and it clearing out the babyback ribs from last week, there's really not much on my mind, right now (I did get kinda dizzy from this morning's experience).

What other things have I learned, other than knowing I can go 42 ribs (possibly more with ample preparation)? I guess, the question "who makes the clown laugh?" wasn't answered in the last three months, and maybe it will be answered in Sydney. I learned a lot about Grant and how the little monkey in his head likes to bang together crazy thoughts, and the consequences of buying faulty scales (he bought scales two months and claims since then that he hasn't gained any weight. I also learned that paying rent is overrated as I haven't been paying rent for the last three months, and my Sydney apt will be paid for the next two months. Oh yeah, I picked up some practical lessons of life as in DON'T titty-twist your driver while he's driving the car (especially if he's bigger than you). I guess not everybody is into homoerotica. But perhaps, more people will be receptive to stand-up poetry as I think I will need to do that; however, I will refrain from combining the words "freshly baked doughnuts" with "death", like when Barry recited his little ditty today. But then again, that's like asking the bird not to fly.

Have a wonderful day and I LOVE YOU ALL.

GOODBYE SYDNEY

Off to Los Angeles again! Reminiscing over the good times in Australia.

Date:	Saturday, March 18, 2000 4:42 AM
To:	All
Subject:	Bye Bye Sydney - Hello Los Angeles

Dear Dear Friends,

About three and a half years ago, I hopped on a plane in pursuit of that brighter day and a better tomorrow. It's been a most exciting 3 years and I must admit, I'm still pretty thrilled to recount the wonderful adventures I've had in Oz.

As you can tell, the mailing list has been changing quite dramatically over the last couple of years, with more and vegemite-lovers joining the honored list of loved ones. Which just goes to show that Australians have contributed greatly to the colorful collection of the Great One's storybook.

The last three years have been somewhat a blur as I've moved around and changed jobs at a more rapid pace. Who can forget Adelaide and my last year with EDS! How I remember all those precious hours I've wasted on the VIM project team by asking them endless Gimme 10 questions and those dastardly and horrible "if you had a gun to your head, and you were given a choice to..." Or how about those black forest cakes, sausage rolls, white chocolate mousse and other fine foods my fellow friends saw me gorge on. No wonder I became a fat bastard in Adelaide.

Which of course forced me to join the gym and scare Aldo with my incredible physique and python arms every morning when I walked in looking all ripped. My gambling habits hadn't reached pandemic proportions yet and so I was content to do paltry bets - like Davide who had the guts and nerve to bet with the Great One on a footy game. I've never seen a grown man plead mercy with his eyes before. How was he supposed to know I was going to take him to the cleaners when I won the "restaurant of your choice" bet? those endless discussions with Simon, Greg and Mark on who was hotter, Michelle Timms or Natasha Stott-Despoja. With exception to that unfortunate incident when EDS made me contribute 5K to the annual corporate budget for emu eggs and boomerangs given to visitors, I quite enjoyed my stint in South Australia.

From then on, I had a brief excursion to the mother country, where I nearly froze to death whilst travelling in a hermetically sealed airconditioned bus for around 300 kms (hey, I was wearing shorts and a t-shirt, it's a tropical country after all!!!). And then it was Sydney! Always the butt of Aldo's jokes that I must be gay for living near Oxford Street but I did like living in the center of the city. I didn't like it though when hail the size of cricket balls came crashing down one night. I somehow got involved with that fascist and elitist bank, Macquarie Bank for a year or so, but luckily, I managed to escape in time. MacBank did provide me with some new compatriots, that crazy guy Grant who has become quite famous (infamous?) now in his own right, good old Dan who lets me spend time with his family even though I'm always telling him that the water system should be poisoned to kill all people over 40 years old, and Derryn, the young fellow who enthralls us with his tall tales of giant fish but we never catch anything. I'm only worried that since lying is a sin that Derryn will end up in hell making charcoal briquets out of donkey poo. But he's a good guy and let me store all my stuff at his house while I was gone.

During the brief period of unemployment, I managed to squeeze in a trip to that great Australian destination Ayers Rock which is a tale in itself. And then it was off with that ever unpredictable GDI Australia, who sent us off to California for 3 months and ended up taking our PCs as hostages and kicking us out of the office. Oh well. Sydney was indeed a very dynamic city - and how about those endless battles with Star City casino? Many a night was spent with my pants down getting spanked by that horrible horrible place. I guess, after a while, you learn to like it.

And the great pathetic CHICK stories that came out of Sydney! But nobody answered the question "who makes the clown laugh?", so I guess I won't be married for a while. Speaking of CHICKS, what would I do without Brooke and Rowena? Thanks to them, I still have faith that not all women are all bad. But Rowena and I are still arguing about who stood up whom, and although we agreed to an armwrestling match to finally settle it, I guess it just won't happen now. I can't really remember everything I did, but I know I must've done a lot because I emailed out so many lengthy discourses on my travels, casino ass-whippings, CHICK action, and every freaking bowel movement I happened to have that morning.

As someone who has no shame when generalizing or stereotyping entire cultures, ethnic groups or races, I do so enjoy the many admirable qualities of the people from Oz. Good-natured, funny, irreverent, caring and loyal camaraderie that is so uniquely Australian - where everyone's a mate or a matey. And they don't work a lot of overtime either, unless you're working for a fascist company.

I apologize already to all the Aussies I didn't mention personally by name - I just don't have enough time to write a little story about everyone, but rest assured since you're on the mailing list (both first and second tiers), you know that you're always welcome to stay at my place wherever I am. I may even lend you money, that's how privileged you are. Unless of course, you become "bad" and I gotta drop you like a bad habit.

So after 3 years, two cities, 3 jobs, 5 apts, I'm off to Los Angeles sometime this week where hopefully I will continue to amuse my dear dear friends with my endless rampages for the next couple of years. I'm leaving behind (in order of importance) all my money (so I may actually come back...), Star City casino, my porno collection and of course all my dear dear friends in Oz.

As a cruel and vindictive person, I'm not one to romanticize friendship for the test of time is often quite harsh and unforgiving, but it would be good if some of you kept in touch and perhaps even visited me in California.

3 years ago I wrote this when I left: "...it is that hope for a brighter day and a better tomorrow that gives us strength to find our place in the sun". I suppose, I still haven't found my place in the sun as I'm still moving around, but today is that brighter day, and tomorrow just seems to keep getting better and better. I'm not one to give advice either, but I reckon it's better to give thanks to all gifts great and small instead of selling your soul for unanswered miracles.

I hope to see you all in Las Vegas someday.

I LOVE YOU ALL!

P.S. Some lessons and thoughts I've come up with in the last three years (no particular order of importance)...

GAMBLING

a) the only reason people lose at the casino is because they didnt bring enough money to win with

b) you should leave the casino as soon as the Good Lord giveth, and not until the Good Lord taketh

PEOPLE

a) sometimes you wonder why evil people get away with so much, but I say not to worry because evil people don't have souls (that's why they're so bad) and can't go to heaven so they're damned to burn in hell for all perpetuity while us heaven-bound people will ride magic ponies senseless around the racetrack and eat ice cream all day in heaven

b) always say sorry if you can, especially if you don't really mean it or if the person youre saying sorry to is pretty

c) it's okay to get rid of bad friends, there's like 6-7 billion other people on this planet, so there's no shortage of people to pick from, besides bad friends are like evil people - they don't have souls

WORK

a) it's usually a bad sign if your boss is a child of Satan

b) as a rule, the older you get, the less you work, and the more you earn (I know, life isn't fair)

c) work is overrated - all you need in life are clowns & farmers, and maybe some teachers and doctors

d) don't work with thin-lipped people - they're naturally cross, surly, aggressive and mean due to their genetic disposition (it may be that thin-lipped people don't have souls as well) - instead work with wonderfully full-lipped, friendly, generous, witty and charming people like myself

FOOD

a) "the least amount of food for the most of amount of money" especially when other people are buying

b) for some crazy reason, chocolate mousse tastes better in a glass instead of a plastic cup

LOVE

a) what's that?

PRETTY & DUMB GIRLS (it's okay, ALL my female friends are PRETTY and SMART, so I'm not offending anyone)

a) I guess they're kinda like polished wood, really nice to look at and touch, but dumb as

PORNO

a) one can never have a big enough porno collection

b) people who say they dont like porno just haven't watched any good porno

INTERNET

a) internet is hell on earth

b) if you are going to go on the net and mess with people's minds, use a nice cute nickname like magic_koala, then you can say all kinds of filthy horrible things but since you have such a cute name everybody still loves you

MONEY

a) money CAN buy happiness

b) people who say money CAN'T buy happiness either 1) don't have enough money or 2) don't know what to buy to make them happy

c) always have 10K of your local currency handy so you can leave the country quickly if you're involved in a serious crime

d) never get your ATM card demagnetized at 2:00 am in the morning at the casino and you have no cash for a taxi back home - it's a long walk home, baby!!!

THAT TIME OF THE YEAR AGAIN

My company folded! I'm off to Fox, another company, another source of stories.

Date:	Friday, May 18, 2001 2:42 PM
To:	Davide; Aldo; Greg; Brooke; Chris; Mark; Rowena; Dan; Karen; Dodge; Roberto; Jun; Maria; Yvette; Eunice; Kirsten; Kevin; Tom; Barry; Bruce; Joe O.; Margaret; Vinh; Nancye; Vahe; Pam; Devin; Nitin; Helen; Debra
Subject:	That Time of the Year Again

Today, I celebrated my last working day in Northridge with some of my dear dear friends. Unfortunately, my beloved Amy-waitress wasn't working at Chi-Chi's so I wasn't able to get a free ice cream from her. The guys and girls will just have to tell her the bad news next week that I won't be having meatball sandwiches at Chi-Chi's anymore. She's such a cutie-pootie!!! Thankfully, my dear dear friends paid for my lunch, so it wasn't too bad. I was planning to kiss Eunice goodbye on the cheek but since I had a pizza with anchovies, I thought better of it.

It was kind of fun working across the parking lot from my old EDS friends, but now it's time to move on to bigger and better things at Fox. Since I signed a 3 year contract with Fox, this will give me plenty of time to shoot the breeze with Rupert, a fellow Adelaidean. The facilities at Fox are actually not that great. I think I will be working in a trailer. Sometimes, I'm asked on why I had to sign a contract and work in a trailer. And the smart-ass answer that always comes out is (while stretching both arms up victoriously): "BECAUSE I'M A PROGRAMMING SUPERSTAR!!!!!".

They've got some pretty neat perks at Fox, but I was asked to get rid of my "Bitch Magnet" bumper sticker prominently displayed on the back of my car. Some of the Fox folks warned me there were some pretty intimidating women who might incorrectly interpret my irreverence . So yesterday I replaced my bumper sticker with "Who's Your Daddy Now?".

Well, I've got a lot of things planned out for this year, especially since I finished the email book and need to sell it. I think it's time for a new Dino-mobile as well (sans bumper sticker), and I need to climb the Mexican pyramids sometime in the summer or fall. I must like to climb high places because everybody looks so tiny and insignificant from that height.

I think I told somebody this is probably my second worst nightmare come true. How much more cliche-ridden is working in California for a major media company on the studio lot? For years, we've made fun of people who are in the "biz", and look where I end up. Of course, my worst nightmare is the one I probably will never wake up from, which is working with computer nerds. Unless of course, more people other than my friends actually read and buy my email book and I can spend the rest of my life travelling the world attending book signing sessions (oh yeah, for all those who've sent in their book comments, thanks for those. I'm still accepting comments if you've got some).

In closing, and because it is appropriate to the subject, I would just like to quote from a Stephen King book:

"Any man fast enough can grab a tiger by it's balls, but only a hero will keep on squeezing".

Bye bye.

THE BOOK

Camarado, this is no book.
Who touches this, touches a man.
Walt Whitman

BOOK IDEA

Wondering if a book about emails has potential...

Date:	Monday, April 09, 2001 12:48 PM
To:	Dale; Joe O.
Subject:	book idea

since you two can consistently high-caliber emails upon demand, what do you think of this idea?

compile a book just about emails

in my case, these would be my mass emails from 1995-2001 (I don't really have a lot 1996 and earlier since we had officevision and that crazy email at OAN). I have enough material to fill 200 pages.

the book would have no point, and the emails wouldn't even be funny necessarily. I guess it has more of a voyeuristic appeal

I could put photos of the people I'd address the emails to, and photos of some of the locations and events I'm referring to.

Some of the replies are actually funny, but I'm not gonna put them in for fear of litigation. Same with emails sent to me versus from me. Personal emails would not make it to the book, either. I don't want to get sued by my friends.

if I became famous, I could go around the world performing book-signings and be invited to morning talk shows promoting my book about nothing

Friendly Encouragement

Friends are like melons.
Shall I tell you why?
To find one good,
You must a hundred try.
Claude Mermet

Want to Write a Book Commentary?

I think accepting comments would be interesting. Naturally, if they take this opportunity to be "bad", they'll be punished severely.

Date:	Wednesday, April 18, 2001 1:57 PM
To:	Greg; Rowena Dan; Joe O.; Eunice; Vahe; Dale; Tom; Barry; Bruce; Maria; Yvette; Davide; Aldo; Kirsten
Subject:	Want to write a book commentary?

I'm 50% done on my email book (I've pretty much done 1999-present, about 80-90 emails), and now I gotta do 1999 and prior (prob back to 1993 but there isn't a lot of pre-1997). I didn't do personal emails and replies, except for a few exceptions. I think it's pretty funny actually. I still think "FW: Lessons", "Fishing Trip 2" and "Movie Review of What Lies Beneath" are classics. I hope I'll be done in 3 weeks. I wonder how I'm going to sell this idea?

If you're interested, just write a couple of sentences or paragraph or longer, and if it's interesting enough I'll stick it in the back of the book. Then you can come with me on book-signing gigs when I tour the world promoting my book.

It's tough going through the document and deleting everybody's last names and email addresses.

ALDO

This makes fun of the Great One yet it doesn't hurt my feelings. Perfect.

Date:	Thursday, April 26, 2001 7:29 PM
Subject:	RE: Want to write a book commentary?

Here Go's

Joe Dino the e-mail pal from hell, Well not quite! Being a bit player in the drama that is the rise and fall of the Mighty One aka Joe Dino mild mannered computer programmer, has provided a welcome diversion from the hum-drum of daily life. The contradictions that are Joe, open new and interesting perspectives. After all how do you explain a man with a childish comic book collection so large it forms a significant fraction of his furniture and personal effects yet is a man who loves porno, strippers and gambling, who however lived 20 metres from the worlds second gay mecca and just up the road from the fag hag frock shop. At least I know where he got his size 14 stiletto's.

From attempting to get Joe to sleep on a mattress, to advice on romance, to the creeping suspicion of gayness (or is that gaiety), to the realisation that Joe is just plain weird, I have been there, e-mailed that. Despite hating people who lecture me I have taken the role of the friend who lectures, a conscience to replace the one Joe lost somewhere between falling in love with the body pierced goddess (Grrr!) and not sleeping in a real bed for a year.

It's just a pity that the conversations that we had when we sat less than a metre apart are not recorded in e-mail. The epic saga of Natasha Stott-Despoya vs Nose Ring girl vs Hoon in the sack would add even more weight and substance to this literary epic. So Joe give me 10 mate and to paraphrase Spike Milligan. JOE DINO (THE MIGHTY ONE) - My part in his downfall.

PS Natasha is now leader of the democrats one step from PM.

YVETTE

Yvette uses this opportunity to remind me of what's really important... her birthday.

Date: Friday, April 27, 2001 2:02 PM
Subject: RE: can you write your email commentary soon

Here is mine....

"Joe is a crazy fool who makes me laugh with his stories. I must admit I'm looking forward to his long emails that are written after a trip, date, party, and...."

My true friends who are not going to see me tomorrow are wishing me happy birthday today either by dropping a note or a present. Are you gonna send an email at least!!!

DALE

I know he's kidding about the eggrolls because I don't make eggrolls. I make wonton.

Date: Friday, April 27, 2001 4:03 PM
Subject: RE: can you write your email commentary soon

Okay, how about:

"Even though the droll, inane, Seinfeld-ish dialogue dispensed in these emails taught me not to take the Dino mind too seriously, it is easy to see that Joe is at once witty, vulnerable, opinionated, brooding, happy-go-lucky, guarded, encouraging, and melancholy. In short, he's very real, and one of the few who can make me laugh. But heck, let's face it, the only reason I like him is because sometimes he makes me free eggrolls."

Okay?

MARGARET

I gave her a copy to read after she gave me her first comment. It's a far cry from "I always enjoy your e-mails. Thanks for making my day a little brighter."

Date:	Tuesday, May 08, 2001 5:10 PM
Subject:	RE: thanks for your comments – here

Joe,

Thanks for sending the book. This is a GREAT idea. I was spending so much of my time today reading it, that I was forced to print out the whole damn thing. I plan on sharing it with everyone I know, so maybe there is hope for you yet, that is to become famous (he-he). Keep sending me your e-mails cause they make me laugh so hard I almost piss my pants.

Margaret

PS Is that a better comment??????

DAN

Dan's experienced many of my casino and work exploits, but sometimes he disagrees with some of my more morally dubious actions. That's okay, he's still my friend.

Date:	Monday, May 07, 2001 5:12 PM
Subject:	RE: hey, where are your email book comments???

Does this makes sense:

Compulsory reading for young and old. Life would be so boring without knowing the world famous emails which go over across continents. Like the writer this email book is unbelievably funny and unpredictable.

I guarantee tears will come out of your eyes, not just because they are funny, but also some stories are just so cunning and sad.

How's that?

TOM

He's only being sarcastic because he's bald and I have lots of hair on my head.

Date: Tuesday, May 08, 2001 11:52 AM
Subject: RE: I thought this was pretty cool

Okay, here you go, you big cry-baby. Tom S.'s sleeve analysis of Joe Dino's email compilation book:

A MASTERPIECE! ... Email after email, Dino keeps you in stitches as only a short, chubby, Filipino can ... I haven't laughed this hard since Old Yeller ... From the author of "Striking Out with Chicks Down Under" and "Livin' with Mom in Monrovia," comes this latest soon to be best seller ... Buckle up for life in the Dino lane ... Set your cruise control for 35 and roll down the windows -- ain't nothin' like gettin' blown in a Nissan Altima ... Baby!

I think it's pretty good. Definitely better than those other two you sent me. I believe I deserve top bill on the jacket sleeve.

Okay, bye-bye now,

Tom

ROWENA

Sheer brilliance. If I didn't know she was married, I would've asked her to marry me.

Date: Tuesday, May 08, 2001 6:01 PM
Subject: RE: hey, where are your email book comments???

How's this?

"A self-confessed, undiscovered genius. The great one provides a valuable insight into the simple yet complex life of a computer nerd-turned-superhero in his thought-provoking emails. What would one pay for such entertainment at the theatre - or circus? But for those of us whom the great one lends a sympathetic shoulder, accepting that the genuine gift he has been born with will never be truely appreciated, we are simply entertained in return for eternal friendship.

For those whose lives have been touched in some way by Joe Dino - a karaoke night, a buy-one-get-one-free dinner date, or just the odd coffee (which you've had to pay for yourself, but knowing you had the opportunity to be spending time with the great one on the occasions that he actually shows up!)- may you reminisce over the memories incorporated into this first chapter of the journey, which is sure to be greater than the trip from LA to Vegas".

EUNICE

Close call right here. I got away safe and sound, so it seems. I did change the title of the story afterwards.

Date:	Tuesday, May 08, 2001 6:42 PM
Subject:	RE: your email book comments please

As I was scanning through the table of contents to pick out the ones I was going to read (as your emails do amuse me), I couldn't help noticing the "date with Eunice ...." as the title was entirely too daring.

Although I'd change it to a better suited title such as "Never invite Eunice to Karaoke practice" or "My DVD player just isn't good enough for Eunice" as it was all about me and my rudeness, it is your book and you can do whatever you want with it. I believe that I do sing "When I need you" better than you and perhaps that's what ticked you off.

I would have to commend you for keeping up with your emails to make your friends laugh and well informed of your activities. Thanks for offering good humor for us!

VAHE

Typical Vahe, I always have communication problems with him. His comments aren't even about my emails. He spelled "right" instead of "write".

Date:	Friday, May 11, 2001 2:59 PM
Subject:	Re: hey, where's your email book commentary?

Here we go.

First you never told me that you need my comments.

Usually it is very hard for a Big Man to right a comment about another Big Man.

We all know that once a while you and your other smart friends are taking IQ tests and also we all know that it is not important whose score is the highest (According to Joe, his score is the highest- at least for the last 30 some years).

ROBERTO

I had warned him explicitly not to write about gay black men having anal sex. I guess he tried really hard.

Date:	Friday, May 18, 2001 3:07 PM
Subject:	RE: email book comment

Joe you are as crazy as before, but I have to say that sometimes I enjoy your weird stories. They make me laugh and I know that it can only happen to you. Always seeking adventures is one good thing; this way, I can tell your stories to my co-workers. So, any more excitement happening ?

JOE O.

I like the contrast between megalomaniac and an insecure child. Brilliant!

Date:	Friday, May 18, 2001 5:39 PM
Subject:	Re: where's your little email book comment?

Here's my addition:

"How does one describe Joe' emails? At once a megalomaniac and a timid, sometimes insecure child, Joe has brought keeping in touch with his friends to a new level. Many a humdrum day was brightened upon receiving yet another email from "The Great One." Joe would keep us informed on his personal philosophies, his "triumphs" with women (the quotation marks are used quite intentionally), his on-going battles with the wagering establishments of the world, his adventures through the wilds of various countries, his trials and tribulations with the working/professional world, and his unwaivering love and affection for his family and his "dear, dear" friends. Quirky, long-winded, hilarious at times, and always unexpected, Joe's emails have become an important, and necessary diversion for his recipients.

Write on, Great One... write on!"

There... what do you think?

DEBRA

I'd rather leave this cryptic message to the wild imaginings of the curious reader. But that's all that really happened. We really did lock our toes together.

Date:	Wednesday, October 03, 2001 11:15 AM
Subject:	RE: 3 more pages

My author comment would be: "Joe Dino is a great story teller and my favorite person to lock toes with."

NANCYE

I pondered over Nancye's profound contribution for many an hour, and I can only speculate that this is the sound of one hand clapping.

Date:	Wednesday, October 03, 2001 11:55 AM
Subject:	RE: 3 more pages

so basically what you're saying is that all the money you collect from the book signing "forced purchasing" will be sent to the Widows and Children's Funds for both the NYC PB and Firefighters Union?

I knew you had a heart in there somewhere.

And I guess since I see my name is in the same distribution as Barry, Bruce, Yegge et al - I must be Tier 1, but geographically impaired....I'm in good company.

As what to contribute... well things are slow at work today as we are all preparing to attend our the memorial service for our employee Sean's beloved wife Melissa who was a victim of the terror of September 11...

In 1991 a mighty corporation rescued a tiny firm in the heart of the other valley

And with this acquisition came a collection of faces new to these sea foam green spaces

To those 36 members of the original tiny firm in the other valley

It meant no more paychecks bouncing down the 405

Or knowing whose direction to follow.

However, the challenge before these folks from the other valley was, not to simply learn CAS,

But to discover what values, ethics, and morals really looked and felt like.

Do not fret, learning experiences were heavy in the air,

Our mighty homogeneous corporation and crew had to learn about and live with diversity from their opening bow.

For those of us eager to befriend these strangers, we were to become acquainted with a thriftiness to make a Scotsman's kilt lose its pleating,

An opposition to challenge personal ritual quite fierce,

That to change the week's lunch schedule could send one seeking a very large dosage of Prozac to cope with.

And as I sit here and write, I must pause and put forth

That no more loyal or trustworthy a gaggle of friends could this girl find

Than those I ate with, drank with, laughed with, danced with, cooked for, cried with and continue to care for

Than the boys and girls that descended on Haskell Ave 10 years ago hence...

For most of use we have moved along to hither and yon

And valley low and valley high

But when reflecting on life and the decade past

I am grateful to say

That we are still truly honest, sometimes glib, always sarcastic and always heartfelt with the slash of our pen (okay keyboard, but it ruins my rhythm) or the shrill of our voice...

Oy, I can write no more, I'm exhausted... Do with it what you will.

KAREN

Always the sophisticated yet fiery redhead that she is, Karen brings a certain class to my circle of friends. Notice the word "puerile".

Date:	Wednesday, October 03, 2001 3:01 PM
Subject:	RE: 3 more pages

joe, I delight in reading your emails, however puerile the topic, your inimitable take on it always amuses me. Your descriptive prose evokes a smile and/or chuckle - humour is a positive power & there should be much much more - so thanks for helping me thru the stresses of daily life.

And yes - let me know your proposed book distribution plan - maybe I should get a donation from other Australians & pop over for a visit & bring back a couple of suitcases of books for your loyal fans here in outpost down under

DAVIDE

A good-natured and fun-loving soul hides in the broad frame of this Italian-Australian mobster (himself a master of interesting predicaments).

Date:	Thursday, October 04, 2001 1:38 AM
Subject:	RE: Want to write a book commentary?

Hi Joe

Now I have to think about this one. I haven't proofed this and feel free to modify it to suit your needs.

Lets see, my thoughts of the man they call Joe Dino.

Well lets just say I first met Joe in Adelaide. I noticed Joe not because of his good looks (his words) but because he was the only other sucker in on weekends when I was trying to finish my STUBS project. I first worked with Joe on the VIM project (I actually cant say I worked on the project, though I was placed on it, but that is another story after my infamous STUBS rubbing). I sat 2 cubicles away from Joe and could always hear Aldo's and Joe's conversations. We nicknamed the isle as the MAFIA isle and made Joe an honorary Italian.

I remember Joe standing up in his cubicle so his head just reached over it, bringing out some classic lines of "How much would you want to sleep with Hoon, or Amanda Vanstone?" or give me 10 items...etc. Joe could pick the women to make your skin crawl that is for sure, though he did get a dollar figure for each.

Other classics of Joe would be:

The old market trips which became an almost daily routine of buying pull-aparts and some very weird patty favourites of Joe. We always discussed how little EDS was paying and how much shafting they could do after splashing out the cash for the new furniture in the managers office.

The how much would it cost to sleep with ... questions

The infamous footy tipping bet which cost me a dinner at the Red Ochre, how could he beat me (I ended winning the competition out of 100 ppl), but he still got me for that one round and it hurt my visa card.

That time I fell asleep on one of the cubicles and Joe could hear some snoring but just couldn't find the source.

The time I went to a conference in Sydney and stayed at Joes place, I came home the first night puking in his toilet twice and falling asleep with all my clothes on, Joe even provided me a drink of water, how sweet. (This also dispelled the theory Joe was gay as I was in a very vulnerable situation and he didn't take advantage of me, maybe he knew where I have been (Hoon???)) The email that went out after this brought tears to my eyes from laughter, right in the middle of Microsoft's tech ED computer pool where I was reading it.

Joe's e-mails are always appreciated as I know each will bring a new laugh and we all know there can never be too much of that. My favourites would have to be his chat scripts, the holy crystals etc.

Well Joe, keeping all your e-mails is certainly one hard task, to make a book even harder, but to sell one copy of this, now that will be impressive.

And remember Joe, who makes the clown laugh?

MARIA

That's all I am to these folks... a clown. Sniff. Did I mention Maria's got really big boobs?

Date:	Thursday, October 04, 2001 11:07 AM
Subject:	RE: 3 more pages

My comment:

To the person who seeks 'Who makes the clown laugh?': the journey in search for the answer is so close and simple. The entertainment you provide to others should fill your life with laugher, for giving others joy by means of words is not a simple task. I congratulate you on your exaggeration and creativity for words.

From your friend who will forever be entertained by you!

We are all here for a spell, get all the good laughs you can.

— Will Rogers

Ordering Information

Sent Items $9.95 (plus $2.00 shipping & handling per book)

You can order *Sent Items* directly from The Sexy Beast Company by mailing this coupon (or copy) to:

The Sexy Beast Company
319 Genoa St. #8
Monrovia, CA 91016

Please send me ___ copies of *Sent Items*. I am enclosing $________.

Please add $2.00 per book for postage and handling. Send check or money order: no cash or CODs.

NAME ____

ADDRESS ____

CITY________________________ STATE ______ ZIP ______________

We cannot ship to post office boxes or addresses outside the United States. Prices are subject to change without notice.